Caring for Preschool Children

A Supervised, Self-Instructional Training Program

Volume I

Diane Trister Dodge
Derry Gosselin Koralek
Peter J. Pizzolongo

Washington, DC

Distributed by

Gryphon House Inc.
P.O. Box 207
Beltsville, MD 20704

Distributed by

Gryphon House Inc.
P.O. Box 207
Beltsville, MD 20704-0207

ISBN: 0-9602892-3-2 (Volume I)
ISBN: 0-9602892-2-4 (Two-Volume Set)

Library of Congress Card Catalog Number: 89-051192

Acknowledgments

This training program is based on several previous efforts. It draws from earlier publications and experiences of the authors, each of whom has provided training and developed materials for use in day care and other early childhood settings. The primary basis for this publication is a training program developed by the authors for the U.S. Navy and the U.S. Army Child Development Services Programs. Carolee Callen, Head of the Navy Child Development Services Branch, originally conceived of the idea of a standardized, self-instructional training program for child care staff. In 1986 the Navy contracted with Creative Associates International, Inc., a Washington, DC-based consulting firm where the authors then worked, to develop a training program and to train child care center directors to implement the program. M.-A. Lucas, Chief of the Child Development Services Division in the U.S. Army, funded an adaptation of the training program to support CDA training in Army Child Development Centers. We are indebted to these two individuals, their headquarters staff, and the staff at Army and Navy child development centers who reviewed all drafts of the materials developed under this contract and provided us with constructive and helpful suggestions that greatly improved the program.

During the development of this training program, in its original format for military child care settings and as revised and expanded in 1989, several early childhood educators worked with us and provided expert advice. In particular, we want to thank Dr. Jenni Klein, whose considerable knowledge and vast practical experience made her contributions exceptionally valuable. Dr. Joan Lombardi reviewed the training materials from the perspective of the Child Development Associate (CDA) Standards and showed us where changes and additions were needed. Her guidance was particularly useful in ensuring that the materials are consistent with the profession's standards for caregiver competencies. On individual modules, we are grateful for the expert assistance we received from Marilyn Goldhammer, Dr. Trudy Hamby, Bonnie Kittredge, Cynthia Prather, and Lillian Sugarman.

The production of a document of this size required the specialized expertise of three dedicated individuals: Martha Cooley, who edited the manuscript; Jennifer Barrett, who designed the cover and graphics; and Frank Harvey, who served as production coordinator. We are indebted to each of them for their substantial contributions.

And finally, we want to acknowledge the many teachers and trainers we have worked with over the years from whom we have learned a great deal. We have undoubtedly adapted and expanded on many of their excellent ideas; this training program is richer as a result.

It is our hope that *Caring for Preschool Children* will support the important role of teachers and trainers and that its implementation in centers across the country will have a positive impact on the quality of early childhood education programs.

Contents

already have acquired many of the relevant skills. Or you might prefer to begin with a module focused on your greatest need for training.

Implementation of the *Caring for Preschool* Training Program will vary from one center to another. However, there is an established sequence of steps you most likely will follow for each of the modules. These steps are described below.

- **Complete the Overview**

    The overview introduces and defines the topic addressed in the module. It explains why the topic is important and gives concrete examples of how teachers demonstrate their competence in that functional area. You will read three short situations and answer questions to help you learn more about the topic. The last activity in the section gives you an opportunity to apply the topic to your own experiences as an adult.

- **Take the Pre-Training Assessment**

    The pre-training assessment is a two- to three-page list of key skills that teachers should possess in each area. You will read each one and indicate whether you do these things regularly, sometimes, or not enough. After you have completed the assessment, you will identify three to five skills you wish to improve or topics you wish to learn more about. Then discuss this assessment with your trainer.

- **Complete Each Learning Activity**

    Each module has a set of four to seven learning activities. Each learning activity begins with objectives—what you will learn—and several pages of information. After completing the reading, you will have an opportunity to apply the information. This may involve responding to questions, trying out suggestions you read, and noting your observations of children. When you have completed each learning activity, arrange a time to meet with your trainer to discuss the activity and to receive feedback.

- **Summarize Your Progress**

    After you have completed all the learning activities in the module, you will be asked to review the pre-training assessment and write a brief summary of what you have learned and the skills you feel you have acquired. Meet with your trainer to review your progress and to determine whether you have successfully completed all the learning activities.

- **Complete the Assessment Process**

  Your trainer will give you the knowledge assessment and the competency assessment. On the knowledge assessment, you must achieve a score of 80 percent before going on to a new module. Your trainer will observe you working with children to assess your competence in the functional area.

Before You Begin

As an early childhood teacher, you are part of an important profession. Teaching is more than a job. It is a profession with an established body of knowledge and a nationally recognized credentialing system. You have a right to take pride in the role you play in the lives of young children.

Take a few minutes to review the glossary of terms that follow this page. This will make you familiar with words and phrases you will find throughout the modules. You will then be ready to take the self-assessment and to begin planning your own training.

Glossary

Child Development | All the stages of growth of a child, including intellectual, physical, emotional, and social growth.

Child Development Associate (CDA) | A person who has been assessed by the Council for Early Childhood Professional Recognition and judged to be a competent early childhood teacher.

CDA Credentialing Program | A process established by the Council to assess the competence of early childhood professionals. Assessment and credentialing are based on performance in 13 functional areas. The CDA Credential is accepted by the early childhood profession nationwide.

Competencies | Those tasks, skills, attitudes, and values that are needed to provide high-quality child care for children. Competencies differ from knowledge in that competencies describe a teacher's actions and performance.

Competency assessments | The performance-based section of the *Caring for Preschool Children's* assessment process. For the competency assessments, teachers will have to plan and implement activities to demonstrate their skills.

Developmentally appropriate | Reflecting children's basic patterns of social, emotional, cognitive, and physical development; referring to an environment, daily routines, interactions and activities that meet the needs of children at their stage of development.

Environment | The physical space, including furniture and materials, in which care is provided for children.

Knowledge assessment | The paper-and-pencil exercises of the *Caring for Preschool Children's* assessment process, testing the teacher's knowledge of the concepts presented in the module.

Observation | The act of systematically watching what a child says and does during everyday activities. Its purpose is to learn more about that child in order to plan activities that reflect the child's needs, strengths, and interests.

Pre-training assessment | Used at the beginning of each module by the teacher and the trainer to identify what skills the teacher has and where more training is needed.

Functional Areas of the Child Development Associate Competency Standards*

Safe

Provide a safe environment to prevent and reduce injuries.

Healthy

Promote good health and nutrition and provide an environment that contributes to the prevention of illness.

Learning Environment

Use space, relationships, materials, and routines as resources for constructing an interesting, secure, and enjoyable environment that encourages play, exploration, and learning.

Physical

Provide a variety of equipment, activities, and opportunities to promote the physical development of children.

Cognitive

Provide activities and opportunities that encourage curiosity, exploration, and problem-solving appropriate to the developmental levels and learning styles of children.

Communication

Communicate with children and provide opportunities and support for children to understand, acquire, and use verbal and nonverbal means of communicating thoughts and feelings.

Creative

Provide opportunities that stimulate children to play with sound, rhythm, language, materials, space, and ideas in individual ways to express their creative abilities.

*The Council for Early Childhood Professional Recognition, (Washington, DC).

**Functional Areas of the Child Development Associate
Competency Standards**

Self

Provide physical and emotional security for each child and help each child to know, accept, and take pride in himself or herself and to develop a sense of independence.

Social

Help each child to feel accepted in the group, help children learn to communicate and get along with others, and encourage feelings of empathy and mutual respect among children and adults.

Guidance

Provide a supportive environment in which children can begin to learn and practice appropriate and acceptable behaviors as individuals and as a group.

Families

Maintain an open, friendly, and cooperative relationship with each child's family, encourage their involvement in the program, and support the child's relationship with his or her family.

Program Management

Use all available resources to ensure an effective operation.

Professionalism

Make decisions based on knowledge of early childhood theories and practices, promote quality in child care services, and take advantage of opportunities to improve competence both for personal and professional growth and for the benefit of children and families.

Bibliography

Janice J. Beaty, *Observing Development of the Young Child* (Columbus, OH: Charles E. Merrill, 1986). Focuses on observing six major aspects of development in children ages two through six: social, emotional, physical, cognitive, language, and creative and includes a skills checklist.

Sue Bredekamp (ed.), *Developmentally Appropriate Practice in Early Childhood Programs Serving Children from Birth Through Age 8* (Washington, DC: National Association for the Education of Young Children, 1987). Defines the profession's standards for quality in early childhood programs. Describes the role of play in children's lives and teaching strategies that support growth and development.

Dorothy H. Cohen, Virginia Stern, and Nancy Balaban, *Observing and Recording the Behavior of Young Children*, 3rd ed. (New York: Teacher's College Press, 1983). Provides an excellent introduction to the purposes and techniques of observing young children in all areas of development.

Louise Derman-Sparks and the A.B.C. Task Force, *Anti-Bias Curriculum: Tools for Empowering Young Children* (Washington, DC: National Association for the Education of Young Children, 1989). Contains many practical suggestions for helping adults understand how biases are unintentionally conveyed to children and how to minimize, deal with, and even eliminate those biases.

Diane Trister Dodge and Laura J. Colker, *The Creative Curriculum for Early Childhood*, 3rd ed. (Washington, DC: Teaching Strategies, 1991). A comprehensive curriculum appropriate for children from three to five years old. Offers practical strategies based on child development theory for setting the stage and promoting learning in ten interest areas: Blocks, House Corner, Table Toys, Art, Sand and Water, Library, Music and Movement, Cooking, Computers, and Outdoors.

Stephanie Feeney, Doris Christensen, and Eva Moravcik, *Who Am I in the Lives of Children? An Introduction to Teaching Young Children*, 4th ed. (Columbus, OH: Charles E. Merrill, 1990). Presents a variety of ways to work with young children to enhance self-concept, to enlarge the ability to make choices and clarify values, and to enhance learning. Addresses CDA competencies in practical terms throughout each chapter.

S. J. Meisels, *Developmental Screening for Early Childhood: A Guide* (Washington, DC: National Association for the Education of Young Children, 1985). A practical, how-to guide on organizing and conducting an early childhood screening program. Reviews four valid and reliable screening instruments.

Karen Miller, *Ages and Stages* (Marshfield, MA: Telshare, 1985). A comprehensive guide to the stages children pass through as they develop physically, emotionally, and intellectually. Offers suggestions for meeting children's needs and encouraging their growth and development.

Specific Competency Areas

Health and Safety

Nancy J. Ferreira, *Learning Through Cooking: A Cooking Program for Children Two to Ten* (Palo Alto, CA: R & E Research Associates, 1982). Offers recipes, explains the skills and concepts learned through cooking, and includes sample forms for planning and evaluating cooking projects.

Martin I. Green, *A Sigh of Relief* (New York: Bantam, 1984). A first-aid resource for child care programs on how to respond to childhood emergencies. Focuses on prevention, includes numerous safety checklists and first-aid instructions that are clearly illustrated.

Barbara Johnson and Betty Plemons, *Cup Cooking* and *Cup Cooking Starter Set* (Lake Alfred, FL: Early Educators Press, 1985). Offers single-serving recipes that children can prepare themselves. Includes illustrations to explain the steps involved in measuring and mixing ingredients.

Abby Shapiro Kendrick, Roxane Kaufman, and Katherine P. Messinger, *Healthy Young Children: A Manual for Programs* (Washington, DC: National Association for the Education of Young Children, 1991). A comprehensive manual, including three separate chapters devoted to maintaining a safe classroom environment, transportation safety, and handling emergencies.

U.S. Department of Health and Human Services, Public Health Service, and Centers for Disease Control, *What You Can Do to Stop Disease in the Child Day Care Center* (Atlanta, GA: Centers for Disease Control, 1984). A handbook for teachers that explains how to protect yourself and children from disease and how to stop disease from spreading within your classroom and program.

U.S. Department of Health and Human Services, Public Health Service, and Centers for Disease Control, *What You Should Know About Contagious Diseases in the Day Care Setting* (Atlanta, GA: Centers for Disease Control, 1984). Contains a practical and descriptive listing of all major childhood illnesses, how they are spread, and measures for prevention.

N. Wanamaker, K. Hearn, and S. Richarz, *More Than Graham Crackers: Nutrition Education and Food Preparation with Young Children* (Washington, DC: National Association for the Education of Young Children, 1979). Includes nutritious and appealing recipes as well as creative ideas on how children can learn to select and prepare good food.

Learning Environment

J.L. Frost and B.L. Klein, *Children's Play and Playgrounds* (Austin, TX: Playground International, 1979). Describes how to design and build safe playgrounds and includes useful checklists with hundreds of photographs and illustrations.

Jim Greenman, *Caring Spaces, Learning Places: Children's Environments That Work* (Redmond, WA: Exchange Press Inc., 1988). Shows how to create environments that make use of space creatively and with attention to children's developmental needs. Richly illustrated with photographs that show children using indoor and outdoor space.

S. Kritchevsky and E. Prescott, with L. Walling, *Planning Environments for Young Children: Physical Space* (Washington, DC: National Association for the Education of Young Children, 1977). Describes how the organization of space can eliminate problems, such as aimless wandering, or children running into each other, and can have a positive effect on children's behavior.

J. Vergeront, *Place and Spaces for Preschool and Primary Indoors and Outdoors* (Washington, DC: National Association for the Education of Young Children, 1988). These two books include sketches and patterns for creating play structures that are safe and creative.

Physical

Sandra Curtis, *The Joy of Movement in Early Childhood* (New York, NY: Teachers College Press, 1982). Offers a framework for planning programs that will enhance motor development in young children. Includes photographs that show children doing a variety of motor skills and offers activity suggestions that challenge and motivate young children.

G. Engstrom (ed.), *The Significance of the Young Child's Motor Development* (Washington, DC: National Association for the Education of Young Children, 1971). Describes the importance of movement and physical activities for preschoolers and how these can be encouraged in the classroom.

P. Skeen, A.P. Garner, and S. Cartwright, *Woodworking for Young Children* (Washington, DC: National Association for the Education of Young Children, 1984). Discusses how to teach woodworking to young children and includes suggestions for materials and approaches that work best.

Molly Sullivan, *Feeling Strong, Feeling Free: Movement Exploration for Young Children* (Washington, DC: National Association for the Education of Young Children, 1982). A step-by-step approach to planning movement activities for three-to eight-year-olds. Describes the value of movement experiences and how to plan and introduce them to young children.

David Thompson, *Easy Woodstuff for Kids* (Mt. Rainier, MD: Gryphon House, 1981). A woodworking primer that shows how young children can be creative using sticks, branches, and wood leftovers and scraps; includes detailed instructions for each project.

Cognitive

LaBritta Gilbert, *I Can Do It, I Can Do It* (Mt. Rainier, MD: Gryphon House, 1984). Includes 135 successful, independent learning activities with specific instructions and photographs showing children involved in many of the recommended activities.

E. S. Hirsch (ed.), *The Block Book* (Washington, DC: National Association for the Education of Young Children, 1984). An illustrated book that describes how and what children can learn using blocks, including math concepts, science, social studies, self-awareness, and more.

Bess-Gene Holt, *Science with Young Children* (Washington, DC: National Association for the Education of Young Children, 1977). Provides teachers with suggestions on how to set up for science experiences and how to guide children's learning.

C. Emma Linderman, *Teachables from Trashables: Homemade Toys That Teach* (St. Paul, MN: Toys 'n Things Press, 1983). Illustrated construction directions for turning "junk" materials into educational and engaging toys.

Karen Miller, *The Outside Play and Learning Book* (Mt. Rainier, MD: Gryphon House, 1989). A comprehensive and creative collection of outdoor activities that include many suggestions for making good use of the outdoor environment in all seasons.

Eugene F. Provenzo, Jr., and Arlene Brett, *The Complete Block Book* (Syracuse, NY: Syracuse University Press, 1983). A beautifully illustrated book with many photographs of children using blocks in various ways. Combines the history of blocks, theory, and their practical use in the classroom.

Rhoda Redleaf, *Teachables II: Homemade Toys That Teach* (St. Paul, MN: Toys 'n Things Press, 1987). Over 75 educational toys to make from common "junk" materials; includes descriptions of the skills children learn while playing with the toys.

Robert E. Rockwell, Elizabeth A. Sherwood, and Robert A. Williams, *Hug a Tree* (Mt. Rainier, MD: Gryphon House, 1983). Each outdoor learning experience has a suggested age level, a clear description of what will be done, and suggestions for follow-up learning.

Barbara Sprung, Merle Frosch, and Patricia B. Campbell, *What Will Happen If...Young Children and the Scientific Method* (New York, NY: Educational Equity Concepts, 1985). A guide to help teachers integrate science and math into the curriculum through developmentally appropriate activities.

Robert A. Williams, Robert E. Rockwell, and Elizabeth A. Sherwood, *Mudpies to Magnets: A Preschool Science Curriculum* and *More Mudpies to Magnets* (Mt. Rainier, MD: Gryphon House, 1987 and 1990). Each book describes numerous hands-on science experiments for young children, including clear directions and materials needed.

Communication

Linda Gibson, *Literacy Learning in the Early Years* (New York: Teachers College Press, 1989). This author is a teacher-researcher who combines a theoretical perspective with examples from observations of teachers and children. Learning to read and write is viewed as an ongoing process that begins in infancy. The book's four parts are organized according to age level.

M. R. Jalongo, *Young Children and Picture Books: Literature from Infancy to Six* (Washington, DC: National Association for the Education of Young Children, 1988). An excellent book for teachers on what constitutes high-quality literature and art for young children and how children benefit from good books.

Shirley C. Raines and Robert J. Canady, *Story S-t-r-e-t-c-h-e-r-s: Activities to Expand Children's Favorite Books* and *More Story S-t-r-e-t-c-h-e-r-s* (Mt. Rainier, MD: Gryphon House, 1989 and 1991). Filled with activities teachers and parents can use to extend children's enjoyment of their favorite books. Five active learning experiences are described for each of the 90 books.

Judith A. Schickedanz, *More Than the ABCs: The Early Stages of Reading and Writing* (Washington, DC: National Association for the Education of Young Children, 1986). A practical book filled with ideas for organizing the environment so that children experience reading and writing as a meaningful part of their lives.

Dorothy S. Strickland and Lesley Mandel Morrow (eds.), *Emerging Literacy* (Newark, DE: International Reading Association, 1989). The 12 chapters in this book are each authored by a different expert on children's literacy development. Literacy is presented as an emerging process that begins when parents and teachers expose infants to oral and written language and continues throughout the toddler and early childhood years.

Creative

Bev Bos, *Before the Basics: Creating Conversations with Young Children* (Roseville, CA: Turn-the-Page Press, 1984). A practical guide for teachers and caregivers on ways to use music and language to enhance creativity and promote children's self-esteem.

Bev Bos, *Please Don't Move the Muffin Tins: A Hands-Off Guide to Art for the Young Child* (Roseville, CA: Turn-the-Page Press, 1984). A wonderful collection of developmentally appropriate art experiences for young children.

Deya Brashears, *Dribble-Drabble Art Experiences for Young Children* (Fort Collins, CO: DMC Publications, 1985). Contains art activities and recipes appropriate for children from age two through preschool and early elementary school.

D. M. Hill, *Mud, Sand and Water* (Washington, DC: National Association for the Education of Young Children, 1977). Describes the value of these natural materials and how they stimulate creativity and learning.

Mary Ann Kohl, *Mudworks, Creative Clay, Dough, and Modeling Experiences* (Bellingham, WA: Bright Ring Publishing, 1989). Over 100 open-ended ways to engage children in modeling experiences; includes clearly written recipes in a format that gives appropriate guidance to adults.

L. Lasky and R. Mukerji, *Art: Basic for Young Children* (Washington, DC: National Association for the Education of Young Children, 1980). A practical, easy-to-read book describing the wonders of art and why it is so valuable for young children.

D. T. McDonald, *Music in Our Lives: The Early Years* (Washington, DC: National Association for the Education of Young Children, 1979). Shows adults how they can plan exciting music activities for young children even if they are not musical themselves.

Mary Salkever, *The Shake, Pluck, Bang Book* (Baltimore, MD: Maryland Committee for Children, 1986). Contains 18 different musical instruments to make with young children. Includes materials needed, directions, and illustrations.

Self and Social

Don Adcock and Marilyn Segal, *Play Together, Grow Together: A Cooperative Curriculum for Teachers of Young Children* (White Plains, NY: The Mailman Press, 1983). Sixty-seven activities that focus on the development of social skills such as sharing, cooperating, playing in a group, and making friends.

Jan Bandich, *Get Ready for Dramatic Play* (Cypress, CA: Creative Teaching Press, 1988). With a minimum number of props and maximum encouragement from teachers, children can project themselves into a variety of roles. Contains 24 kit ideas to assemble for role playing indoors and outdoors.

Nancy Balaban, *Starting School: From Separation to Independence* (New York: Teacher's College Press, 1985). Explains how young children experience separation and provides practical suggestions for supporting children in the child care setting.

Dorothy Corkille Briggs, *Your Child's Self-Esteem* (Garden City, NY: Dolphin Books, 1975). Focuses on the importance of self-image, how it develops, and how adults can support children's self-esteem.

Harris Clemens and Reynold Bean, *How to Raise Children's Self-Esteem* (Los Angeles, CA: Price/Stern Sloan, 1986). A practical description of self-esteem; why it is important; why children act the way they do; and how parents and teachers can help children to develop a positive sense of self.

J. B. McCracken (ed.), *Reducing Stress in Young Children* (Washington, DC: National Association for the Education of Young Children, 1986). Contains a series of articles from *Young Children* covering the major issues that today's young children face in growing up. Provides adults with useful ways to help children cope successfully with stress while reducing stress in the classroom environment.

Bonnie Neugebauer (ed.), *Alike and Different: Exploring Our Humanity with Young Children* (Redmond, WA: Exchange Press, 1987). Each of the five chapters contains a series of articles on different aspects of children's self-image: bringing the world into your curricula; meeting the needs of all children; providing a diverse staff; learning from parents; and living in a changing world.

J. K. Sawyers and C. S. Rogers, *Helping Young Children Develop Through Play: A Practical Guide for Parents, Caregivers, and Teachers* (Washington, DC: National Association for the Education of Young Children, 1988). Overview of the role of play that is easy to read, with practical suggestions on how to foster play in preschool children.

Rita Warren, *Caring, Supporting Children's Growth* (Washington, DC: National Association for the Education of Young Children, 1977). Provides suggestions for teachers and parents on how to help young children cope with the many challenges in social development, such as death, child abuse, divorce, and so on.

Dennie Palmer Wolf (ed.), *Connecting: Friendship in the Lives of Young Children and Their Teachers* (Redmond, WA: Exchange Press, 1986). A collection of articles that address the many aspects of children's social development and friendships. Offers teachers practical ideas on how to facilitate relationships for both children and adults in the early childhood classroom.

Marilyn Segal and Don Adcock, *Your Child at Play: Three to Five Years* (New York: Newmarket Press, 1985). Presents detailed information on how children use their play to make sense of the world, express creativity, and establish friendships.

Guidance

Clare Cherry, *Parents, Please Don't Sit on the Kids* (Belmont, CA: David S. Lake Publishers, 1985). Contains many practical suggestions for guiding children's behavior, explaining techniques that work with young children and those that don't.

Grace Mitchell, *A Very Practical Guide to Discipline with Young Children* (Marshfield, MA: Telshare Publishing Co., 1982). Describes an approach for guiding children's behavior that leads to the goal of self-discipline.

Jeannette Galambos Stone, *A Guide to Discipline* (Washington, DC: National Association for the Education of Young Children, 1978). Addresses questions teachers and caregivers often ask about discipline in the classroom. Explains how adults can guide children's behavior by avoiding potential problems in advance through words and manner.

Families

E. H. Berger, *Parents As Partners in Education: The School and Home Working Together* (St. Louis, IL: The C. V. Mosby Co., 1981). A hands-on approach for preschool teachers and parents to develop a partnership that enables them to work together.

Ellen Galinsky, *Between Generations: The Six Stages of Parenthood* (New York: Times Books, 1981). Outlines the predictable stages that parents go through in raising their children and shows how parents change and grow as their children develop.

Jeannette Galambos Stone, *Teacher-Parent Relationships* (Washington, DC: National Association for the Education of Young Children, 1987). Describes how parents and teachers can develop mutual respect and work together in support of young children's development.

Alice S. Honig, *Parent Involvement in Early Childhood Education* (Washington, DC: National Association for the Education of Young Children, 1984). Gives some good ideas of ways to involve parents meaningfully in early childhood programs.

J. B. McCracken, *So Many Goodbyes: Ways to Ease the Transition Between Home and Groups for Young Children* (Washington, DC: National Association for the Education of Young Children, 1986). How teachers and parents can work together to ease children's adjustment to preschool programs.

Program Management, Advocacy and Professionalism

Childcare Employee Project, *Working for Quality Child Care* (P.O. Box 5603, Berkeley, CA, 94705). A guide for early childhood educators on how to become effective advocates for improving quality, salaries, and working conditions in early childhood programs.

Sydney G. Clemens, *The Sun's Not Broken, A Cloud's Just in the Way* (Mt. Rainier, MD: Gryphon House, 1986). A teacher's personal account of how to create a learning environment for young children.

Stephanie Feeney and Lynda Sysko, "Professional Ethics in Early Childhood Education: Survey Results," *Young Children* (Washington, DC: National Association for the Education of Young Children, 1986), pp.15-20. Discusses the ethical issues facing early childhood professionals today as identified by a survey conducted by NAEYC.

Stacie G. Goffin and Joan Lombardi, *Speaking Out: Early Childhood Advocacy* (Washington, DC: National Association for the Education of Young Children, 1988). Helps demystify advocacy by providing practical ideas and examples of how to influence policies for young children, families, and the early childhood profession.

Joanne Hendrick, *Why Teach?* (Washington, DC: National Association for the Education of Young Children, 1987). Provides a realistic picture of the rewards and challenges of being an early childhood teacher. Photographs of children with teachers reinforce the content.

James L. Hymes, *Year in Review* (Washington, DC: National Association for the Education of Young Children, yearly). NAEYC publishes Dr. Hymes' annual summaries of the issues and highlights in the early childhood field.

Self-Assessment

SKILL	I DO THIS REGULARLY	I DO THIS SOMETIMES	I DON'T DO THIS ENOUGH
1. SAFE			
a. Providing safe indoor and outdoor environments.			
b. Responding to accidents and emergencies.			
c. Helping children develop safe habits.			
2. HEALTHY			
a. Providing healthy indoor and outdoor environments.			
b. Helping children develop good health habits.			
c. Recognizing and reporting child abuse and neglect.			
3. LEARNING ENVIRONMENT			
a. Organizing indoor and outdoor areas that encourage play and exploration.			
b. Selecting and arranging appropriate materials and equipment that foster growth and learning.			
c. Planning and implementing a schedule and routines appropriate to the ages of the children.			

SKILL	I DO THIS REGULARLY	I DO THIS SOMETIMES	I DON'T DO THIS ENOUGH
4. PHYSICAL			
a. Reinforcing and encouraging physical development.			
b. Providing equipment and activities for gross motor development.			
c. Providing equipment and activities for fine motor development.			
5. COGNITIVE			
a. Providing opportunities for children to use all their senses to explore their environment.			
b. Interacting with children in ways that help them develop confidence and curiosity.			
c. Providing opportunities for children to develop new concepts and skills.			
6. COMMUNICATION			
a. Interacting with children in ways that encourage them to communicate their thoughts and feelings.			
b. Providing materials and activities that promote communication skills.			
c. Helping children develop listening and speaking skills.			

SKILL	I DO THIS REGULARLY	I DO THIS SOMETIMES	I DON'T DO THIS ENOUGH
7. CREATIVE			
a. Arranging the learning environment to support children's creative development.			
b. Providing a variety of activities and experiences to promote creative development.			
c. Interacting with children in ways that encourage creative expression.			
8. SELF			
a. Developing a positive and supportive relationship with each child.			
b. Helping children accept and appreciate themselves and others.			
c. Providing children with opportunities to feel successful and competent.			
9. SOCIAL			
a. Helping children learn to get along with other members of the group.			
b. Helping children understand and express their feelings and respect those of others.			
c. Providing an environment and experiences that help children develop social skills.			

SKILL	I DO THIS REGULARLY	I DO THIS SOMETIMES	I DON'T DO THIS ENOUGH
10. GUIDANCE a. Providing an environment that encourages children's self-discipline.			
b. Using positive methods to guide individual children.			
c. Helping children understand and express their feelings in acceptable ways.			
11. FAMILIES a. Communicating with family members often to exchange information about the child at home and at the center.			
b. Providing a variety of ways for family members to participate in the child's life at the center.			
c. Providing support to families.			
12. PROGRAM MANAGEMENT a. Observing and recording information about each child's growth and development.			
b. Working as a member of a team to plan an individualized program.			
c. Following administrative policies.			

SKILL	I DO THIS REGULARLY	I DO THIS SOMETIMES	I DON'T DO THIS ENOUGH
13. PROFESSIONALISM a. Continually assessing one's own performance.			
b. Continuing to learn about caring for children.			
c. Applying professional ethics at all times.			

Module Completion Plan

Review your responses to the self-assessment with your trainer. What do you feel are your strengths, interests, and needs? Decide which areas you would like to work on first. Select three modules to begin with and set target dates for their completion. (Your trainer can let you know how much work is involved for each module.) Record the module titles and target completion dates below. You may also wish to determine a tentative schedule for completing *Caring for Preschool Children*.

	Module	**Target Completion Date**
1.	_____	_____
2.	_____	_____
3.	_____	_____

Tentative schedule for completion of the *Caring for Preschool Children* Training Program:

Module	**Date**
_____	_____
_____	_____
_____	_____
_____	_____
_____	_____
_____	_____
_____	_____
_____	_____
_____	_____
_____	_____
_____	_____
_____	_____

Teacher	Date	Trainer	Date

Module 1
Safe

What Is Safety and Why Is It Important?

Safety is freedom from danger, and danger is minimized by reducing hazards. You feel safe when you know that:

- no great harm will come to you;

- you can do something to prevent dangerous situations; and

- those around you share your concern for safety and act in a cautious way.

Adults feel safe when they are in control of situations. They are in control when they prevent accidents and injuries and when they know what to do if accidents and injuries occur.

Children begin to learn about safety from the time they are infants. They learn to trust their parents and other important adults. This lets children know that they are safe and that no harm will come to them. Children also learn that the important adults in their lives know what to do when accidents occur. Eventually, children learn that they can take part in controlling their world, that they can explore their world in a safe way, and that they can stay free from danger.

As a teacher, you play an important role in keeping children safe. Young children are often unaware of and unable to avoid the possible dangers in their environment. Therefore, you set up a room that is free from or reduces these dangers. Your room is designed so active preschoolers can explore and take risks. You also handle emergencies in a calm way. Through your actions, you help children develop attitudes about safety and learn how to keep themselves safe.

Keeping children safe involves:

- providing safe indoor and outdoor environments;

- responding to accidents and emergencies; and

- helping children develop safe habits.

Listed below are examples of how teachers demonstrate their competence in keeping children safe.

Providing Safe Indoor and Outdoor Environments

Here are some examples of what teachers can do.

- Check indoor and outdoor areas for debris, poisonous materials, sharp objects, and any other dangerous objects. Remove any they find.

- Check the room daily to be sure all electrical outlets are covered.

- Check materials and equipment daily for broken parts or jagged edges and make sure they are repaired or replaced.

- Arrange the room to allow for clear fire exits.

- Supervise children at all times.

- Respond quickly to children in distress.

- Take safety precautions in a calm and reassuring manner without overprotecting children or making them fearful.

Responding to Accidents and Emergencies

Here are some examples of what teachers can do.

- Help develop and post accident and emergency procedures.

- Know and follow established emergency procedures.

- Know where to find parents' emergency telephone numbers.

- Follow established procedures for conducting children to safety during fire and other hazard drills and in real emergencies, should they occur.

Helping Children Develop Safe Habits

Here are some examples of what teachers can do.

- Convey to children in actions and words that the center is a safe place and that they will be protected. "Johnny, I'll stand next to the slide if that will help you feel better about going down."

- Use diagrams, pictures, and words understood by children as reminders of safety rules and emergency procedures. "Susan, please walk in the room. If you run inside you might get hurt."

- Model taking risks. "I'm cutting with a sharp knife, so I make sure my other hand is away from the blade."

- Teach children how to observe safety rules on neighborhood walks and field trips. "Let's make sure everyone has a partner and knows which group they are in for our trip."

- Use positive guidance techniques to keep children safe. "That hurts Teresa when you drive your trike into the back of her ankles. Ask her to please move off the path and onto the grass."

- Remind children of safety rules. "Hold your funnel over the water table so the water doesn't spill on the floor. When the floor is wet, someone might slip and fall."

Keeping Children Safe

In the following situations, teachers are ensuring children's safety. As you read each one, think about what the teachers are doing and why. Then answer the questions that follow.

Providing Safe Indoor and Outdoor Environments

Ms. Kim notices three-year-old Jill across the room climbing on a box where balls are kept. It is sagging with her weight. "Ms. Richards," Ms. Kim says, alerting the teacher on that side of the room. Quickly, Ms. Richards moves to Jill's side. "Jill," she says in a calm voice, "I'm going to help you climb down off that box. It isn't a safe place for climbing, because it isn't strong enough to hold you." Jill looks startled as she finds her feet on the ground. "You know what?" Ms. Richards asks. "I am going to put this box in the closet so children won't climb on it. Do you want to help me?" As they carry the box, Ellen comes to help. "Thank you for helping make our room safer," says Ms. Richards. "Now, would you like to climb on the climber? It's a good place for climbing."

1. How did Ms. Kim and Ms. Richards work together to make the center a safe place?

_____

_____

_____

2. What do you think Jill learned from this experience?

_____

_____

_____

Responding to Accidents and Emergencies

The fire drill is over. Mr. Lopez and his group of four-year-olds are coming back into the building when Andy trips and scrapes his knee. "You scraped your knee a little," explains Mr. Lopez as he helps Andy to his feet. When they get back to the room, Mr. Lopez takes Andy to the office while the other teachers take care of the children. They get the first-aid kit off the shelf. A chart telling how to treat minor injuries is taped to the inside lid of the kit, where Mr. Lopez can easily find it. He reviews it quickly, then washes off Andy's knee with soap and water. Andy winces. "You're being brave," says Mr. Lopez. "I know this stings a bit, but your knee needs to be clean to get better." At Andy's request, he puts a bandage on the scrape. Andy helps stick it in place. Finally, Mr. Lopez takes Andy back to the room. "You're all set," he says. He fills out an accident report form and writes a note on the daily chart so at the end of the day he will remember to tell Andy's parents to read and sign the accident report.

1. **What resources did Mr. Lopez have available to help him know what to do?**

_____

_____

_____

2. **What did Mr. Lopez do after taking care of Andy's injury?**

_____

_____

_____

Helping Children Develop Safe Habits

Five-year-old Kirsten has recently learned to balance the unit blocks as she builds with them. Today she builds a structure as high as her head. "I want to build my house bigger than I am," she says to the other children in the block area. She continues to stack the blocks. Ms. Williams hears Kirsten's announcement and walks to the block area. "No one here has built a building taller than she is, yet, Kirsten. Let's talk about how to do that safely," she says. She sits with Kirsten and the other children who are in the block area, and they discuss how to build things high in a safe way. They also decide that they need to write a "Safety in the Block Area" chart, with pictures and words, so all will know the guidelines. Kirsten says, "Let's talk about what we put on our safety chart at circle time today."

1. **How did Ms. Williams let the children know that the center is a safe place?**

_____

_____

_____

2. **How were the children learning to keep themselves safe?**

_____

_____

_____

Compare your answers with those on the answer sheet at the end of this module. If your answers are different, discuss them with your trainer. There can be more than one good answer.

Your Own Need for Safety

Safety is a basic need we all share. We particularly want to feel safe in our own environments —where we live and work. When we know that we are protected from harm, we can function. When we do not feel protected, we are fearful and anxious.

When you are in charge of your environment, you can make it a safe one. You probably have experienced times when you were doing something that was potentially dangerous, and you did things to make that activity safer. Do you remember times when you:

- climbed a ladder while someone held it to keep it stable;
- drove a car slowly on a slippery road; or
- carefully unplugged a lamp with a frayed cord and had the wiring replaced?

You have learned about safety through experience. When you were an infant and toddler, the important adults in your life controlled your environment to keep it safe. They helped you develop an attitude and habits concerning safety. As you grew older, they helped you learn what you could do to minimize dangerous situations.

Think of a situation where you didn't feel safe and describe it below.

_____

_____

_____

What did you want to happen?

_____

_____

_____

What can you learn from this experience that will help you keep young children safe?

_____

_____

_____

As you work through this module you will learn how to set up and maintain a safe environment. Safety is important in all areas of child development—whether you are guiding children's learning, building their self-esteem, or promoting their self-discipline. Keeping children safe is one of your most important responsibilities.

When you have finished this overview section, you should complete the pre-training assessment. Refer to the glossary at the end of this module if you need definitions of the terms that are used.

Pre-Training Assessment

Listed below are the skills that teachers use to make sure children are safe. Think about whether you do these things regularly, sometimes, or not enough. Place a check in one of the columns on the right for each skill listed. Then discuss your answers with your trainer.

SKILL	I DO THIS REGULARLY	I DO THIS SOMETIMES	I DON'T DO THIS ENOUGH
PROVIDING SAFE INDOOR AND OUTDOOR ENVIRONMENTS 1. Supervising children at all times.			
2. Checking indoor and outdoor areas daily for safety hazards.			
3. Conducting monthly safety checks to discover if any equipment or toys need to be repaired.			
4. Organizing indoor and outdoor areas so children can move freely without bumping into anything.			
5. Arranging the room to allow for clear exits.			
RESPONDING TO ACCIDENTS AND EMERGENCIES 6. Responding quickly to children in distress.			
7. Taking safety precautions in a reassuring way, without over-protecting or scaring the children.			
8. Helping develop and post accident and emergency procedures.			

SKILL	I DO THIS REGULARLY	I DO THIS SOMETIMES	I DON'T DO THIS ENOUGH
9. Knowing location of first-aid supplies and following accident and emergency procedures.			
10. Knowing where to find parents' emergency telephone numbers.			
HELPING CHILDREN DEVELOP SAFE HABITS 11. Establishing rules for safe field trips and teaching them to children.			
12. Following a daily schedule that includes times for active and quiet play.			
13. Showing children, by words and actions, that the center is a safe place.			
14. Using diagrams, pictures, and words to remind children of safety rules and emergency procedures.			
15. Showing children how to be careful while taking risks.			

Review your responses, then list three to five skills you would like to improve or topics you would like to learn more about. When you finish this module, you will list examples of your new or improved knowledge and skills.

_____

_____

_____

_____

Now begin the learning activities for Module 1, Safe.

I. Using Your Knowledge of Child Development to Keep Children Safe

In this activity you will learn:

- to recognize some typical behaviors of preschool children; and

- to use what you know about children to keep them safe.

Preschool children like to be busy and active most of the time. They also like quiet times when they can get away and be by themselves. By understanding what to expect from preschool children, you can ensure that the environment is safe and that children are free from harm.

You expect preschoolers to run, climb, jump, and hop whenever they have a chance to do so. Sometimes they will perform these actions on a dare: "Who can jump farthest...run fastest...climb highest?" To allow them to do these things safely, your indoor and outdoor play areas must be set up for active play. Your schedule must provide times and places for active play to occur. Dangerous obstacles must be removed from both indoor and outdoor areas. And active play must be continually supervised to prevent accidents.

Preschool children are curious. They like to take things apart and put them back together. The objects in your room must be selected with safety in mind. Toys and other items should be well-constructed and durable enough to withstand children's play and explorations.

Preschool children often like to play by themselves. A child may sit alone, exploring and experimenting with a toy. Children need to know the rules for exploring ("Little pieces stay in our hands, not our mouths," for example). Children's quiet play, like their active play, must be supervised at all times.

Learning what preschool children are like at this stage of development can help you set up a safe room. It can also help you anticipate play that might be unsafe.

The chart on the next page identifies some typical behaviors of preschool children. Included are behaviors relevant to safety. The right column asks you to identify ways that teachers can use this information about child development to keep children safe. Try to think of as many examples as you can. As you work through the module you will learn new strategies for keeping children safe, and you can add them to the child development chart. You are not expected to think of all the examples at one time. If you need help getting started, turn to the completed chart at the end of the module. By the time you complete all the learning activities, you will find that you have learned many ways to keep children safe.

Using Your Knowledge of Child Development to Keep Children Safe

WHAT PRESCHOOL CHILDREN ARE LIKE	HOW TEACHERS CAN USE THIS INFORMATION TO KEEP CHILDREN SAFE
They have lots of energy and like to run around.	
They hop and jump over objects.	
They ride tricycles and other moving equipment.	
They slide, swing, and climb on equipment.	

WHAT PRESCHOOL CHILDREN ARE LIKE	HOW TEACHERS CAN USE THIS INFORMATION TO KEEP CHILDREN SAFE
They throw, kick, and catch objects.	
They build block towers.	
They use hammers, saws, and other woodworking equipment.	
They show their curiosity by manipulating, poking, handling, or squeezing everything.	

WHAT PRESCHOOL CHILDREN ARE LIKE	HOW TEACHERS CAN USE THIS INFORMATION TO KEEP CHILDREN SAFE
They can cut with scissors and knives.	
They use the toilet independently.	
They share toys and take turns with some assistance.	
They begin to understand cause and effect.	

When you have completed as much as you can do on the chart, discuss your answers with your trainer. As you proceed with the rest of the learning activities, you can refer back to the chart and add more examples of how teachers keep children safe.

II. Creating a Safe Environment for Children

In this activity you will learn:

- to choose safe toys and equipment; and

- to set up a safe learning environment for preschool children.

One of the major ways you can keep children safe is by creating a safe environment. Your choice of toys, materials, and equipment and the way you arrange your space can prevent dangerous situations from occurring. In a safe room you can focus on what the children are doing, confident that electrical outlets are childproof and that toys and equipment are sturdy and in good repair.

Preschoolers are capable of many physical feats. Most preschoolers walk, run, jump, and climb. In setting up a safe environment, remember that the children are rapidly developing new skills. You must be prepared for the unexpected. Because children don't always think ahead and see the consequences of their actions, you must do it for them as you set up your space.

Here are some general rules to follow in setting up a safe preschool environment.

- Set up activity areas using low dividers so that you can easily see all children at all times.

- Store dangerous substances, such as cleansers and medicines, in a locked cabinet out of children's reach.

- Keep electrical cords out of children's reach and make sure electrical outlets are childproof.

- Know where the fire extinguishers are located and how to use them.

- Inspect equipment and toys regularly for splinters, rough edges, broken safety straps, and chipped paint, and see that repairs are made.

- Secure furniture that could fall or be pulled over, or remove it from the room.

- Use low, open shelves for storage. Do not store toys in chests with heavy lids that can fall on children.

- Arrange toys on shelves so that the heaviest toys are on the bottom shelves. That way, children won't pull heavy things down on themselves.

- Include in your written plans a schedule of when each teacher will supervise a particular activity or area.

- Set up the room for easy exiting in case of fire or other emergencies.

- Examine toys and equipment regularly to make sure they are:

    - in good repair
    - nonflammable
    - nontoxic
    - free of sharp edges, points, and splinters
    - nonbreakable
    - free of lead paint
    - hypo-allergenic
    - free of small movable parts that might be swallowed.

- Plan ways to control spills from water and sand play. Use newspapers, drop cloths, or towels, and limit the number of children using the area at one time.

Knowing what preschool children are like and being able to anticipate dangerous situations will help you set up a safe environment. In this learning activity you will observe a child for five minutes and try to identify hazards in your environment. Take notes on all the things the child does—index cards are handy for this. Then use your observation notes to answer the questions that follow. Begin by reviewing the example on the next page.

Identifying Dangers and Creating a Safe Environment
(Example)

Child: _____Bernard_____ **Age**: ___4 years___ **Date**: _April 12_____

Setting: __Table Toys_____

What is the child doing?

Bernard is stacking table toys. He's rough with the toys, banging one on top of another—Ring-a-Majigs, plastic cars, bingo chips, plastic chain links, and others.

What dangers exist in the environment?

Thin brittle plastic could break or chip, leaving sharp edges. He may injure himself or another child.

What can you do to make the environment safer for this child?

Because Bernard and other children are rough with toys, I can make sure the plastic toys we use are flexible and well-made. I can also teach them how to use the materials more carefully.

Identifying Dangers and Creating a Safe Environment

Child: _____   **Age:** _____   **Date:** _____

Setting: _____

What is the child doing?

_____

_____

_____

_____

What dangers exist in the environment?

_____

_____

_____

_____

What can you do to make the environment safer for this child?

_____

_____

_____

_____

_____

_____

Discuss your answers with another teacher in your room. Then examine all the materials in your room and use the form on the next page to list possible dangers and changes to be made.

UNSAFE MATERIALS	CHANGES TO BE MADE

Discuss your ideas with your trainer and make the changes you identified.

III. Maintaining a Safe Environment

In this activity you will learn:

- to recognize how your daily actions help make your environment safe for children; and

- to use a safety checklist to keep your room and outdoor play area safe.

Now that you have identified ways to make your environment safe, the next step is to keep it that way. Maintaining a safe environment is up to you and the other teachers in your room.

Preschool children often act before thinking about what might happen. They may run without seeing everything in their paths. They may climb without testing the sturdiness of the "mountain" they are climbing. They may grab and handle objects without looking for jagged edges and splinters. They may lose patience with poorly working toys and handle them roughly.

As teachers work regularly with preschool children, they become aware that preschoolers can't always tell what is safe and what is dangerous. The children rely on your good judgment to protect them. One way to protect them is to set up hazard-free indoor and outdoor play areas by carefully arranging the furniture and equipment. Another way is to anticipate children's actions and prevent accidents from happening.

A safety checklist is a good tool for identifying hazards. Using such a checklist can help you maintain a safe environment. Because children use the indoor and outdoor materials and equipment continuously as they play, wear and tear may cause a once-safe space to become dangerous. Scheduling times to routinely check your areas is important. Some areas must be checked daily for unlocked cabinets, broken glass, broken toys, and wet spots. Some things should be checked monthly: blocks in need of sanding, table screws in need of tightening, or hinges and bolts that should be replaced.

In this learning activity you will assess the safety of your indoor and outdoor spaces using the two safety checklists that follow this page. Then you will identify items that need your attention and what precautions you can take to improve the safety of your indoor and outdoor areas.

Indoor Safety Checklist

SAFETY CONDITIONS	SATISFACTORY OR NOT APPLICABLE	NEEDS ATTENTION
CHECK DAILY		
1. The lesson plan allows for supervision of children at all times.		
2. Electrical outlets are childproof.		
3. Cleaning materials and other poisons are stored only in locked cabinets or out of the room.		
4. Furniture has no sharp edges or corners at children's eye level.		
5. Inclines are clearly marker.		
6. Steps and platforms are padded and have protective railings.		
7. Pillows, mattresses, or mats are below high places where children might climb.		
8. Teachers' scissors, knives, and other sharp objects are out of children's reach.		
9. The room contains no highly flammable furnishings or decorations.		
10. Children have enough space to play in each area.		
11. Timers, signs, and other items that help children play safely are in their appropriate places.		
12. Floors are dry.		

Indoor Safety Checklist (Continued)

SAFETY CONDITIONS	SATISFACTORY OR NOT APPLICABLE	NEEDS ATTENTION
13. Children are supervised at all times; required child-adult ratios are maintained; teachers interact with children rather than congregating with each other.		
CHECK MONTHLY		
14. Blocks are smooth and splinter-free.		
15. Toys' moving parts (wheels, knobs) are securely fastened and working properly.		
16. Children's scissors and food preparation knives are sharp enough for children to use them easily.		
17. Hinges, screws, and bolts on furniture and equipment are securely fastened.		
18. Electrical wires are not frayed.		
19. Radiators and hot water pipes are covered or insulated.		
20. Smoke detectors and fire extinguishers are working properly.		
21. The fire exit plan is posted.		
22. A fire drill is held every month.		

Outdoor Safety Checklist

SAFETY CONDITIONS	SATISFACTORY OR NOT APPLICABLE	NEEDS ATTENTION
CHECK DAILY		
1. The area is securely fenced, and gate latches are locked and may be opened only by adults.		
2. Play equipment surfaces are smooth and splinter-free.		
3. There is enough cushioning material under climbers, slides, and swings.		
4. No objects or obstructions are under or around equipment where children might fall.		
5. There are no frayed cables, no worn ropes, and no chains that could pinch.		
6. No broken glass or debris is present.		
7. Stay-clear zones around swings and slides are marked. Teachers are there to remind children what the marks mean.		
8. Riding paths are clearly marked, gently curved, and separate from large group areas.		
CHECK MONTHLY		
9. Screws, nuts, and bolts on climbing and other equipment are securely fastened and recessed.		
10. Tricycles and other riding toys are in good repair (screws tightened, etc.)		

Review the items on each of the checklists that you feel need attention and list them below. Then identify what steps you can take to improve the safety of your environment.

ITEMS NEEDING ATTENTION	STEPS TO IMPROVE THE SAFETY OF THE ENVIRONMENT	DATE COMPLETED

Discuss what steps you noted with your trainer. Make these changes in your room and check them off when they have been completed. Schedule times for daily and monthly safety checks throughout the year.

IV. Knowing and Following Emergency Procedures

In this activity you will learn:

- to be prepared for accidents and other emergencies; and

- to follow the center's established procedures for dealing with emergency situations.

Emergencies often happen at the worst possible moments, so the time to get ready for emergencies is before they happen. As the person responsible for the safety of the children in your care, you must know your center's emergency policies and procedures. You must also follow the procedures in a calm and clearheaded way. The greater your awareness of the procedures, the more quickly and effectively you can act when an emergency occurs.

Although you work hard to make your environment safe, some emergencies are caused by events outside your control. Fires, floods, tornadoes, and other catastrophes may happen with little or no warning. If you know what to do when they happen, you can act swiftly. Participating in emergency drills helps everyone to be ready. You should also post the emergency procedures so all adults can assist you in getting the children to safety.

Preschool children are very active, and because of this they sometimes have accidents. In these situations you must quickly assess how serious an injury is and respond correctly. Most injuries require only soothing words and perhaps bandages. Others require first aid at the center and perhaps taking children to the hospital.

Parents must be told about their children's injuries. For minor injuries (cuts and bruises), teachers can inform parents when they pick up their children at the end of the day. For more serious accidents, the parents should be contacted immediately.

The teacher's role in emergencies is important. You must know the proper procedures. You must remain calm. You must notify your supervisor that an accident has occurred and inform the child's parents, if necessary. And you must document, on the appropriate form, what has happened.

In this learning activity you will read "Emergencies and First Aid." Then you will review the established procedures at your center for evacuating children and staff in case of fire or other emergencies. Also review your center's accident procedures. Then answer the questions on emergency procedures that follow.

Emergencies and First Aid[1]

A child falls from the climber on your playground. You suddenly lose your electrical power during a winter storm. You smell gas in the kitchen. A child starts to choke during snack time. Would you know what to do?

No matter how careful and safety-conscious you are, there will be times when emergencies occur. If your center has a comprehensive, written emergency policy, you will be better prepared to handle such situations. Your center's policy needs to answer questions such as
- Who will give first aid?
- Who will take the attendance list if the building needs to be evacuated?
- What will you do if some of the children panic?

Your policy should clearly state the roles and responsibilities of the children and each staff member in an emergency. Parents, too, need to be informed of your emergency policy and their roles in it.

Preparing for emergencies

In the event of an emergency in your program, remember these three important things:
- **KEEP CALM**—if you panic, the children are likely to panic, too.
- **FOLLOW YOUR EMERGENCY PROCEDURES**
- **ACT QUICKLY**

Figure 8-1 outlines emergency procedures you can adapt to fit your program, based on its size, location, and children's ages. This and all other figures referred to in this chapter are located at the end of the chapter.

In addition to specifying emergency procedures, you should also take these steps to prepare for potential emergencies.
- **Train staff in first aid and CPR.** Make sure staff receive training and certification in first aid and

CPR and renew this certification annually. Require that at least one certified staff person be in attendance at all times.
- **Maintain a first-aid kit.** Figure 8-2 lists the contents for first-aid kits. Pack your kit in any lightweight, convenient container (a lunch box, hand-

Nancy P. Alexander

Develop a standardized form for reporting all injuries or illnesses that require first aid or additional care.

---

[1]Reproduced with permission from Abby Shapiro Kendrick, Roxane Kaufmann, and Katherine P. Messenger, editors, *Healthy Young Children, A Manual for Programs* (Washington, DC: NAEYC, 1988), pp. 93-105.

bag, or shopping bag). Keep **at least one** first-aid kit available at all times including neighborhood walks and trips. Locate it near high-risk areas such as the kitchen or playground. Have another kit available for field trips or walks. Store your first-aid kit **out of the reach of children** but easily accessible in case of an emergency. Make sure that someone on the staff inspects the kit each month and replaces supplies. Keep a list of contents for the kit, as well as a record of the monthly inspections.

- **Keep information where you need it.** Place a list of emergency phone numbers (Figure 8-5) and a copy of your emergency procedures near each phone for quick reference. Keep an extra list with you on field trips.
- **HAVE IMPORTANT FORMS AVAILABLE**

Parental permission forms—Hospitals and emergency rooms will not give emergency treatment to any minor child, except in a life-threatening situation, without parental informed consent at the time of treatment. Ask parents to complete emergency transportation permission forms (Figure 8-3) before enrollment, and keep these on file. Take a copy of all permission forms with you on field trips.

Injury report forms—Your program should develop a standardized form for reporting all injuries or illnesses that require first aid or additional care (Figure 8-4 presents a sample). Give one copy of the report to the child's parents and keep another copy in the child's folder. Find out which incidents or injuries must be reported to state or local authorities. Maintain a master listing or injury log so that patterns of injury or other incidents can be monitored and safety in your program improved.

Getting help

Most of us assume that we can use a telephone to call for help. Usually we can, but it is important to think about alternatives in case a telephone is not available. Know the locations of nearby pay phones, fire alarm boxes, or places you could go for help. Make sure that the phone in your program can be reached easily.

Keep a phone emergency list posted by every telephone (Figure 8-5). Usually you can reach emergency assistance by dialing 911. If 911 is not available in your area, refer to your phone list for specific numbers for police, fire, and ambulance. You can also call the operator, but this is a slower way to get help.

Be sure you know the location of phones in parks, playgrounds, and other places you visit with the children.

Your phone list should include your program's address, description of the building, and directions to it from a major road since these may be hard to remember in a crisis.

Find answers to these questions about your local emergency and medical services.

- Who answers the emergency phone? (Police, fire, ambulance, dispatcher?)
- What steps does the dispatcher have to take before sending the ambulance? (Call another dispatcher? Call Emergency Medical Technicians?)
- Who provides the ambulance service? (Police, fire, volunteer, private companies, another town?)
- How far do they have to travel to get to your program? Where is the station?
- How long will it usually take them to get to your program?
- Where are the nearest emergency rooms?

Try to visit your local helpers **before** you need them in a crisis. Most ambulance services are happy to show groups of visitors around their office, and some will even come visit you if you ask. Emergency rooms are harder to tour, but you can at least visit the waiting area and become familiar with how to get checked in. Familiarity with helpers now will come in handy when you need them later. These visits will also help reassure children.

Emergency evacuation plans

Evacuation procedures

Saving lives is the first priority in the event of any emergency. Saving property should be considered **only** when all lives are safe.

Planning, preparation, and practice are the essential ingredients of a successful evacuation plan. Develop a written procedure that includes routes, assignments for all staff, and location of nearest alarm that alerts the fire department.

When your program has an emergency that requires evacuation, follow these steps.

- Sound alarm—notify everyone in building.
- Evacuate—use exit routes or alternate routes previously marked and practiced in drills.
- Eliminate drafts—close all doors and windows.
- Take a head count—make sure everyone is safely out of the building.

- Call fire department **after** leaving the building—call from nearest alarm box or phone if building alarm is not connected to the fire department.

Prepare for emergencies in advance by taking these important actions.

- Keep up-to-date emergency information for children and staff. Make a specific person responsible for having this information on hand in emergencies, on trips, and in the event of program site evacuation. Ask parents to update emergency contact information every 6 months, and verify it by phone or mail.
- Know where you are going to stay if the building has to be evacuated. Families must know where to look for their children. Prearrange an emergency shelter where you will stay and inform parents by letter.
- Record daily attendance of staff and children. Designate a staff member to carry the list out of the building so that complete evacuation is assured.
- Post emergency telephone numbers (police, fire, rescue or central emergency code, and poison control) beside every phone. All individuals using the building should be familiar with these numbers and the procedures to be used in an emergency.
- Plan two exit routes from every area of the building. Post emergency evacuation exit instructions in every room where they can be seen easily.
- Have unannounced evacuation drills monthly. Evacuation should include use of alternative exit routes in case of blockage. Time should vary to include all activities (naptime too) and when the fewest adults are at the center.
- Maintain logs of evacuation drills for on-site inspection and review by the building inspector. **For most buildings, evacuation in less than 2 minutes is possible.** Fire-resistant exit routes in large buildings are usually required to provide enough time to exit safely.
- Contact the public education division at your local police and fire departments and ask them to arrange on-site visits to help staff make appropriate emergency plans.

Fire preparedness procedures

- Keep the phone number of the fire department and heating service company by your telephones (see Figure 8-5).
- Post a diagram showing the main shut-off switches for electricity, gas, and water.

- Test fire and smoke alarms at least once each month to be sure they are working. Have fire extinguishers inspected annually.
- Place fire extinguishers where they can be reached easily.
- Post diagrams of exits and escape routes in each room. Mark exits clearly, and do not block them with furniture or other objects.
- Practice leaving the building with the children once each month so that they know the sound of the alarm and where to go.
- Include fire and burn prevention in children's curriculum.

Knowing when and when not to use a fire extinguisher is an important part of fire preparedness. Use your extinguisher only if

- You are nearby when a fire starts or the fire is discovered in its early stages.
- Other staff **get all children out of the building and call the fire department.**
- The fire is small (confined to its origin—in a wastepaper basket, cushion, or small appliance).
- You can fight it with your back to an exit.
- Your extinguisher is in working order, and you
  —Stand back about 8'.
  —Aim at the base of the fire, not the flames or smoke.
  —Squeeze or press the lever while sweeping from the sides to middle.
- You can get out fast if your effort is failing.

If the fire spreads beyond the spot where it started or if the fire could block your exit, don't try to fight it. **If you have the slightest doubt about whether to fight or not to fight—don't.** Get out and call the fire department.

Helping children during emergency or evacuation procedures

To calm a group of panicked children. Remove them from the scene (if a child has been injured), and reassure them. Explain simply and carefully what has happened and what will happen. Answer their questions truthfully. Then redirect their attention—a game or quiet activity. Most important: **STAY CALM.** If you panic, the children will panic, too. If you need to evacuate the building, and children are frightened, have them hold each other's hands. Human touch is very reassuring in scary situations.

To get non-ambulatory children out of the building. Carry two or three infants at the same time. Use a large wagon to quickly transport toddlers or severely disabled children outdoors (if your building has ramps) or at least to the door where someone else can take them.

To get a child who is too scared to move to leave the building. Use your legs to press gently on the back of the child's knees to push him forward or hold his hands with one of your arms across his back. Having everyone join hands can also help the child feel less frightened.

First-aid procedures

First aid is the immediate care for persons who are injured or ill. All staff must be trained in first-aid procedures and have access to a first-aid guidebook at all times.

Emergency situations are always upsetting. Being upset makes it difficult to think clearly. In these situations, it is particularly important to follow a system so you will be able to react quickly and correctly. First aid is a way to manage an illness or injury until further medical care can be obtained, if necessary. When giving first aid, there are two ways you can harm someone. The first is by not treating an injury, and the second is by further damaging the injury.

Remember these two very important rules of first aid:
• **Do no harm.**
• **Never move a hurt child except to save a life.**

When you provide first aid, it is absolutely critical that you remain calm and reassure the victim. A calm attitude will allow you to think clearly and act appropriately. At the time of an emergency injury or illness, ask other adults to remove the other children to an area away from the victim. This will clear the area so you can carry out the necessary first aid. It will also create a calmer atmosphere for the other children. Later, when the situation is taken care of, you and all others involved (including other children) will need the opportunity to work through your feelings about what happened.

Assess the injury

Follow these steps whenever you are faced with an emergency situation. If more than one person is injured, start with the one who appears to be in greatest danger.

1. **Find out what happened.** What caused the injury? How? Who is hurt? Is there still danger?

Remember, never move a victim except to save a life. Am I calm and reassuring to the children? Who can help?

2. **Check for life-threatening problems.** Is the child conscious?

If the child is not conscious, is the child breathing (chest moving, air coming out of nose or mouth)? If not, lift only the jaw of child and give four quick breaths of mouth-to-mouth resuscitation. Is there a pulse in the neck? If not, start CPR.

If the child is conscious and old enough, ask questions such as, "What's your name?" to help determine the child's condition. Keep checking breathing and pulse as you proceed.

Wash any wounds to reduce chances of infection.

3. **Call an ambulance if you have any doubt about the situation.** Ask another adult to call the emergency number first and then the person legally responsible for the child.

4. **Check for injuries.** Start at the head and work down unless the place of injury is obvious.

Eyes. Pull eyelids open and look at the pupils (dark circle in middle). Are they the same size? Are the child's eyes looking in the same direction?

Ears. Look for blood or fluid (don't be fooled by tears).

Scalp. Feel gently (without moving child's head) for bumps, dents, bleeding, or anything unusual.

Nose and mouth. Look for bleeding or tooth injury.

Neck. Recheck pulse and breathing. Feel for bleeding, swelling, or stiffness.

Chest. Feel gently for swelling, unusual position or motion of bones.

Back. Slide your hands under the child to check for bleeding or pain.

Abdomen. Check for bleeding, pain, or tight muscles.

Arms. Start at the shoulder and feel carefully along both arms. Check for bleeding, swelling, pain, or any unusual shape or motion. Check pulse at the wrist (if it is not strong, check pulse at neck again). Feel hand bones. Check skin temperature.

Hips and legs. Are knees the same distance from the hips? Are feet warm or cold?

Keep the victim comfortable and warm with a clean blanket or clothing until help arrives. Provide detailed information to the emergency crew.

If you are handling the situation, administer the appropriate first aid.

5. **Regroup.** Check the condition of any other injured children. Talk with all present in calm, reassuring tones about how you are taking care of the injured child. Complete an injury report form (Fig-

ure 8-4). Give one copy to the parents the day of the incident, put one copy in the child's file. Note the incident in the injury log.

First aid for common situations

Choking

If an infant younger than 1 year of age chokes and is unable to breathe, place the baby face down over your arm with the head lower than the trunk. Rest your forearm on the infant's thigh. Deliver four measured blows rapidly with the heel of your hand between the infant's shoulder blades (see illustration A). If breathing does not start, roll the infant over and compress the chest four times rapidly as for CPR (see CPR section in next column).

If a child older than 1 year of age chokes, place the child on her or his back. Kneel down and place the heel of your hand on the child's abdomen in the midline between the navel and the rib cage. Apply a series of 6 to 10 abdominal thrusts (as with Heimlich maneuver—rapid inward and upward thrusts) until the foreign body is expelled (see illustration B). With an older child, you can apply the thrusts with two hands while the child is sitting, standing, or lying down (see illustration C).

If the child does not start to breathe, open the mouth and place your thumb over the child's tongue, with your fingers wrapped around the lower jaw. If you see a foreign body, remove it with a finger sweep.

Rapid transport to a medical facility is urgent if these emergency first-aid measures fail.

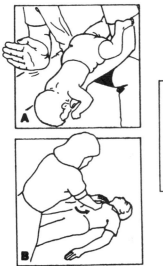
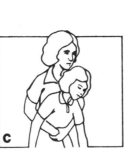

Cardiopulmonary resuscitation (CPR)

To be used in situations such as drownings, electric shock, and smoke inhalation. Technique of pulmonary support

- Clear the throat (see section on choking in left column) and wipe out any fluid, vomitus, mucus, or foreign body.
- Place victim on back.
- Straighten neck (unless neck injury suspected) and lift jaw.
- Give slow, steady breaths into infant's nose and mouth and into larger child's mouth with nostrils pinched closed.
- Breathe at 20 breaths per minute for infants and 15 breaths per minute for children, using only enough air to move chest up and down.

Technique of cardiac support (if no pulse or heartbeat)

- Place victim on firm surface.
- In the infant, using two fingers depress breastbone ½″ to 1″ at level of one finger's breadth below nipples. Compress at 100 times per minute.
- In the child, depress lower ⅓ of breastbone with heel of hand at 80 compressions per minute. There should be 5 compressions to one respiration.
- Learn and practice CPR.

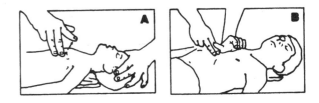

First-aid instructions from the *AAP First Aid Chart*, AAP Committee on Accident and Poison Prevention, revised 1988.

Bites and stings

Snake (non-poisonous)
- Treat as a puncture wound. Consult physician.

If poisonous
- Put patient and injured part at rest. Keep quiet.
- Do not apply ice. May use cool compress for pain.
- Immediate suction without incision may be beneficial.
- Apply loose (allow two fingers under) constricting band above the bite (not around fingers or toes) if cannot get to medical help in 1 hour.
- Transport victim promptly to a medical facility.

Insects. Spiders, scorpions, or unusual reaction to other stinging insects such as bees, wasps, or hornets.
- Remove stinger if present with a scraping motion of a plastic card or fingernail to reduce injection of more toxin. Do not pull out.
- Use cold compresses on bite area to relieve pain.
- If victim stops breathing, use artifical respiration and have someone call rescue unit and physician for further instructions.
- If any reactions such as hives; generalized rash; pallor; weakness; nausea; vomiting; "tightness" in chest, nose, or throat; or collapse occur; get patient to physician or emergency department immediately.
- For scorpion sting, get immediate medical advice.
- For spider bites, obtain medical advice. (Save live specimen if safe and possible.)

Ticks
- Always thoroughly inspect child after time in woods or brush. Ticks carry many serious diseases and must be completely removed. Use tweezers or protected fingers placed close to the head to pull tick away from point of attachment.
- If the tick's head breaks off, the child should be taken without delay for medical removal of the tick.

Animal. Bat, raccoon, skunk, and fox bites, as well as unprovoked bites from cats and dogs (may be from a rabid animal).
- Call physican or medical facility.
- Wash wound gently but thoroughly with soap and water for 15 minutes.

Marine animals (poisonous). Stingray, lionfish, catfish, and stonefish stings.
- Put victim at rest and submerge sting area in hot water.
- Call physician or medical facility.

Marine stings (non-poisonous)
- Flush with water, remove any clinging material.
- Apply cold compress to relieve pain.
- Call physician or medical facility.

Burns

Protection against tetanus should be considered in all burns and whenever the skin is broken.

Burns of limited extent. If caused by heat
- Immerse extremity burns in cool water or apply cool (50° to 60° F.) compresses to burns of the trunk or face for pain relief.
- Do not break blisters.
- Nonadhesive material such as household aluminum foil makes an excellent emergency covering.
- Burns of any size of the face, hands, feet, or genitalia should be seen immediately by a physician.

Extensive burns
- Keep patient in a flat position.
- Remove non-adherent clothing from burn area— if not easily removed, leave alone.
- Apply cool, wet compresses to injured area (not more than 25% of the body at one time).
- Keep patient warm.
- Get patient to hospital or physician at once.
- Do not use ointments, greases, or powders.

Electric burns
- Disconnect power source if possible, or pull victim away from source using wood or cloth.
- Do not use bare hands.
- Electric burns may require CPR to be administered.
- All electric burns must be evaluated by a physician.

Sunburn. Children younger than 1 year of age may suffer serious injury and should be examined by a physician.

Convulsions

Seek medical advice. Lay the patient on side, with head lower than hips. Put nothing in mouth. Sponge with cool water if fever is present.

Eye irritants

- Hold lids open and flush out eye immediately with water.
- Remove contact lenses, if worn.
- Irrigate eye for 15 minutes with a gentle, continuous stream of water from a pitcher.
- Never rub the eye, or use eye drops.
- Call physician, poison control center, or emergency department for further advice.

Eye pain

Do not apply pressure to eye or instill medications without physician's advice.

- Attempt removal of foreign body by gentle use of moist cotton swab. If not immediately successful, obtain medical assistance. Pain in eye from foreign bodies, scrapes, scratches, cuts, etc., can be alleviated by bandaging the lids shut until aid from a physician can be obtained.
- For chemicals splashed in eyes, flush immediately with plain water and continue for 15 minutes. Do not use drops or ointments. Call physician or poison control center.
- If eye is perforated by a missile or sharp object, do not apply pressure to lids. Avoid straining. Consult ophthalmologist immediately.
- If eye received blunt trauma, consult a physician if in doubt, especially if there is blurring or double vision, flashing lights, or floating specks.

Fainting

Keep patient in a flat position. Loosen clothing around neck. Turn head to one side. Keep patient warm and mouth clear. Give nothing to swallow. Obtain medical aid.

Fractures and sprains

Any deformity of an injured part usually means a fracture has occurred. Do not move the person without splinting. A suspected neck or back injury should only be moved with medical assistance to avoid causing paralysis.

Elevate sprains and apply only cold compresses. If marked pain or swelling is present, seek medical advice.

Head injuries

Provide complete rest. Consult physician. Obtain additional consultation if

- there is a loss of consciousness at any time after injury
- you are unable to arouse the child from sleep. (You should allow the child to sleep after the injury but check frequently to see whether the child can be aroused. Check at least every 1 to 2 hours during the day, and 2 to 3 times during the night.)
- there is persistent vomiting
- the child is unable to move a limb
- there is oozing of blood or watery fluid from the ears or nose
- the child has a persistent headache lasting more than 1 hour. The headache will be severe enough to interfere with activity and normal sleep.
- the child experiences persistent dizziness for 1 hour after the injury
- the child's pupils are unequal
- the child is pale and does not regain normal color in a short time

Poison emergencies

We usually think of poisoning as swallowing a toxic substance. However, chemicals in the eyes or on the skin and the breathing of toxic fumes are also considered poison emergencies. Do not rely on antidote charts or first-aid information on product labels. They are sometimes incorrect or out of date and can cause additional damage.

In all cases of poisoning, call your local poison control center. When you call, be sure to give specific information about

- the product the child was exposed to (have container with you when you call)
- the amount
- the time of exposure

Include **syrup of ipecac** in your first-aid kit. Swallowing ipecac is the most effective way to cause vomiting. **Do not use ipecac unless told to do so by the poison center or physician.** Some poisons, such as drain cleaner or lye, can cause serious damage to the esophagus if vomited.

Phone number of local poison control center:

Shock

Speak reassuringly to the victim. Keep the victim at a comfortable temperature—cover if the environment is cool; cool if the environment is warm.

Skin wounds

Protection against tetanus should be considered in all burns and whenever the skin is broken.

Bruises. Rest injured part. Apply cold compress for 30 minutes (no ice next to skin). If skin is broken, treat as a cut. For wringer injuries and bicycle spoke injuries, always consult physician without delay.

Scrapes. Use wet gauze or cotton to sponge off gently with clean water and soap. Apply sterile dressing, preferably non-adhesive or "film" type (Telfapad).

Cuts

Small. Wash with clean water and soap. Hold under running water. Apply sterile gauze dressing.

Large. Apply dressing. Press firmly and elevate to stop bleeding—use tourniquet only if necessary to control bleeding. Bandage. Secure medical care. Do not use iodine or other antiseptics without medical advice.

Puncture wounds. Consult physician.

Slivers. Wash with clean water and soap. Remove with tweezers or forceps. Wash again. If not easily removed, consult physician.

First-aid education

Staff

All staff must be trained in basic first-aid procedures, including choking, seizures, and resuscitation. This training, done by qualified instructors, should be repeated at least yearly, or more often if necessary to train new staff. The first-aid training should include a developmental approach to young children and injury prevention as well as how to handle emergencies appropriately from both a medical and psychological viewpoint. All staff must know your program's policies for emergencies in addition to basic first aid.

Children

Young children can begin to know how and from whom to get help. Teach children these basic, helpful concepts.
● Follow all safety rules.
● Tell an adult right away if something is wrong (someone is hurt or sick).
● Some things are dangerous (e.g., poisons, matches, tiny objects in the mouth).
● A person who is very hurt or sick may need to be alone with a helper.

Older preschool children also can be taught about basic care concepts such as cuts need to be cleaned with soap and water, direct pressure helps stop bleeding, burns should be treated with cold water. This information may help children to be more cooperative if they can understand why certain first-aid procedures are necessary.

Parents

Set up a program to help parents refresh their first-aid skills. You may consider inviting parents to your staff training or having a special meeting to review home first-aid procedures. You might want to put brief articles in your newsletter, if you have one. Keep parents informed when you hear about community education programs. First-aid resources are a great addition to a parent lending library, too.

Figure 8-1. Emergency procedures

1. Remain calm. Reassure the victim and others at the scene.

2. Stay at the scene and give help at least until the person assigned to handle emergencies arrives.

3. Send word to the person who handles emergencies for your program. This person will take charge of the emergency, assess the situation, and give any further first aid, as needed.

4. Do not move a severely injured or ill person except to save a life.

5. If necessary, phone for help. Give all the important information slowly and clearly. To make sure that you have given all the necessary information, **wait for the other party to hang up first.** Arrange for transportation of the injured person by ambulance or other such vehicle, if necessary. Do not drive unless accompanied by another adult. Bring your emergency transportation permission form (Figure 8-3) with you.

6. Do not give aspirin or other medications unless authorized by your local poison control center (for poisonings) or physician (for other illnesses).

7. Notify parent(s) of the emergency and agree on a course of action with the parent(s).

8. If parent cannot be reached, notify parent's emergency contact person and call the physician shown on the child's emergency transportation permission form.

9. Be sure that a responsible individual from the program stays with the child until parent(s) take charge.

10. Fill out an injury report (Figure 8-4) within 24 hours. File in the child's folder. Give parent(s) a copy, preferably that day. Note injury information in central injury log.

Figure 8-2. First-aid kit contents

These items should be included in a basic first-aid kit.
- a quick-reference first-aid manual (e.g., *A Sigh of Relief—The First Aid Handbook for Childhood Emergencies* [Green, 1984])
- index cards and pens
- thermometer
- flashlight
- blunt-tip scissors
- tweezers
- 10 2" × 2" gauze pads
- 10 4" × 4" gauze pads
- 1 roll 2" flexible gauze bandage
- 1 roll 4" flexible gauze bandage
- 25 1" and 25 assorted small bandages
- 1 roll 1" bandage tape

- 2 triangular muslin bandages
- syrup of ipecac (at least 10 1-oz. bottles)
- a large (1 to 2 quart) clean container for use in flushing eyes
- plastic bags (for ice pack)
- rubber gloves
- tissues
- safety pins
- in your field trip kit—coins for pay phones, soap for washing wounds, alcohol-based wipes, synthetic ice packs

Note: If a child has a special health need, you will want to include additional supplies in your kit; e.g., bee sting kit or antihistamine for a child with a severe allergy, sugar or honey for a child with diabetes, or inhalator for a child with asthma.

Figure 8-3. Emergency transportation permission form

Child's name _____

    I understand that no emergency treatment may be given without parental consent except in a life-threatening situation. Because informed consent must be given at the time of the incident, I agree to leave numbers where I (or my spouse or a responsible adult designated by me) can be reached promptly if the numbers below do not apply for any given day.

    In case of a medical emergency while my child is attending _____
                                                                         (program name)

_____

I understand that the following procedure will be followed:

1. The program will contact parent(s):

Mother can be telephoned at _____-_____ during _____.
                                                                                     (hours/days)
                                       _____-_____ during _____.
                                                                                     (hours/days)
Father can be telephoned at _____-_____ during _____.
                                                                                     (hours/days)
Father can be telephoned at _____-_____ during _____.
                                                                                     (hours/days)

2. If neither parent is available in an emergency, the program will contact these people:

Name _____ can be reached at _____-_____.

Relationship to child _____

Name _____ can be reached at _____-_____.

Relationship to child _____

Name _____ can be reached at _____-_____.

Relationship to child _____

3. The program will arrange for emergency transportation to _____
    or the nearest emergency medical facility, if necessary. At no time will a staff member drive with my child unless accompanied by another adult. My child will be transported by an ambulance or other such vehicle when necessary.

4. The program may contact my child's medical care provider _____

    who can be telephoned at _____-_____.

I hereby authorize the program to follow this procedure.

Parent's signature _____ Date _____

Figure 8-4. Injury report form

SUBMIT WITHIN 24 HOURS OF INJURY

_____ File in child's folder.

_____ Give copy to parent.

_____ Enter data into injury log.

Child's name _____ Age _____ Date _____

Time of injury _____ a.m./p.m. Witnesses _____

Parent(s) notified by _____ Time _____

Location where injury occurred _____

Equipment/product (if any) involved _____

Description of injury (specify body part) and how it occurred _____

_____

_____

First aid given at the program _____

_____

_____

Other action taken by medical personnel (specify hospital, clinic, or physician) _____

_____

Diagnosis/follow-up plan _____

_____

_____

_____

Corrective action needed to prevent reoccurence _____

_____

_____

Signature of staff member _____ Date _____

Signature of parent _____ Date _____

Figure 8-5. Phone emergency list

This phone is located at _____

Phone number _____-_____-_____
　　　　　　　　　Area code

Program name _____

Description of building _____

Directions for reaching this location from a major road _____

_____

_____

Emergency numbers

Ambulance _____　　Battered women's shelter _____

Poison control center _____　　Suicide prevention hotline _____

Police _____　　Gas company _____

Fire _____　　Water company _____

Health consultant _____　　Heating equipment service _____

Hospital _____　　Electric company _____

Nearest emergency facility _____　　Plumber _____

Local board of health _____　　Taxi _____

State dept. public health _____　　Parents Anonymous _____

Child abuse reporting _____　　Alcoholics Anonymous _____

Rape crisis center _____

Always give this information in emergencies:
1. Name
2. Nature of emergency
3. Telephone number
4. Address
5. Easy directions
6. Exact location of injured person
   (e.g., backyard behind parking lot)

Optional information:
7. Help already given
8. Ways to make it easier to find you
   (e.g., standing in front of building,
   waving red flag)

DO NOT HANG UP BEFORE THE OTHER PERSON HANGS UP!

Emergency and Accident Procedures

What is your emergency evacuation plan?

_____

_____

_____

What would you do if a child cut his or her leg during outdoor play?

_____

_____

_____

What would you do if a child had a seizure?

_____

_____

_____

Who informs parents if their child has had a minor accident?

_____

_____

_____

Who calls for emergency medical assistance and contacts parents when a serious accident occurs?

_____

_____

_____

What hospital would you go to in an emergency and how would you get there?

_____

_____

_____

_____

Discuss your answers with your trainer. If you have questions about what to do in an emergency, review your center's emergency procedures and discuss them with your supervisor.

V. Ensuring Children's Safety Away from the Center[2]

In this activity you will learn:

- to provide for children's safety in traffic; and

- to take safe field trips with children.

The preschool years are a time when young children expand their understanding of the world around them. One of the ways you support children's growing interest in their extended environment is by planning field trips and walks in the neighborhood. Taking children away from the center and into traffic, or transporting them in motor vehicles to locations that are new and unfamiliar involves an element of risk. You can minimize the risks to children's safety by planning ahead of time, establishing rules for field trips, and teaching children how to behave safely in traffic.

Walking Safely Near Traffic

There are many reasons you might need to take children into traffic. One reason would be to visit a neighborhood park that offers the children a new and challenging environment for their growing skills. You might plan walks to explore new concepts or skills: a listening walk; a walk to collect seeds in the fall; or a visit to local stores to purchase something the group needs or to learn about the community.

Preschool children must be carefully supervised by adults when they are walking across streets. They are also capable of learning rules about walking in traffic safely. Here are some suggestions for ensuring children's safety when they are in traffic.

- To keep the group together, use a clothesline or rope with knots tied in it. Children can hold onto the knots as they walk together.

- Make the walk fun by singing a song, looking for objects or shapes, or playing follow the leader.

- Explain the rules for crossing the street safely—look to the left, look to the right, look to the left again, wait for the green light—and follow the rules consistently.

- Post pictures of traffic warning signs (stop lights, stop signs, crosswalks) in the classroom and discuss them with the children. Point out these signs when you are on a walk and talk about how they help keep people safe.

---

[2] Strategies in this section are based on Abby Shapiro Kendrick, Roxane Kaufmann, and Katherine P. Messenger, editors, *Healthy Young Children, A Manual for Program* (Washington, DC: National Association for the Education of Young Children, 1988), pp. 57 and 85-90.

- Know which children may need close attention on a walk and be sure one adult is assigned to be close by at all times.

Planning Safe Field Trips

Field trips are special events that expose children to new and unfamiliar places. As a result, young children are likely to be excited when a field trip is planned. Some children may be fearful about leaving the center, breaking the normal routine, and going to a strange place. They may worry that their parents won't know where to find them. The drivers may not be familiar with the route or with the children. For all these reasons, it is important to plan ahead and take precautions to ensure children's safety on field trips.

In preparing for a field trip, you can avoid problems and unnecessary risks by taking the following steps.

- Recruit additional help—parents, senior citizens, students from early childhood programs at a local college or high school—to help supervise the children.

- Obtain signed permission slips for each trip so parents know their children will be leaving the center and where they will be going.

- Go over the route to be sure you have correct directions and have allocated adequate time for travel and the visit.

- Prepare children for the trip. Discuss what you will see and the rules for safety. Involve children in making rules that will keep everyone safe.

- Prepare for an emergency by bringing a first-aid kit with you if one is not already on the bus.

- Put together a folder with a list of emergency phone numbers, copies of emergency forms, and signed permission slips.

- If you will be traveling by car, make sure you will have enough seat belts for each child and adult.

- Prepare tags for each child to wear that state the name and the telephone number of your center.

The planning you do before a field trip goes a long way in making you feel relaxed and in control. Children will sense this and be reassured by your calm manner. You also set an example for children by following safety rules yourself. Here are some suggestions for traveling safely with preschool children.

- Place each child in a securely adjusted seat belt and use one yourself. Never put two or more children in the same belt.

- Keep sharp or heavy objects in the trunk. They can become deadly projectiles in a sudden stop.

- Do not let children put their arms or heads out of the windows.

- Use travel time to talk about scenes along the way and what you expect to see when you arrive at your destination, and to remind children of the safety rules.

- If children become unruly or remove their seat belts, pull off the road and stop. Do not try to discipline children when you are driving. Let children know that the rules must be followed.

- Never leave children alone in a vehicle.

- Make sure all children are accounted for at all times.

Ensuring children's safety is especially challenging when you are away from the center. Following the suggestions listed above will make your job a little easier.

In this learning activity, you will review your center's policies and procedures for ensuring children's safety on field trips and when walking in traffic. After recording them in this notebook, you will compare them to the suggestions above and identify any additional safety precautions you want to add to ensure children's safety away from the center.

Protecting Children Away from the Center

What rules and procedures does your program have for taking children on walks away from the center?

_____

_____

_____

_____

What does your program require you to do before taking a field trip?

_____

_____

_____

_____

What are the rules and procedures for ensuring children's safety while on a field trip?

_____

_____

_____

_____

How can you improve the procedures and planning process to more effectively ensure children's safety away from the center?

_____

_____

_____

_____

Discuss your answers with your trainer and implement ideas you feel are needed to ensure children's safety away from the center.

VI. Helping Children Learn to Keep Themselves Safe

In this activity you will learn:

- to maintain a safe environment through supervision; and

- to develop safety rules with children.

The first step in teaching children safety is to show them, by your actions, how you prevent accidents. Children need to see adults acting in safe ways:

- walking, not running, in the room;

- sitting, not standing, on chairs;

- using a step stool to reach a high cupboard; and

- keeping their hands away from sharp objects during woodworking and food preparation.

It is the job of each teacher in the room to make sure that all areas of the room and the outdoor area are supervised. When one teacher is busy with a group in the woodworking area, another adult should keep an eye on the rest of the room. Some activities require closer supervision than others. Two teachers who are moving around to different areas could agree to divide the room or yard between them. Teachers must also be aware of how the children are feeling. If activities are too long, children may tire, and tired children often have accidents. If an activity is too demanding, preschoolers may get frustrated, and frustrated children also tend to have accidents.

You should be aware of the possible hazards for each activity area, as described in Learning Activities II and III of this module. When you know what to look for when supervising the areas, you can prevent accidents. The children should be made aware of safety limits for the room and outdoor area and traffic rules to follow on field trips, so they can stay safe.

Preschool children have reached an age where they begin to understand cause and effect. Using simple language, you can talk with the children about dangerous situations. You can also demonstrate, using concrete objects and experiences, the correct use of materials and ways to play.

To develop safety rules with children, you might start a discussion by saying:

- "Tell me about …"

- "What could happen when…?"

- "What might happen if…?"

For example, you might want to talk with children about using an electric skillet safely. If you ask them to tell you about cooking with skillets, they could have several answers. One child might say, "It's fun," and another might say, "It gets really hot." You could then ask, "What might happen if you put your hand on a hot skillet?" "You would get burned," a child might answer. You could then ask the group to develop rules for using the skillet. The rules might include the following:

- keep your hands off the skillet;

- use a pot holder; and

- one child uses the skillet at a time.

By participating in this discussion, children will learn that there are things they can do to keep themselves safe. You can remind them of these safety rules while you supervise activities. Children will then begin to develop skills and sound judgment to keep themselves safe.

In this learning activity you will work with the children in your room to develop safety limits for one activity area or outdoor area. First complete the reading, "Prevent Unnecessary Accidents," beginning on the next page. Then review the example and answer the questions that follow the reading.

Prevent Unnecessary Accidents[3]

Be Alert to Safety Hazards

Preschoolers are very busy. They are always running wherever they go. They are quick in their movements and changeable in their activities, and they know definitely what they want to do and how they want to do it. All this is normal. Their activity and changing interests are the signs of healthy children.

Accidents among preschool children are common. The safety and protection of these children from accidents is the responsibility of every member of the staff. Anything, including the "safe" toys at the center, can become dangerous if used the wrong way. The so-called "safe" toys can hurt children if:

- the large, hollow, wooden blocks are allowed to be stacked higher than the shoulders of the children;

- the swings are placed where children run too closely in front or behind them; and

- the slick part of the slides are climbed instead of the ladder.

Only your well-trained eyes can protect the child from water spilled on the floor, sharp edges, loose parts of toys, slivers, and broken toys.

Take Preventive Steps

The primary way to avoid accidents is to remain alert to what children are doing and how they are feeling. Notice what is happening with the children, and take steps to keep things flowing smoothly and safely.

When children have become tired from too much active play or overly excited by too many other children, too much noise, or activities that are too long, accidents happen. Children are not attentive; they lose control over their bodies and feelings, and in a moment they can hurt themselves or others.

Preschoolers are socially active, too. Almost always, they are busy with each other. This social activity takes energy, just as physical activity takes energy. All this activity will tire any child, especially the young child for whom it is a new experience. The teacher can arrange the day's activities to keep children from becoming too tired. One way to do this is to alternate quiet activities with more active or vigorous ones. Changing activities from active play to quiet play will help the child avoid tiring. Another way to keep children from tiring is to keep them in small groups.

---

[3]Adapted from Department of Defense, *Caring for Preschoolers* (Washington, DC: Government Printing Office, April 1982), pp. 95-96.

Remember:

- Accidents happen when the child is tired.

- Accidents happen when the child is overly excited.

- Accidents happen when the teacher is not paying attention.

- Accidents can be prevented through planning.

Help Children Learn to Do Things the Safe Way

Preschool children can learn rules of safety and take an active part in teaching others these same rules. Here are some steps to follow in teaching children to do things the safe way:

- Explain rules simply and repeat them often. "This is the trike riding path. You can kick your ball on the grass."

- Be consistent in following rules and offer praise to the children who follow them.

- When necessary, step in and assist a child in following the rules. "I cannot allow you to build blocks any higher than this because they might fall down on top of you or the other children."

- Remove the child from the situation if he or she continues to break a safety rule, and explain to the child why he or she is being removed.

Even three-year-olds can know and understand safety rules, but they may be in such a hurry that they will trip over objects on the floor. While a four-year-old can understand safety rules and can even remind others of the rules, he or she cannot be trusted to remember them every minute. Constant supervision and frequent, firm reminders are necessary for preschool children's protection. Some five-year-olds can help you by reminding the younger children of the necessary safety rules. They may also encourage younger children to follow the safety rules.

Developing Safety Rules with Children
(Example)

Area: <u>*Woodworking*</u>   Age(s): <u>*4-5 years*</u>   Date: <u>*September 10*</u>

What do you think are the safety hazards in this area?

Children could be cut with saws. Fingers could be pinched by hammers, vises, pliers. Children could swallow nails.

How did the children answer your "tell me about..." questions?

John said, "It's fun." Susan said, "You can hammer your finger." Kim said, "You can make things." Cynthia said, "You can saw something you shouldn't."

How did the children answer your "what might happen if..." and "what could happen when..." questions?

Susan said, "You could hammer your finger, if you're not watching what you're doing." Cynthia said, "You could cut your finger with the saw, if your hands aren't in the right place."

What safety limits did you and the children develop for this area?

Only two children may be in the woodworking area at a time.

One adult must be in the area when children are working.

When sawing, one hand holds the saw and the other holds the wood but stays away from the blade.

When hammering, use the pad to hold the nail still.

Developing Safety Rules with Children

Area: _____ **Age(s):** _____ **Date:** _____

What do you think are the safety hazards in this area?

_____

_____

_____

How did the children answer your "tell me about..." question?

_____

_____

_____

How did the children answer your "what might happen if..." and "what could happen when..." questions?

_____

_____

_____

What safety limits did you and the children develop for this area?

_____

_____

_____

_____

_____

_____

Discuss your responses with your trainer.

Summarizing Your Progress

You have now completed all of the learning activities for this module. Whether you are an experienced teacher or a new one, this module has probably helped you develop new skills for keeping children safe. Before you go on, take a few minutes to summarize what you've learned.

- Turn back to Learning Activity I, Using Your Knowledge of Child Development to Keep Children Safe, and add to the chart specific examples of what you learned about keeping children safe while you were working on this module. Compare your ideas to those in the completed chart at the end of the module.

- Next, review your responses to the pre-training assessment for this module. Write a summary of what you learned, and list the skills you developed or improved.

_____

_____

_____

_____

_____

_____

_____

_____

_____

_____

_____

_____

_____

If there are topics you would like to know more about, you will find recommended readings listed in the orientation.

Your final step in this module is to complete the knowledge and competency assessments. Let your trainer know when you are ready to schedule the assessments. After you have successfully completed these assessments, you will be ready to start a new module. Congratulations on your progress so far, and good luck with your next module.

Answer Sheets

Keeping Children Safe

Providing Safe Indoor and Outdoor Environments

1. How did Ms. Kim and Ms. Richards work together to make the center a safe place?

    a. Ms. Kim spotted Jill climbing on the box. She calmly alerted Ms. Richards, who was closer.

    b. Ms. Richards responded quickly to Ms. Kim's warning and calmly moved in to keep Jill safe.

    c. Ms. Richards put the box in the closet so children wouldn't climb on it.

2. What do you think Jill learned from this experience?

    a. She learned that the box was not a good thing to climb on but the climber was safe.

    b. She learned that Ms. Richards would keep her safe.

    c. She learned that she could help Ms. Richards do important and real work to make the room safer.

Responding to Accidents and Emergencies

1. What resources were available to Mr. Lopez to help him know what to do?

    a. He had a first-aid chart taped on the lid of the first-aid kit, where he could find it easily.

    b. The center had accident report forms and a daily chart to record information.

2. What did Mr. Lopez do after taking care of Andy's injury? Why?

    a. He reassured Andy that his injury had been taken care of and that he was now safe.

    b. He filled out an accident report form and made a note so he would remember to tell Andy's parents what had happened and ask them to sign the form.

Helping Children Develop Safe Habits

1. **How did Ms. Williams let the children know that the center is a safe place?**

   a. She walked calmly to the block area.

   b. She let Kirsten know that she wanted her to build in a safe way.

   c. She asked the children to help think of safe ways to build high.

2. **How were the children learning to keep themselves safe?**

   a. They learned that there are safe ways to do things.

   b. They helped develop a safety chart for the block area.

   c. At circle time they talked about the safety rules they made.

Using Your Knowledge of Child Development to
Keep Children Safe

WHAT PRESCHOOL CHILDREN ARE LIKE	HOW TEACHERS CAN USE THIS INFORMATION TO KEEP CHILDREN SAFE
They have lots of energy and like to race around.	Set up the outdoor area with space to run. Organize the indoor environment so children don't run and bump into each other or the furnishings.
They hop and jump over objects.	Organize indoor and outdoor areas where children can move freely without knocking into each other or the furniture and equipment. Set up an obstacle course outdoors where children can hop and jump safely.
They ride tricycles and other moving equipment.	Use hard surfaces outdoors (and indoors, if possible) for riding. Help children take turns with the equipment so they don't fight over it. Discuss safe riding practices with children.
They slide, swing, and climb on equipment.	Allow sliding, swinging, and climbing only on sturdy equipment where adequate cushioning is provided. Remind children of safety guidelines. Mark off areas around swings and at the base of slides that must be kept clear so children aren't knocked down.
They throw, kick, and catch objects.	Allow children to throw and kick soft objects only in safe areas where others won't be hurt. Provide balls and bean bags for kicking and throwing so children don't throw sand, toys, and other items that could cause injury.
They build block towers.	Set up a building-block area in a large carpeted space. Limit the number of children allowed in the area at one time so there is room to play safely. Set guidelines for the height of structures.

WHAT PRESCHOOL CHILDREN ARE LIKE	HOW TEACHERS CAN USE THIS INFORMATION TO KEEP CHILDREN SAFE
They use hammers, saws, and other woodworking equipment.	Set up the woodworking area away from the line of traffic so children don't knock into those using saws. Use sturdy, real tools so children can hammer and cut with success. Store the tools when they're not in use. Limit the number of children allowed in the area and establish clear rules.
They show their curiosity by manipulating, poking, handling, or squeezing everything.	Cover exposed radiators. Remove toys and other items with jagged edges or splinters. Keep sharp materials (knives, teacher's scissors) out of children's reach. Lock cleaning materials and medicines in cabinets.
They can cut with scissors and knives.	Use sharp, blunt-end, child-sized scissors for right- and left-handed children so they can cut easily and with success. Use butter knives for spreading and cutting at mealtimes, to reduce the possibility that children will cut themselves. Use sharp child-sized knives for supervised food preparation activities so children can cut easily.
They use the toilet independently.	Supervise toileting. Be sure water in the center is hot enough for handwashing but not so hot that it burns.
They share toys and take turns with some assistance.	Provide duplicates of popular toys to prevent fighting over toys. Help children take turns by using timers, clocks, or planning boards. Anticipate fights and give children words to use when they are having difficulty sharing and taking turns.
They begin to understand cause and effect.	Discuss playing safely with individuals and in small groups so children know what they can do. Use circle time to involve children in establishing classroom limits. Remind children of their limits as they play, to prevent accidents and injuries.

Glossary

Emergency	Unplanned or unexpected situation in which children or adults are harmed or may be harmed.
Precaution	Step taken to prevent accidents or to ensure safety.
Safety	Freedom from danger.

Module 2
Healthy

What Are Good Health and Nutrition and Why Are They Important?

Good health is a state of well-being—physical, mental, and social well-being—not simply the absence of disease. One area of development affects every other area of development. People who are healthy feel good about themselves.

- They are well-rested, energetic, and strong.

- They eat the right foods.

- They avoid, or use only in moderation, alcohol, cigarettes, and caffeine.

- They exercise regularly.

- They get along well with others.

- They have high self-esteem.

Each of us has certain health and nutrition routines that are part of our daily lives. Some of these routines may be good for us, and some may not. Because most of us want to become and remain healthy, we try to increase the number of good routines and decrease the number of bad ones.

Young children learn about good health and nutrition by following our lead. We try to maintain environments that promote wellness and prevent illness and abuse. We also model and encourage good health and nutrition habits for children. When good habits are developed at an early age, they usually continue throughout a person's life.

As a teacher, you play a key role in keeping children healthy. Children under five have more illnesses related to infection than any other age group. Those in group care tend to be exposed to more diseases than those cared for at home. Therefore, teachers need to know how to prevent diseases from spreading. In addition, you teach about good health and nutrition in the course of daily life at the center. You do this when you wash your hands before eating and after toileting, when you serve and eat nutritious foods, and when you clean a soiled table top.

The emotional tone you create in your environment affects the health of everyone who spends their day in it. A positive, relaxed atmosphere encourages a sense of well-being in children and teachers.

Keeping children healthy involves:
- providing healthy indoor and outdoor environments;
- helping children develop good health habits; and
- recognizing and reporting child abuse and neglect.

Listed below are examples of how teachers demonstrate their competence in keeping children healthy.

Providing Healthy Indoor and Outdoor Environments

Here are some examples of what teachers can do.

- Check the room daily for adequate ventilation and lighting, comfortable room temperature, and good sanitation.

- Open windows daily to let in fresh air.

- Provide tissues, paper towels, and soap in places children can reach.

- Plan a daily schedule consistent with children's activity levels and their need for quiet times and rest. "We did a lot of climbing and running in the playground today! Now let's sit quietly and look through our books before we get ready for lunch."

- Take children outdoors daily for exercise and fresh air.

- Complete a daily health check on each child to discover symptoms of illness.

- Recognize symptoms of common childhood diseases and stay in regular contact with parents.

Helping Children Develop Good Health Habits

Here are some examples of what teachers can do.

- Help children develop and provide opportunities for them to use self-help skills in toileting, handwashing, and toothbrushing.

- Talk with children about ways to stay healthy. "Rochelle, I'd like you to rest now because you had a very busy morning."

- Serve age-appropriate, nutritious meals and snacks.

- Encourage children to taste new foods by serving as models and offering verbal encouragement. "I'm going to taste the squash, and I want you to taste it too, Ralph."

- Help children learn to recognize that their bodies need rest, food, and movement. "Kegan, it looks as if you need to stretch your body and get the wiggles out."

Recognizing and Reporting Child Abuse and Neglect

Here are some examples of what teachers can do.

- Recognize the symptoms of physical, sexual, and emotional child abuse and neglect.

- Respond to children in a caring way while avoiding situations that might be questioned by others.

- Follow required procedures to report suspected child abuse and neglect.

Promoting Good Health and Nutrition

The following situations show teachers promoting good health and nutrition for preschoolers. As you read, think about what the teachers in each scene are doing and why. Then answer the questions following each episode.

Providing Healthy Indoor and Outdoor Environments

Ms. Williams enters her room and opens several windows. It is a cool day, so she raises them only a few inches. She checks the area around the children's sink and notices that the soap dispenser is full but the towel supply is low. As she puts out a stack of paper towels, the children begin to arrive. She greets each child warmly, checking to see if the flu that has been running through the center has made any children in her group sick. "You have the sniffles today, David. Please blow your nose with a tissue from the box next to the sink," she says. David is having some difficulty with this task, so Ms. Williams asks if she can help him. "It's hard," he says. "I'm blowing through the tissue!" She doubles the tissue and helps him blow his nose. After dropping the used tissue into the waste can, she says, "Now let's both wash our hands to make sure all the germs are gone."

1. **What are three things Ms. Williams did to maintain a healthy room?**

_____

_____

_____

2. **What did Ms. Williams do to keep germs from spreading?**

_____

_____

_____

Helping Children Develop Good Health Habits

"What a delicious lunch we're having. Will you please pass me the apples?" Mr. Lopez asks Jerry. Jerry hands the bowl of apple slices to Mr. Lopez. "I like crunchy, juicy apples," Mr. Lopez says. Jerry watches Mr. Lopez eat his apple. He reaches for an apple slice, too. "Eating apples is good for us," Mr. Lopez says. After lunch, Mr. Lopez and his assistant clear the table with the children. Then Mr. Lopez says, "Now it's time to brush our teeth." He helps three children at a time choose their toothbrushes from the egg-carton holder. "Remember to brush up and down," says Mr. Lopez. He brushes his teeth, too. Sandy watches Mr. Lopez, her toothbrush in hand. "I'm brushing my teeth," she says proudly, smiling at him.

1. What three healthy things did Mr. Lopez do with the children?

_____

_____

_____

2. How did Mr. Lopez teach the children ways to keep themselves healthy?

_____

_____

_____

Recognizing and Reporting Child Abuse and Neglect

Carolyn has just upset her pudding, spilling it down the front of her shirt. Ms. Kim quickly moves to help Carolyn and suggests they find a clean shirt for her. As Ms. Kim helps Carolyn take off her soiled shirt, she sees that the child's back is criss-crossed with bruises. The bruises are loop-shaped. Some look fresh; others seem older. Ms. Kim asks Carolyn what happened, and Carolyn replies, "I was bad, so I got whipped."

Ms. Kim tells Ms. Lee, the director, what she has seen and heard. They discuss the cues to possible child abuse and decide that Ms. Kim should write down her observations and concerns. Ms. Lee reminds Ms. Kim to keep the information confidential. Ms. Lee reports the incident to the Child Protective Services, which sends someone to the center to investigate.

1. What are the clues to possible child abuse in this situation?

_____

_____

_____

2. How did Ms. Lee support Ms. Kim?

_____

_____

_____

Compare your answers with those on the answer sheet at the end of this module. If your answers are different, discuss them with your trainer. There can be more than one good answer.

Your Own Health and Nutrition

Most of us know that good health and proper nutrition are important. The national focus on staying fit—which is stressed in the media, in schools, and at the workplace—has provided much useful information and has led to an increased motivation to stay healthy. We have learned that staying healthy improves the quality of life and can actually prolong life.

Most of us know what to do to stay healthy. We try to improve our health by doing the right things—and when we do, we tend to feel better about ourselves. Perhaps you have done some of the following things to improve your health.

- You began walking or jogging more often.

- You joined an aerobics class or exercise program.

- You quit smoking or vowed never to start.

- You increased the variety of foods in your diet to include more vegetables, fruits, and whole-grain products.

- You lost weight using a sensible diet.

- You began eating more starchy foods and less sugar, fats, and salt.

- You decreased the amount of unnecessary stress in your life.

- You discovered the positive effects of relaxation techniques.

You may have found, though, that changing too much too quickly led to failure. Have you found yourself saying these things?

- "I tried quitting smoking but I felt like I was going crazy and I couldn't stop eating!"

- "I don't have time to jog and still manage to go to work, cook for my family, and keep the lawn mowed."

- "Well, I'd like to cook healthier foods for my family, but it takes so long to plan and prepare. It's just easier to get fast foods."

Changing our health and nutrition habits can be hard. It is one thing to know what to do; it is something quite different actually to do it. Being judgmental and critical of ourselves only makes us feel worse.

A very old proverb states, "If we don't change our direction, we will very likely end up in the place we are headed." We might as well do all we can to ensure our own success by being gentle with ourselves and appreciating each step we take in our desired direction. Since doing everything "right" is very hard, you might think in terms of more and less. You want to do more of certain good things, such as:

- exercising;
- eating foods low in fats, salt, and sugar; and
- getting enough sleep.

You want to do less of certain unhealthy things, such as:

- smoking;
- eating fattening, salty foods; and
- drinking alcohol.

Keeping in mind your whole state of well-being—physical, mental, and social—take time to answer the questions below.

What healthy habits do you want to maintain or improve?

_____

_____

_____

_____

What unhealthy habits do you want to decrease?

_____

_____

_____

_____

How do you feel your health affects your work?

_____

_____

_____

_____

List three concrete and specific steps you will take to maintain healthy or change unhealthy habits.

1. _____

   _____

   _____

2. _____

   _____

   _____

3. _____

   _____

   _____

Give yourself the positive support and appreciation you would give your best friend, and you are very likely to succeed!

As a reference, we have included a summary of the *Dietary Guidelines for Americans* from the U.S. Department of Agriculture and the U.S. Department of Health and Human Services. You will find this resource on the following pages.

When you have finished this overview section you should complete the pre-training assessment. Refer to the glossary at the end of this module if you need definitions of the terms that are used.

Dietary Guidelines for Americans[1]

Eat a Variety of Foods

- Eat a variety of foods daily in adequate amounts, including selections of the following:

  - fruits
  - vegetables
  - whole-grain and enriched breads, cereals, and other foods made from grains
  - milk, cheese, yogurt, and other products made from milk
  - meats, poultry, fish, eggs, and dry beans and peas

- Women and adolescent girls should eat calcium-rich foods such as milk and milk products for strong bones.

- Young children and women should eat iron-rich foods such as beans, cereals, and grain products.

Maintain Healthy Weight

- Eat a variety of foods that are low in calories and high in nutrients, as follows:

  - Eat more fruits, vegetables, and whole grains.
  - Eat less fat and fatty foods.
  - Eat less sugar and fewer sweets.
  - Drink fewer alcoholic beverages.

- Increase your physical activity.

- Eat slowly.

- Take smaller portions.

- Avoid second helpings.

Choose a Diet Low in Fat, Saturated Fat, and Cholesterol

- Choose lean meat, fish, poultry, and dry beans and peas as protein sources.

- Use skim or low-fat milk and milk products.

---

[1] Based on the U.S. Department of Agriculture and U.S. Department of Health and Human Services, *Dietary Guidelines for Americans*, 3rd edition (Washington, DC: U.S. Government Printing Office, 1990).

- Moderate your intake of egg yolks and organ meats.

- Limit your intake of fats and oils, especially those high in saturated fat, such as butter, cream, lard, heavily hydrogenated fats (some margarines), shortenings, and foods containing palm and coconut oils.

- Trim fat off meats.

- Broil, bake, or boil rather than fry.

- Moderate your intake of foods that contain fat, such as breaded and deep-fried foods.

- Read labels carefully to determine both the amount and type of fat present in foods.

Choose a Diet with Plenty of Vegetables, Fruits, and Grain Products

- Choose foods that are good sources of fiber and starch, such as whole-grain breads and cereals, fruits, vegetables, and dry beans and peas.

- Eat at least three servings of vegetables and two servings of fruits daily.

- Have six or more servings of grain products (breads, cereals, pasta, and rice) daily.

- Substitute starchy foods for those with large amounts of fats and sugars.

Use Sugar in Moderation

- Use less of all sugars and foods containing large amounts of sugars, including white sugar, brown sugar, raw sugar, honey, and syrups. Examples include soft drinks, candies, cakes, and cookies.

- Avoid eating sweets between meals. How often you eat sugar and sugar-containing food is even more important to the health of your teeth than how much sugar you eat.

- Read food labels for clues on sugar content. If the word sugar, sucrose, glucose, maltose, dextrose, lactose, fructose, or syrup appears first, then the food contains a large amount of sugar.

- Eat fresh fruits or fruits processed without syrup or with light rather than heavy syrup.

- Brush with a fluoride toothpaste and floss regularly.

Use Salt in Moderation

- Learn to enjoy the flavors of unsalted foods.

- Cook without salt or with only small amounts of added salt.

- Try flavoring foods with herbs, spices, and lemon juice.

- Add little or no salt to food at the table.

- Limit your intake of salty foods such as potato chips, pretzels, salted nuts and popcorn, condiments (soy sauce, steak sauce, garlic salt), pickled foods, cured meats, some cheeses, and some canned vegetables and soups.

- Read food labels carefully to determine the amounts of sodium they contain. Use lower-sodium products when available.

Pre-Training Assessment

Listed below are the skills that teachers use to promote good health and nutrition for preschool children. Think about whether you do these things regularly, sometimes, or not enough. Place a check in one of the columns on the right for each skill listed. Then discuss your answers with your trainer.

SKILL	I DO THIS REGULARLY	I DO THIS SOMETIMES	I DON'T DO THIS ENOUGH
PROVIDING HEALTHY INDOOR AND OUTDOOR ENVIRONMENTS 1. Checking the room daily for adequate ventilation and lighting, comfortable room temperature, and good sanitation.			
2. Providing tissues, paper towels, and soap in places children can reach.			
3. Planning a daily schedule consistent with children's activity levels and their need for quiet times and rest.			
4. Completing a daily health check on each child to discover symptoms of illness. into anything.			
5. Washing hands upon arrival for work, before preparing and serving food, after helping with toileting or wiping a nose, and cleaning up after messes.			
6. Conducting activities in a positive, relaxed, and pleasant atmosphere to reduce tension and stress.			

SKILL	I DO THIS REGULARLY	I DO THIS SOMETIMES	I DON'T DO THIS ENOUGH
HELPING CHILDREN DEVELOP GOOD HEALTH HABITS			
7. Talking with children about ways to stay healthy.			
8. Serving nutritious family-style snacks and encouraging children to taste new foods.			
9. Helping children brush their teeth after eating.			
10. Providing frequent opportunities for children to dress themselves; reminding them to wear jackets outdoors when it is cold.			
11. Planning and implementing health and nutrition education activities on a regular basis.			
12. Being a good role model for children.			
RECOGNIZING AND REPORTING CHILD ABUSE AND NEGLECT			
13. Recognizing the signs of possible physical, sexual, and emotional child abuse and neglect.			
14. Responding to children in caring ways while avoiding questionable situations.			
15. Being alert to changes in behavior that may signal abuse or neglect.			
16. Knowing and following state laws and the program's policies for reporting suspected abuse and neglect.			

Review your responses, then list three to five skills you would like to improve or topics you would like to learn more about. When you finish this module, you will list examples of your new or improved knowledge and skills.

_____

_____

_____

_____

_____

Now begin the learning activities for Module 2, Healthy.

I. Using Your Knowledge of Child Development to Promote Good Health and Nutrition

In this activity you will learn:

- to recognize some typical behaviors of preschoolers; and

- to use what you know about preschoolers to promote good health and nutrition.

Preschool children can do many things for themselves, but they need assistance from adults to keep their environment and themselves healthy. You need to be aware of what children do so you can plan activities to meet their health and nutrition needs.

Most children need many opportunities to exercise by running, jumping, climbing, throwing, and catching. This type of play provides a safe release of energy as well as an opportunity to exercise developing muscles.

Of course, children need to rest after active play. A balanced program of active and quiet times, and indoor and outdoor activities, allows them to get the rest they need. Most preschool children in full-day programs need to nap or rest quietly for at least two hours in the afternoon.

Preschool children acquire many self-help skills. They put on their jackets, brush their teeth, use the toilet, wash their hands, and blow their noses. Encouraging the use of these skills helps children learn to keep themselves healthy. Serving as a model for appropriate health habits teaches them the importance of preventing illness and disease.

Children can also learn to prepare, select, and eat nutritious foods. Food-preparation activities and family-style eating allow preschoolers to learn about good nutrition.

The chart on the next page identifies some typical behaviors of preschool children. Included are behaviors relevant to children's health and nutrition. The right column asks you to identify ways that teachers can use this information about child development to promote good health and nutrition. Try to think of as many examples as you can. As you work through the module you will learn new strategies for ensuring children's health, and you can add them to the child development chart. You are not expected to think of all the examples at one time. If you need help getting started, turn to the completed chart at the end of the module. By the time you complete all the learning activities, you will find that you have learned many ways to promote children's health and nutrition.

Using Your Knowledge of Child Development
to Promote Good Health and Nutrition

WHAT PRESCHOOL CHILDREN ARE LIKE	HOW TEACHERS CAN USE THIS INFORMATION TO PROMOTE GOOD HEALTH AND NUTRITION
They can run, jump, hop, kick, climb, throw, and use indoor and outdoor large muscle equipment.	
They can dress themselves.	
They understand relationships expressed by "if…then" or "because" clauses.	
They ask questions for information.	
They can learn by observing and imitating adults.	

WHAT PRESCHOOL CHILDREN ARE LIKE	HOW TEACHERS CAN USE THIS INFORMATION TO PROMOTE GOOD HEALTH AND NUTRITION
They are beginning to blow their own noses.	
They can use the toilet and wash their hands.	
They can pour from small pitchers and use utensils properly.	
They can use knives with assistance.	
They develop feelings of self-esteem, good or poor, related to how people respond to and treat them.	

When you have completed as much as you can do on the chart, discuss your responses with your trainer. As you proceed with the rest of the learning activities, you can refer back to the chart and add more examples of how teachers promote good health and nutrition for preschool children.

II. Maintaining an Environment That Promotes Wellness

In this activity you will learn:

- to provide and maintain a hygienic environment; and

- to recognize symptoms of illness in preschool children.

What can you do to promote health? First, you can check the room daily to see that it is clean and uncluttered. Even when custodial staff do the cleaning, you will need to check the room each day. You should report any problems to your supervisor. It is your job to be sure that your room promotes wellness and minimizes or reduces the incidence of illness or disease.

You can also keep your room in good condition during the day. You do this by cleaning spills as they happen; wiping off tables before and after eating, after painting, and so forth; storing food and bottles properly; and throwing away garbage promptly. Whenever possible, the children can assist with these chores. You should keep paper towels within their reach.

In addition, you can ensure that your room is sanitary. Bacteria, parasites, or viruses can be left on tables, toys, and equipment by sick children or can grow on perishable food. To disinfect toys and equipment, thoroughly wash surfaces with soap and water. Then wipe the surfaces with a bleach solution or a commercial disinfectant. If you make your own solution, mix 1/4 to 1/2 cup of bleach per gallon of water (or 1 tablespoon of bleach per quart of water). Use this solution to sanitize mops, brooms, dustpans, table tops, and other soiled surfaces after each use. Wash and disinfect surfaces in easy reach of children (floors, doorknobs, climbers, etc.) at least weekly.

To make sure the room remains hygienic, work with children and other adults to minimize germs and keep them from spreading. Toothbrushes should be stored in sanitary receptacles, such as upside-down egg cartons or slotted plastic milk containers. Toothbrushes should be allowed to air dry. Tissues should be placed where children can reach them. Each child should have a sheet and blanket for napping. These must be laundered at least once per week.

The bathroom is a major source of germs. You should check this room daily to make sure it is clean and well stocked with paper supplies. Report problems and missing items to your supervisor. When you help children use the toilet, wash your hands afterward.

The most effective way to reduce illness and disease is to wash your hands properly throughout the day. Encouraging preschoolers to do so also prevents germs from spreading.

You should wash your hands:

- when you arrive for work in the morning;

- before you prepare or serve food;

- after you help a child use the toilet, or wipe a nose;

- after you clean up messes; and

- after you use the bathroom.

Of course, germs are present even in an apparently spotless room. Preschool children may come to the center with a variety of illnesses. You must be aware of the symptoms and incubation periods for common childhood illnesses. The chart on the next page summarizes this information.[2]

If a child in your group has a severe cold or the symptoms of another illness noted in the chart, he or she should not come to the center while ill. Also, parents need to inform you if their child has recently been exposed to one of these illnesses. Then you can be careful to ensure that all children and staff take necessary precautions to keep the illness from spreading.

---

[2] Based on Centers for Disease Control, *What You Should Know About Contagious Diseases in the Day Care Setting* (Atlanta, GA: Centers for Disease Control, December 1984).

Contagious Diseases in Day Care

INFECTION	SYMPTOMS	INCUBATION PERIOD
Hepatitis A	Fatigue, loss of appetite, yellowish skin and whites of the eyes, dark-brown urine, light-colored stool	A month or longer
Chicken pox	Itchy rash of small red bumps on the stomach or back before spreading to the face	11-21 days
Colds and flu	Stuffy or runny nose, sneezing, coughing, sometimes a fever	The first days, when symptoms may or may not be visible, are the most infective. Symptoms may linger for 1-1/2 weeks.
Strep throat	Red and painful throat, often accompanied by fever	1-5 days
Impetigo	Flat, yellow, crusty, or oozing patch on the skin	5 days
Measles	Fever, upper-respiratory illness, red-brown blotchy rash on the face and body	14 days
Mumps	Swelling of the glands at the jaw angle	14-21 days
Rubella (German measles)	Fever and a red rash (in children, usually a milder illness than measles)	14-21 days

What Teachers Need to Know About HIV

HIV (Human Immunodeficiency Virus) is the virus that causes AIDS (Acquired Immune Deficiency Syndrome). HIV attacks the white blood cells in the immune system that normally protect the body from viruses and bacteria. This makes it difficult and gradually impossible for the body to fight off infection.

HIV is not transmitted through casual contact or from being around someone who is infected. It cannot be transmitted by mosquitos or pets. The virus does not live by itself in the air. You cannot get it by:

- Being in the same room with someone
- Sharing drinks or food
- Being near when someone coughs or sneezes
- Hugging, shaking hands, or kissing as friends do
- Sharing a swimming pool, bath, or toilet
- Sharing bed linens or towels

HIV is transmitted through blood, semen, and vaginal secretions. A person can become infected:

- **From mother to child (perinatal).** Most children with HIV infection under 13 years of age are infected this way. If the mother has HIV, her blood can transmit the virus to the baby during pregnancy or delivery. Because HIV has been found in breastmilk, mothers with HIV infection are discouraged from breastfeeding.

- **Through sexual intercourse** with a man or woman who has HIV. Sexually abused children are at risk for HIV infection.

- **By sharing intravenous needles** that contain infected blood from a previous user.

- **From blood and blood product transfusions prior to 1985,** before blood was tested for HIV infection. Many children were infected this way, including those with hemophilia.

Children with HIV infection can remain healthy for long periods of time. They have AIDS when the virus has severely damaged the immune system. Because children with HIV infection are more susceptible to germs, good hygiene is very important. Washing hands vigorously with soap and warm water for 15 seconds is one of the best ways to prevent the spread of germs. Since HIV is carried in the blood, you should always create a "barrier" between yourself and someone's blood when cleaning a cut or applying pressure to a bloody nose. A towel, rolled cloth, paper towel, or disposable gloves can be a barrier.

Children with HIV infection may have special nutrition and therapy needs. If you are caring for a child with HIV infection, find out if specific training in these areas is available.

This learning activity will help you maintain an environment that promotes wellness. Begin by reading "Communicable Diseases in the Day Care Setting" on the following pages. Then complete the Health Checklist. After reading the example that follows it, record your answers to the questions on the form provided.

Communicable Diseases in the Early Childhood Setting: Help for Staff[3]

Most childhood diseases need to be carefully monitored because they tend to be highly contagious. In an early childhood setting, it is likely that what is contracted by one child will be transmitted to others. In order to minimize the spread of communicable diseases, teachers and parents should follow simple hygienic guidelines in a consistent manner. Studies have suggested that the number of illnesses in early childhood settings can often be reduced by half when such practices are followed.

Although people are aware of the most common contagious diseases, such as chicken pox, many do not realize that diarrhea, hepatitis, and impetigo can also be spread. Even a few germs on a hand or a toy may be enough to spread a disease. Disease can be spread through body secretions, by direct contact, and even when no illness is apparent.

Germs Spread Through Body Secretions

Both intestinal and respiratory-tract infections may spread through body secretions. Intestinal-tract infections usually show up as diarrhea. Diarrhea is actually a symptom of infection caused by several kinds of germs—either bacteria (like Salmonella or Shigella); parasites (like Giardia); or certain types of viruses. Hepatitis A (infectious hepatitis) is also caused by a virus that spreads through the intestinal tract. Very young children infected with the disease may not seem sick at all or may appear to have a mild "stomach flu."

Respiratory-tract infections spread through coughing, sneezing, and runny noses, and also through speaking and singing. For this reason, children can easily spread colds, flu, strep throat, and even bacterial meningitis (spinal meningitis) through sharing food, touching, or kissing another child. Viral rashes, such as chicken pox, measles, roseola, and mumps, are also transmitted through oral and nasal secretions. Respiratory-disease germs can live on cloth, tissues, toys, and any other surface for hours or even days. These germs are often spread during the incubation period (that is, before symptoms appear).

Certain diseases can be contracted simply by touching the infected area of another person's body. The most common diseases in this group are head lice, impetigo, scabies, and ringworm. Rabies, a very rare disease, can result from direct contact with the saliva of an infected animal.

A person harboring a disease is often contagious before he or she develops symptoms. Sometimes, people spread germs without even getting sick themselves. Therefore, procedures designed to prevent the spread of contagious diseases must be followed always—not just when a person is already ill.

---

[3]From Maryland Committee for Children, Inc., *Maryland Child Care* (Baltimore, MD: Maryland Committee for Children, Inc., Spring 1985).

The possibility of spreading disease is greater when the same teacher is responsible for multiple duties, such as helping children use the toilet and food preparation. Also, germs are spread more easily when there is improper ventilation, overcrowded conditions, unsanitary food storage and preparation (such as lack of hot and cold running water in the area or poorly sealed garbage bags and lids), and an unstable population (children who drop in to a program). Another major factor is the presence of children with "borderline" or emerging symptoms.

The best way to protect the health of children and teachers is by establishing policies that prevent the spread of disease.

Recommended Handwashing Procedures

The surest, most highly recommended way to reduce disease is to encourage staff and children to follow recommended handwashing procedures as outlined below:

- Using soap and running water, rub your hands vigorously.
- Wash all surfaces—backs of hands, wrists, between fingers, under fingernails.
- Rinse your hands well.
- While leaving the water running, dry your hands with a disposable paper towel.
- Turn off the water using a paper towel instead of bare hands.

Liquid soaps from dispensers are more sanitary than bar soaps, which can harbor germs.

Staff should be sure to wash their hands:

- when arriving for work in the morning;
- before preparing or serving food;
- after nose wiping or cleaning up messes; and
- after using the bathroom, with a child or by themselves.

Children should wash their hands especially:

- when arriving at the program in the morning;
- before eating or drinking;
- after using the toilet; and
- after touching a child who may be sick.

When children forget to wash their hands or are not washing them correctly:

- tell them to wash their hands correctly;
- show them how to wash their hands thoroughly if they do not know how; and
- remind them that washing their hands correctly will help keep them healthy.

Children's Symptoms That Require Attention

When children arrive in the morning, check to see if they have any of the following symptoms:

- severe coughing (red or blue in the face, high-pitched croupy or whooping sound);
- difficulty breathing;
- yellowish skin or eyes;
- pinkeye (tears, redness of eyelid lining, irritation, swelling, discharge of pus);
- unusual spots or rashes;
- infected skin patches or crusty, bright-yellow dry or gummy skin areas;
- feverish appearance; or
- unusual behavior (child is cranky, less active than usual or cries more than usual; child feels general discomfort or just seems unwell).

During the day, check for these signs that signify illness:

- gray or white stool;
- unusually dark, tea-colored urine;
- sore throat or trouble swallowing;
- headache or stiff neck;
- nausea and vomiting;
- loss of appetite; and
- diarrhea.

Also watch for frequent scratching of the body or scalp. This may be a sign of lice or scabies.

If a child exhibits any of these symptoms, separate him or her from the other children and take his or her temperature. Make sure to inform your supervisor. A separate area should be designated where children can be cared for until taken home.

Organize Space, Equipment, and Supplies to Prevent Disease Transmission

If possible, arrange to have separate classrooms and play areas for each group of children, as small groups and less mixing will help prevent germs from spreading. Younger children, especially those in diapers, should be separated from older children, as infants and toddlers are at especially high risk for spreading hepatitis A and diarrheal diseases.

Keep sufficient quantities of facial tissues, paper towels, linen and mattress covers, and supplies for handwashing, diapering, and cleaning readily available.

Teachers in groups with diapered children should not prepare food, or as a minimum precaution should not serve food to children outside their group. If they must prepare food, they should be sure to wash their hands.

If potty chairs are used, they should be kept in bathrooms and out of a child's reach. Potty chairs should be rinsed in a sink used only for this purpose. If this is not possible, wash the sink and disinfect all exposed surfaces.

Wash and Disinfect Surfaces

Disinfecting is effective only when surfaces are thoroughly washed first. Be sure all facilities and supplies are washed with soap and water and then disinfected with either a bleach solution or a commercial disinfectant designed to kill bacteria, viruses, and parasites such as Giardia.

Make an effective bleach solution by mixing 1/4 to 1/2 cup bleach per gallon water or 1 tablespoon bleach per quart of water. A spray bottle is easy to use and handy for storage. Fresh bleach solution should be made and used daily. Keep this out of the reach of children.

Handle Soiled Clothing Carefully

Take special care with children's soiled clothing. Clothing should not be washed in the center. When children have accidents, empty the stool into the toilet, and put the clothes in sealed plastic bags to be picked up by the child's parent at the end of the day. Hands should be washed thoroughly after handling soiled clothing.

Exchange Important Information with Parents

Parents and teachers can help promote good health of children and staff in the center by sharing important information. Infection control policies and procedures used in the setting, as well as immunization requirements, should be explained to parents. Phone numbers of parents, family physician, hospital, and a contact person (in case parents cannot be reached) along with significant medical information about each child should be given to the teacher. In particular, ask parents to inform the staff if their child has recently been exposed to the following diseases:

- bacterial meningitis;
- chicken pox;
- diarrheal diseases;
- diphtheria;
- hepatitis;
- measles;
- mumps;
- pertussis (whooping cough);
- rubella (German measles); or
- pneumonia, epiglotitis (swelling of the back of the throat), acute infectious arthritis.

The staff can then be especially careful to ensure that the child maintains good health precautions, such as handwashing, while being aware of any unusual changes in the child's behavior or the appearance of symptoms that may indicate illness. If the child is then diagnosed as having a contagious disease, the center can take full precautions to protect the health of the other children. Heeding the previously described precautions can help eliminate common childhood illnesses that are easily transmitted.

(The information on communicable disease and prevention was excerpted from the Centers for Disease Control [CDC] handbooks.)

Health Checklist

Look at your room and think about your routines. Use this health checklist to assess your environment.

THINGS YOU CAN DO TO MAINTAIN A HEALTHY ENVIRONMENT	ROUTINE IS SATISFACTORY	ROUTINE NEEDS IMPROVEMENT
1. Let in fresh air daily by opening windows or doors.		
2. Check the room daily to make sure it is clean. Report problems to your supervisor.		
3. Ask children to wipe off tables after eating and messy activities and to wash their hands.		
4. Store food so that it doesn't spoil.		
5. Put garbage in metal or plastic pails with lids.		
6. Keep tissues where children can reach them.		
7. Store toothbrushes without touching each other. Allow bristles to air dry.		
8. Check the bathroom daily to make sure it is clean and well-stocked with toilet paper, paper towels, and soap; report problems and missing items to your supervisor.		
9. Wash your own hands whenever necessary.		
10. Encourage children to wash their hands when they arrive in the morning, before and after eating or drinking, after using the toilet, and after touching a child who may be sick.		

THINGS YOU CAN DO TO MAINTAIN A HEALTHY ENVIRONMENT	ROUTINE IS SATISFACTORY	ROUTINE NEEDS IMPROVEMENT
11. Conduct a health check each day to see if children have: • severe coughing, difficulty breathing, or sore throat; • yellowish skin or eyes; • pinkeye (tears, redness of eyelid lining, irritation, swelling, and discharge of pus); • infected skin patches; • nausea, vomiting, or diarrhea; • loss of appetite; or • unusual behavior.		
12. Separate sick children from others and ask your supervisor to see that they are cared for until taken home.		
13. Report symptoms of possible illness to your supervisor.		
14. Avoid touching body fluids when helping children use the toilet, and wash hands immediately after.		
15. Place children's wet or soiled clothes in plastic bags for parents to launder at home.		
16. Rinse brooms, dustpans, mops, and rags in a disinfectant solution after cleaning body fluid spills.		
17. Send children's clothes and blankets home for laundering once a week.		
18. Launder dress-up clothes and disinfect supplies and equipment handled often by children.		

Use your responses on the checklist to complete the blank chart. Read the example below first.

ITEMS NEEDING IMPROVEMENT	WHAT I INTEND TO DO
I don't always let in fresh air in the winter.	*I will raise two windows just a little to let in fresh air.*
I don't wash my hands when I arrive at work.	*I will wash my hands before the children arrive.*
I don't always do a health check.	*I will make the health check part of my children's arrival routine.*
We don't disinfect mops and brooms.	*I will ask my supervisor to order disinfectant and bleach. I will store them in a locked cabinet.*

Now identify the items in your environment that need improvement.

ITEMS NEEDING IMPROVEMENT	WHAT I INTEND TO DO

Discuss these precautions with your trainer. Make the needed changes in your room and check them off when they have been completed.

III. Helping Children Develop Good Health Habits

In this activity you will learn:

- to provide a model for good health habits in the course of daily life in your room so that children can learn by your example; and

- to plan and conduct health education activities for children.

In Learning Activity II, Maintaining an Environment That Promotes Wellness, you learned that health education works best in a healthy environment where teachers display healthy behaviors. Through routines such as regular toothbrushing, handwashing, using and discarding tissues, and careful food handling, preschoolers can learn good health habits. Adults serve as models to help children learn these habits.

In addition, teachers can conduct health education activities throughout the year. These activities can focus on things preschool children can do to keep themselves healthy. Like other experiences planned for children, these activities should be conducted in a way that matches children's learning styles. That is, they should be:

- based on concrete experiences, using actual objects as much as possible;

- geared to help children move from the simple to the complex;

- matched with children's interests and skill levels;

- conducted when children can play with objects and answer open-ended questions asked by teachers; and

- repeated several times so all can participate.

A number of health education topics lend themselves to appropriate activities in a preschool classroom. These topics, and suggested objectives for children, are outlined in the following chart.[4]

---

[4]Based on Judith L. Pokorni and Roxane K. Kaufmann, *Health in Day Care—A Training Guide for Day Care Providers* (Washington, DC: Georgetown University Child Development Center, 1986), pp. 79-80 and 159-161.

TOPIC	OBJECTIVES FOR CHILDREN
Identifying body parts	Identifying body parts and functions Accepting and understanding growth Taking care of yourself through rest, food, exercise, and cleanliness Being curious about your body
Preventing poisoning and choking	Keeping unknown substances and objects out of your mouth
Health-care providers	Identifying doctors, nurses, dentists, and other health-care providers Accepting care from health-care providers
Germs and hygiene	Covering your mouth when sneezing Using tissues Handwashing correctly
Dental health	Knowing why teeth are important Toothbrushing Identifying foods that help prevent tooth decay Visiting the dentist regularly

Many of the activities you normally provide for preschool children can also be used for health education. These include:

- **Dramatic play.** Set up the house corner as a hospital or dentist's office.

- **Water play.** Have children bathe dolls or wash clothes.

- **Field trips.** Visit a dentist's office, hospital, exercise class, or zoo (to see how animals chew their food with different kinds of teeth).

- **Puppet shows.** Have doctor or nurse puppets and put on a show about caring for someone who is sick.

- **Finger plays and songs.** Include activities related to health topics, such as washing hands, brushing teeth, and so on.

- **Children's books.** Read books such as *Morris Has a Cold* by Bernard Wiseman, *Bread and Jam for Frances* by Russell Hoban, and *Clean as a Whistle* by Aileen Fisher.

- **Table toys.** Have children put together body-part puzzles or health care provider puzzles.

- **Art activities.** Trace children's bodies on large pieces of newsprint to show body image and body parts.

- **Visitors to the classroom.** Invite a dental hygienist to visit the classroom. She or he can talk with small groups of children and demonstrate toothbrushing during free play.

In this activity you will learn how to plan and conduct health education activities. First read "Good Food...Healthy Teeth," and "Dental Health and Sugar" on the following pages. Read the example that follows the articles, then plan and conduct a small group activity to teach a health concept. After conducting the activity, answer the questions on the blank form.

Good Food...Healthy Teeth[5]

This guide will help you select nutritious snacks that are good for children's teeth as well as their general health. Choose foods without added sugars.

Fresh Fruits

Apples	Plums
Oranges	Pears
Tangerines	Peaches
Tangelos	Pineapple
Grapefruit	Cantaloupe
Grapes	Berries

Fresh Vegetables

Broccoli	Peas
Carrots	Asparagus
Celery	Radishes
Cauliflower	Turnips
Cucumbers	Lettuce
Green peppers	Tomatoes

Protein Foods

Chicken	Cheese
Turkey	Cottage cheese
Liver	Yogurt (plain)
Fish	Peanuts
Nuts	Sunflower seeds
Eggs	Pumpkin seeds

Thirst Quenchers

Milk (low-fat, skim)
Buttermilk
Tomato juice
Fruit juice (canned, fresh, frozen
    no sugar added)

Caution: Sweet and sticky foods should not be served as between-meal snacks. Examples of such foods include candy, cake, cookies, cupcakes, pie, jelly, jam, soft drinks, fruit punch, or fruit drinks.

The following foods should not be eaten as snacks because they stick to the teeth. Eat them at mealtimes instead.

Apricots (dried)	Figs
Bananas	Peanut butter
Bread (except 100% whole wheat)	Prunes
Canned fruit (packed in light syrup)	Raisins
Crackers	

Be sure that each child:

- eats foods that don't cause tooth decay,
- is taught to floss and brush teeth (by parent and teacher), and
- has regular dental checkups beginning at age two and a half to three years.

---

[5]Reprinted with permission from Elaine McLaughlin, Nancy Goldsmith, and Peter Pizzolongo, *Living and Teaching Nutrition* (College Park, MD: Head Start Resource and Training Center, 1983), p. 5-B.

Dental Health and Sugar[6]

What Do You Need For Tooth Decay?

- Teeth: They are yours for life if you take care of them.
- Sugar-rich foods: Sticky, sugary foods cause cavities.
- Bacteria: Bacteria and sugar-rich foods produce an acid that causes cavities.

Is Sugar Bad For You?

- Sugar contains 15 calories per teaspoon.
- Sugar in sticky foods is harmful to teeth.
- Sugar contains no protein, vitamins, or minerals.
- Sugar can contribute to obesity and may replace more nutritious food such as fruits, vegetables, and whole grains.

Sugar is Associated with the Following Dangers

- Obesity

    - Fat children often become fat adults (10 to 50 percent of the population is overweight).
    - Concentrated sweets lack fiber, don't give a feeling of fullness, and are easy to overeat.

- Dental Decay

    - Almost everyone (98 percent of the population) gets cavities.
    - Sweet, sticky foods provide a medium for cavity development.
    - For tooth decay the number of times sugar is eaten is more important than the amount.

---

[6]Reprinted with permission from Elaine McLaughlin, Nancy Goldsmith, and Peter Pizzolongo, *Living and Teaching Nutrition* (College Park, MD: Head Start Resource and Training Center, 1983), p. 5-C.

Health Activity
(Example)

Health education concept: _Germs can be airborne._

Date: _February 6_

What did you want the children to learn from this experience?

How far a sneeze travels.

How important it is to cover their nose and mouth when they sneeze.

What resources did you use for this activity?

A recycled spray bottle filled with red-colored water.

A large sheet of white paper.

How did you conduct the activity?

I noticed that one child was sneezing frequently. I invited him to do an experiment with me. I suggested that squirting the spray bottle was like sneezing a sneeze and asked him how far he thought the spray would go. He guessed. I held up the white paper and he squirted the bottle. He was surprised when the red spots of water showed on the white paper. He experimented with different distances. He invited his friends to see.

What if anything will you do differently when you repeat this activity?

Next time I will record the distance the spray bottle "sneeze" travels, and write about our experiment in the parent newsletter. Maybe parents will help encourage their children to cover their sneezes and coughs.

Health Activity

Health education concept: _____

Date: _____

What did you want the children to learn from this experience?

_____
_____
_____
_____

What resources did you use for this activity?

_____
_____
_____
_____

How did you conduct the activity?

_____
_____
_____
_____

What if anything will you do differently when you repeat this activity?

_____
_____
_____
_____

Discuss your answers with your trainer. Talk with other teachers about ways to provide health education activities throughout the year.

IV. Helping Children Develop Good Nutrition Habits

In this activity you will learn:

- to provide experiences that demonstrate that food is important and that a healthy body needs a variety of foods every day; and

- to help children select and enjoy nutritious foods for snacks and meals.

Teaching children good nutritional habits is a wise investment in their future. The food children eat affects their well-being, their physical growth, their ability to learn, and their overall behavior. Attitudes about food develop early in life and last a long time.

We have an opportunity to help children learn about foods, to enjoy a variety of foods from their own culture and others, and to begin to appreciate that their bodies need to be strong, flexible, and healthy.

Eating is a nurturing activity. Eating moderately, eating a variety of foods and eating in a relaxed, pleasant atmosphere are healthy habits for young children to develop.

There are many resources to help us learn about good nutrition. The Departments of Agriculture and Health and Human Services dietary guidelines for Americans are included in the overview section of this module. You may want to post the following guidelines in your kitchen area for you and parents to refer to.

- Eat a variety of foods.
- Maintain desirable weight.
- Avoid too much fat, saturated fat, and cholesterol.
- Eat food with adequate starch and fiber.
- Avoid too much sugar.
- Avoid too much salt.

This information is valuable for adults who want to stay healthy and to teach good nutrition habits to preschool children. It is also valuable as a basis for a nutrition education program.

Just as health education is best acquired when teachers display healthy behavior, nutrition education works best in a healthy environment. When teachers eat nutritious foods, children are more likely to do so as well. When teachers taste all the foods served, they encourage children to try new foods. When teachers treat mealtimes as a chance to talk with other children while eating, children will use this time for relaxed conversation. Nutrition education takes place throughout the day.

Family-Style Eating

One way to make mealtimes more relaxed and pleasant is to serve and eat meals family-style. This means that a teacher sits with a group of children at each table. Everyone eats the same foods, serves themselves, and enjoys pleasant conversation. After experiencing family-style eating at the center, children are more likely to try new foods because they serve themselves. They can decide for themselves whether to put one pea on their plate, or a spoonful. The following tips can help you start family-style eating in your room.[7]

Before the Meal

- Provide or encourage food service staff to provide nutritious foods, including dessert. Desserts could include fresh fruit, blueberry muffins, applesauce, fruit juice, gelatin, or cornbread.

- Arrange the furniture so that tables are far enough apart to walk between but close enough for quiet conversation.

- Plan to seat seven or eight children and one teacher at each table.

- Ask children who are helpers to set the tables. Glue a place setting on a piece of cardboard for the helpers to use as a model.

- Provide child-sized utensils, cups, plates, and pitchers.

- Serve the food in serving bowls or on platters.

- Leave the salt and sugar off the table.

- Lead a quiet activity while small groups of children are toileting and handwashing. After handwashing, children can return to the activity.

- Invite everyone to sit down after the tables are set.

- Suggest that everyone take a deep breath, relax, and think about how this food will make our bodies strong and healthy.

During the Meal

- Ask children and teachers to begin serving as soon as everyone is seated.

- Allow children to pour their own drinks using small covered pitchers.

- Maintain a leisurely mealtime pace.

---

[7] Adapted from Elaine McLaughlin, Nancy Goldsmith, and Peter Pizzolongo, *Living and Teaching Nutrition* (College Park, MD: Head Start Resource and Training Center, 1983), p. 5-D.

- Allow children to refuse food, but encourage them to taste a little of everything.

- Show children how to use utensils if they need help.

- Encourage children to serve themselves only as much as they can eat. If they can't finish what's on their plate, don't force them.

- Model good hygiene, safety practices, and manners.

- Observe the children's mealtime behaviors. Record your observations after the meal.

- Ask children to clean up their own spills.

- Encourage conversation. You can talk about the foods served, where the foods come from, and who prepared them for the children. Also talk about the events of the day, families, or other topics of interest to the children.

- Respect cultural traditions and beliefs regarding mealtime rituals. For example, in some cultures, a respectful silence honoring animals and plants is appropriate and talking during meals is considered inappropriate.

After the Meal

- Remain relaxed.

- Allow children to leave the table when they are finished. They can clean up their dishes, then go to a quiet activity.

- Have small groups of children brush their teeth. Teachers should brush their teeth with the children.

- Ask helpers to clean up and wash the table.

Goals for Nutrition Education

As teachers plan and conduct activities during free play, group times, and mealtimes, they can meet the following nutrition education goals for preschool children.[8]

GOALS	ACTIVITIES
Identifying physical and sensory characteristics.	Eating a variety of foods. Preparing food with children. Dramatic play with plastic foods in the house corner. Matching food picture cards. Playing food bingo with picture cards. Using a "feely" bag with food inside.
Knowing that people of varied cultures, upbringing, and geographic locations have different eating patterns.	Preparing and eating foods from a variety of cultures and regions, such as stir-fry vegetables with rice, arroz con pollo, adobo, and fried bread.
Realizing what happens when too much fat, salt, and sugar is eaten.	Reading stories about eating the wrong kinds of foods, such as *The Snacking Mouse* by Pat and Kim Wilhite.
Developing skills and attitudes that help children enjoy a nutritious diet.	Tasting all foods at snacktimes and mealtimes.
Accepting the rules and limits for eating and consideration of self and others.	Eating with other children and adults in small groups.
Selecting and enjoying nutritious foods for snacks.	Preparing food using single-portion recipe cards. Growing and tasting sprouts. Tasting new foods at snack and meal times. Cooking and eating vegetables and fruits.

---

[8] Adapted from Christine Olson with Jill Randall and Linda Moriss, *The Early Childhood Nutrition Program—Food Experiences for Young Children* (Ithaca, NY: Cornell University Press, 1979), and Elaine McLaughlin, Nancy Goldsmith, and Peter Pizzolongo, *Living and Teaching Nutrition* (College Park, MD: Head Start Resource and Training Center, 1983).

GOALS	ACTIVITIES
Learning where foods come from.	Growing foods from seeds and seedlings. Taking trips to the farm, farmer's market, supermarket, and grocery store. Reading stories about farms and supermarkets. Playing with food and cooking props in the house corner. Putting together farm and supermarket puzzles.
Knowing that food is important and that a healthy body needs a variety of foods daily.	Cutting and eating raw vegetables and fruits. Grinding wheat and making bread. Preparing and eating foods low in fat, salt, and sugar, such as apple salads and raw vegetables. Creating healthy food/junk food collages.

The best way to teach children about food is to use real food. Preschool children can prepare their own snacks and sit with other children and adults to share a relaxed meal. For this learning activity you will plan and conduct a food-preparation activity that uses healthy ingredients for a small group during free play. On 5" x 8" cards or half sheets of paper, describe and illustrate each step in the recipe. Lay out the picture cards left to right on the table so that children can complete one step at a time. Gather food and equipment, and conduct the activity in your room during free play. After conducting this activity, complete the blank form that follows. Begin by reading the example on the next page.

Food Preparation Activity

Children: _Carlos, Deena, Troy_   **Ages:** _4 to 4 1/2 years_   **Date:** _April 23_

What you made: _Cheese burritos_

How did you involve the children in the cooking activity?

I set up the picture cards for making cheese burritos on the table next to the electric fry pan. I laid out the ingredients—flour tortillas, cheese, oil for the pan, salsa—and utensils—cheese grater, spatula, spoon, pot holder, knives, and so on. Carlos came over first. He wanted to grate some cheese. While I was showing him how to hold the grater so he wouldn't grate his fingers Deena and Troy joined us. They wanted their own graters and cheese. I had plenty of equipment so the children didn't have to share.

What did the children learn from this activity?

They learned that cheese melts when it is heated.

They learned how to use the grater.

Deena and Troy tried a new food—the salsa.

We talked about how tortillas are made even though we used store-bought ones.

We talked about how eating cheese helps children develop strong bodies.

When you repeat this activity, what changes, if any, would you make?

I would put out some other ingredients in case children wanted to invent different kinds of burritos.

I would simplify the recipe cards—they were too detailed for the children to follow.

Food Preparation Activity

Children: _____   Ages: _____   Date: _____

What you made: _____

How did you involve the children in the cooking activity?

_____

_____

_____

_____

_____

What did the children learn from this activity?

_____

_____

_____

_____

_____

When you repeat this activity, what changes, if any, would you make?

_____

_____

_____

_____

_____

Discuss your answers with your trainer. Talk with other teachers about ways you can provide nutrition education activities throughout the year.

V. Recognizing Child Abuse and Neglect[9]

In this activity you will learn:

- to identify the four types of child abuse and neglect; and

- to recognize the signs of child abuse and neglect.

Child abuse and neglect cases are often first identified in a child development program. Teachers who have ongoing, daily contact with children are often able to detect and report suspected child maltreatment that otherwise might go unnoticed. Teachers are responsible for knowing how to identify signs of possible child abuse or neglect and to report their suspicions to the appropriate authorities. The first step is to know the definitions of child abuse and neglect. Each state in the United States has its own legal definitions, most of which include the elements listed below.

Child abuse and neglect includes physical abuse, neglect, sexual abuse, and emotional abuse of a child under the age of 18 by a parent, guardian, or any other person who is responsible for the child's welfare.

- **Physical Abuse**—nonaccidental injury, which may include severe beatings, burns, strangulation, or human bites.

- **Neglect**—failure to provide the child with food, clothing, medical attention, or supervision.

- **Sexual Abuse**—the exploitation of a child for the sexual gratification of an adult, as in rape, incest, fondling of the genitals, or exhibitionism.

- **Emotional Maltreatment**—behavior that places unreasonable demands on a child to perform above his or her capabilities and does so in an excessive or aggressive manner. Examples include constant teasing, belittling verbal attacks, and a lack of love, support, or guidance.

Children who are being abused or neglected may exhibit physical and/or behavioral signs of their maltreatment. Physical signs are those you can actually see. Whether mild or severe, they involve the child's physical condition. Frequently physical signs are skin or bone injuries, or evidence of lack of care and attention manifested in conditions such as malnutrition. Behavioral clues may exist alone or may accompany physical indicators. They range from subtle changes in a child's behavior to graphic statements by children describing physical or sexual abuse.

---

[9] Based on materials included in Derry G. Koralek, *A Guide for Early Childhood Professionals on Preventing and Responding to Child Maltreatment* (Washington, DC: National Center on Child Abuse and Neglect, In Press, 1991).

Teachers play an important role in preventing or stopping child maltreatment by identifying and reporting signs of possible abuse or neglect. It is your responsibility to report your suspicions to the director of your center and to the agency designated by your state's law as the recipient of these reports. To fulfill this duty, you must be able to recognize the relevant signs.

Clues to abuse and neglect may be found in how a child looks and acts, what the parent says, how the parent relates to the child, and how the parent and child behave when they are together. No single sign or clue proves abuse or neglect, but repeated signs or several signs together should alert you to the *possibility* that a child is being abused or neglected.

Signs of Possible Physical Abuse

Physical abuse of children includes any nonaccidental physical injury caused by the child's caretaker in single or repeated episodes. Although the injury is not accidental, the adult may not intend to hurt the child. The injury might be the result of overdiscipline or physical punishment that is inappropriate to the child's age. This usually happens when an adult is angry or frustrated and strikes, shakes, or throws a child. Occasionally physical abuse is intentional, such as when an adult burns, bites, pokes, cuts, twists limbs, or otherwise harms a child.

Young children frequently fall down and bump into things. These accidents may result in injuries to their elbows, chins, noses, foreheads, and other bony areas. Bruises and marks on the soft tissue of the face, back, neck, buttocks, upper arms, thighs, ankles, backs of legs, or genitals, however, are more likely to be caused by physical abuse.

When you are helping a child change clothes or go to the bathroom you might see bruises or burns that are covered by clothing. Often abusive parents are consciously or unconsciously aware that the signs of their abuse should be concealed, so they dress their children in long sleeves or long pants. Another sign to look for is bruises that are at various stages of healing, as if they are the result of more than one incident.

Injuries to the abdomen or head, which are two particularly vulnerable spots, often go undetected until there are internal injuries. Injuries to the abdomen can cause swelling, tenderness, and vomiting. Injuries to the head may cause swelling, dizziness, blackouts, retinal detachment, and even death.

In addition to the physical signs that a child has been physically abused, the child might also exhibit behavioral signs. Here are some examples:

- Jackie (3 years) runs to her cubbie to get her blanket whenever she hears another child crying. She clutches her blanket and rocks back and forth, saying, "No hitting. No hitting."

- When she notices the big bruise on his leg, Troy (4 1/2 years) tells his teacher, "Mommy hit me real hard and I fell off my chair."

- Daniel (3 1/2 years) is usually picked up by his mother. When his father comes to get him, he screams and hides behind his teacher's legs. Earlier that day his teacher overheard him playing with the dolls. He said, "I told you to keep those pants dry. Now you're going to get a beating."

Signs of Possible Neglect

Child neglect is characterized by a failure to provide for a child's basic needs. Neglect can be physical (for example, refusal to seek health care when a child clearly needs medical attention), educational (for example, failure to enroll a child of mandatory school age), or emotional (for example, chronic or extreme spouse abuse in the child's presence). Neglect results in death as frequently as abuse. While physical abuse tends to be episodic, neglect tends to be chronic. Neglectful families often appear to have many problems that they are not able to handle.

When considering the possibility of neglect, it is important to look for consistencies. Do the signs of neglect occur rarely or frequently? Are they chronic (present almost every day), periodic (happening after weekends, vacations, or absences), or episodic (for example, seen twice during a period when the child's mother was in the hospital).

Some examples of signs that might indicate that a child is being neglected include the following:

- Sara (4 years) falls down outside and badly scrapes her knee. The center's nurse cleans and bandages it and prepares an accident report for Sara's parents, including information on how to care for the wound. Four days later Sara complains to her teacher that her knee hurts. The teacher takes her to the nurse who notices that the bandage has not been changed and the wound is becoming infected.

- Five-year-old Andrea tells her teacher she is tired this morning because her brother Max (6 months) woke her up in the night. She says, "My mommy wasn't home yet so I made Max a bottle and gave it to him. Then he finally went back to sleep."

Signs of Possible Sexual Abuse

Sexual abuse includes a wide range of behavior: fondling a child's genitals, intercourse, rape, sodomy, exhibitionism, and commercial exploitation through prostitution or pornography. These behaviors are contacts or interactions between a child or adult in which the child is used for the sexual stimulation of the perpetrator or another person. Sexual abuse may be committed by a person under the age of 18 when that person is either significantly older than the victim or when he or she is in a position of power or control over another child. For example, if a 14-year-old volunteer strokes the genitals of a 4-year-old who is in his or her care, this would be considered sexual abuse.

Recently, media attention has focused on incidences of sexual abuse that have occurred in child care centers and family child care homes. Individuals who sexually abuse young children in child care settings might be family child care providers, teachers, directors, support staff, bus drivers, or volunteers—in short, anyone who has access to children. Abuse occurs most frequently in bathrooms while children are being assisted with toileting. For this reason many centers have removed the walls from toilet stalls in bathrooms used by children ages 5 and under.

The physical signs of sexual abuse include some that a teacher would notice while routinely caring for young children. For example, you might notice a child's torn, stained, or bloody underclothing while helping the child use the bathroom. At these same times you might notice bruises or bleeding in the child's external genitalia, vaginal, or anal areas. If a child says that it hurts to walk or sit, or if he or she complains of pain or itching in the genital area, you should take note and watch to see if this is a recurring condition.

Young children who have been sexually abused may also exhibit behavioral signs of their abuse. They might act out their abuse using dolls, or you might overhear them talking with other children about sexual acts. Their premature sexual knowledge is a sign that they have been exposed to sexual activity. They might show excessive curiosity about sexual activities or touch adults in the breast or genitals. Some children who have been sexually abused are very afraid of specific places, such as the bathroom or a bed.

Some examples of behavioral signs that might indicate that a child is being sexually abused include the following:

- A teacher is helping Jason (4 years) get to sleep at nap time. For several weeks Jason has been having a hard time settling down. When he does fall asleep, he sometimes wakes up crying about monsters. Today he turns to his teacher and says, "I've got a secret, but I can't tell you what it is."

- The children in the preschool room are sitting at the table with their teachers eating lunch. Nancy (3 1/2 years) is wiggling around in her seat a lot. Her teacher asks her if she needs to go to the bathroom. Nancy says, "No, it's not that. My bottom hurts where Gary poked me." Gary is her 12-year-old brother.

- The children and teachers are outside on the playground. Simone (4 1/2 years) needs to go inside to the bathroom. Ms. Fox says, "I'll take her." The other teacher, Ms. Young, says, "But it's my turn." Ms. Fox insists that she will take the child. Simone says, "I don't have to go any more." Ten minutes later Simone comes up to Ms. Young and says, "I want you to take me. You don't hurt me."

Signs of Possible Emotional Maltreatment

Emotional maltreatment includes blaming, belittling, or rejecting a child; constantly treating siblings unequally; or a persistent lack of concern by the caretaker for the child's welfare. This type of abuse is the most difficult form of child maltreatment to identify, as the signs are rarely physical. The effects of mental injury, such as lags in physical development or speech disorders, are not as obvious as bruises and lacerations. Some effects might not show up for many years. Also, the behaviors of emotionally abused and emotionally disturbed children are often similar.

Although emotional maltreatment does occur alone, it often accompanies physical abuse and sexual abuse. Emotionally maltreated children are not always physically abused, but physically abused children are almost always emotionally maltreated.

The following are examples of signs that might indicate a child is being emotionally maltreated:

- Each time he comes to pick up Nathan (5 years), Mr. Wheeler makes fun of his son's efforts. Typical comments include: "Can't you button that coat right? You never get the buttons lined up with the holes. You look like an idiot." "What's that a picture of? Is that the only color you know how to use?" "Can't you climb to the top of the climber yet? All those other kids climbed to the top. What's the matter with you, are your legs too short?"

- A teacher is making her first home visit to the Peterson family: Mrs. Peterson and her three young children. She rings the door bell and waits a long time for Mrs. Peterson to come to the door. She can hear lots of noise inside the apartment: loud music, adults arguing, and children crying. She rings the bell again, thinking that perhaps they did not hear her. Finally the door opens and a man pushes his way past her. She looks inside and sees Mrs. Peterson bent over, holding her stomach. The three children are standing in the kitchen doorway holding onto each other. They look very scared, but they are not crying.

Recognizing Signs of Possible Child Abuse and Neglect Through Conversations and Interviews

Early childhood programs are generally family oriented, encouraging a great deal of formal and informal communication between program staff and families of the children in the program. You may gather important information about families from routine conversations with parents and children. During daily drop-off and pick-up times and at scheduled conferences, parents provide details of family life, discuss discipline methods, or ask for help with problems. Young children enjoy talking about their families, so they too may provide information about the family's interactions and home life.

Conversations with parents can provide clues to how the parent feels about the child. The presence of child abuse and neglect may be indicated if the parent constantly:

- blames or belittles the child ("I told you not to drop that. Why weren't you paying attention?");

- sees the child as very different from his or her siblings ("His big sister Terry never caused me these problems. She always did exactly what she was told to do.");

- sees the child as "bad," "evil," or a "monster" ("She really seems to be out to get me. She's just like her father, and he was really an evil man.");

- finds nothing good or attractive in the child ("Oh well. Some kids are just a pain in the neck. You can see this one doesn't have anything going for her.");

- seems unconcerned about the child ("She was probably just having a bad day. I really don't have time to talk today.");

- fails to keep appointments or refuses to discuss problems the child is having in the program ("That's what I pay you for. If she's getting into trouble, it's your job to make her behave."); or

- misuses alcohol or other drugs.

When you know a family well, you are in a better position to gauge whether a problem may be child abuse and neglect or something else; a chronic condition or a temporary situation; a typical early childhood problem that the program can readily handle or a problem that requires outside intervention. Family circumstances may also provide clues regarding the possible presence of abuse or neglect. The risk of abuse or neglect increases when families are isolated from friends, neighbors, and other family members, or if there is no apparent "lifeline" to which a family can turn in times of crisis. Marital, economic, emotional, or social crises are some causes of family stress that can lead to child abuse or neglect.

This activity will help you learn more about how an abused or neglected child might look and behave and about the importance of knowing what is typical behavior for the children in your care. Changes in a child's behavior can be a sign of abuse or neglect. In addition, children who are abused or neglected may express their emotions in a variety of ways. Select two children in your group who you think have different ways of showing when they are happy, sad, or afraid. Observe them for two to three days. Have handy a pencil and something small to write on (index cards work well). Jot down how these children show that they are happy, sad, or afraid. Read the example that follows, and use your notes to answer the questions on the blank form.

Observation Summary
(Example)

Dates: _March 27-29_

	Child: _Juana_ Age: _5 years_	Child: _Alex_ Age: _4-1/2 years_
How does this child look and act when happy?	She leads activities in the house corner.	He laughs loudly and joins in play with other children.
What makes the child happy?	Almost everything, especially riding a Big Wheel.	Making roads in the sand; seeing his father at the end of the day.
How does this child look and act when sad?	Her eyes tear.	He sits by himself and looks at books.
What makes the child sad?	Sad stories at circle time.	Saying good-bye to his friends.
How does this child look and act when frightened?	Says "I'm afraid" and runs to an adult to be held.	His eyes open wide and he shakes.
What frightens this child?	Scary stories.	Being yelled at by other children or adults.

Observation Summary

Dates: _____

	Child: _____ Age: _____	Child: _____ Age: _____
How does this child look and act when happy?		
What makes the child happy?		
How does this child look and act when sad?		
What makes the child sad?		
How does this child look and act when frightened?		
What frightens this child?		

Discuss your answers with your trainer.

VI. Reporting Suspected Cases of Child Abuse and Neglect[10]

In this activity you will learn:

- to identify your state requirements for reporting suspected cases of child abuse and neglect; and

- to overcome emotional and other barriers to reporting.

If you suspect or have reason to believe that a child might have been abused or neglected, you are ethically and legally required to report that information so that action can be taken to help the child and the family. As a teacher you have a professional responsibility to know and understand your program's reporting requirements and those of your state or local government. You must also follow your program's procedures for reporting suspected cases of abuse and neglect. In most instances you will report your suspicions to your supervisor. She or he will then advise you about the appropriate actions to be taken.

Each state law specifies one (or more) agencies that receive reports of suspected child abuse and neglect. Usually reports are made to the Department of Social Services, the Department of Human Resources, the Division of Family and Children's Services, or Child Protective Services. In some states the police department may also receive reports of child maltreatment. It is important to know who receives reports of suspected child abuse and neglect in your jurisdiction. The state reporting statute includes this information.

Some states require that either a written or an oral report be made to the responsible agency. In other states an oral report is required immediately, and a written report must follow in 24 to 48 hours. You or your program will need to check your state law for the specific requirements.

Usually the state requires reporters to provide the following information:

- Child's name, age, and address

- Child's present location (for example, at the child care center)

- Parent's name and address

- Nature and extent of the injury or condition observed

- Reporter's name and location (sometimes not required, but extremely useful for the agency conducting the investigation)

Many programs have established policies defining the duties and responsibilities of all staff in reporting child abuse and neglect. Your orientation training probably includes this information.

---

[10]Based on materials included in Derry G. Koralek, *A Guide for Early Childhood Professionals on Preventing and Responding to Child Maltreatment* (Washington, DC: National Center on Child Abuse and Neglect, In Press, 1991).

If you don't have a copy of your center's child abuse and neglect reporting procedures, ask your supervisor for one. Use it to complete the following chart.

Program Policy on Child Abuse and Neglect

I report suspected child abuse and neglect to:

_____

_____

_____

I must give the following information:

_____

_____

_____

My report must be:

    Oral: _____

    Written: _____

    Both: _____

Getting Ready to Report

Once you suspect that a child is being maltreated, you must waste no time in reporting. Taking this action will probably make you feel at risk, confused, and generally uncomfortable. It is not a pleasant task. To alleviate at least some of your discomfort, you can use the following checklist to prepare for the report.

- Have you documented your suspicions and reviewed your observation notes and anecdotal records? _____

- Have you analyzed your information to define what causes you to suspect abuse/neglect? Have you made a list of the physical and behavioral signs you have observed? _____

- Have you described the parent and child interactions you observed? Have you noted instances when the parent indicated that he or she finds the child difficult, worthless, or impossible to handle? Do you have examples of the parent's lack of interest in the child? _____

- Have you spoken to any of your colleagues concerning the physical and behavioral signs you have documented? If they have reason to suspect abuse or neglect, have you discussed these reasons? _____

- Have you talked with your supervisor about the support he or she will provide once you file the report and the steps the program will take if the parents try to remove the child from the program? Will you have the program's support? _____

- Have you set up a support system for yourself? (After the report is made, you may feel vulnerable and need to talk with others about your feelings and concerns.) _____

- Have you reviewed the program's reporting policy? _____

- Do you have the information needed to file the initial report? _____

- Do you have the exact telephone number and address of the agency to which you should report? _____

- If a written report is required, do you have reporting forms, or will you use a piece of paper?

You might not be able to wait until your answers to these questions are all in the affirmative. Instead, you must report your suspicions immediately. This checklist can help you organize your thoughts and secure the support you will need once the report is filed.

Overcoming Barriers to Reporting

When you suspect that a child in your care is being abused or neglected, you may feel very reluctant to report your suspicions. It helps to remember that a report of child maltreatment is not an accusation; rather, it is a request to begin the helping process. But the reporting process does not always go smoothly. You may encounter difficulties that will discourage you from making future reports. If you are aware of these difficulties beforehand and plan ways to overcome them, you will be better able to fulfill your legal and ethical responsibilities to the children in your care.

Some teachers find that their personal feelings are a barrier to reporting child abuse or neglect. They simply prefer not to get involved. They are afraid that they have made a mistake and that there is a perfectly good explanation for the child's injuries or behavior. They may fear that other parents will think them incompetent or an alarmist. It is important for teachers to remember that while they wait for positive proof of a child's maltreatment, the child is vulnerable to continued incidences of maltreatment.

Another potential barrier to reporting is the special relationship that parents and a teacher develop over months or years, which may hinder teachers from reporting suspected cases of child maltreatment. At times, when teachers observe signs of abuse or neglect, they may give parents the benefit of the doubt. Even when they do suspect child maltreatment, teachers may fear that confronting the parents would result in a hostile, indignant, or distressed reaction or retaliation. It may help to remember that as an early childhood professional, your primary responsibilities are to protect the children in your care and to support their families. By reporting your suspicions to the appropriate authorities, you are protecting children as well as helping their families get the assistance they need to change their behavior.

This activity will help you understand your responsibilities for reporting child abuse and neglect. Answer the following questions, then meet with your trainer to review the answers provided at the end of the module. There can be more than one good answer to each question.

Teacher Responsibilities for Reporting Child Abuse and Neglect

1. Why do child maltreatment laws exist?

   _____

   _____

   _____

2. How do maltreated children get assistance?

   _____

   _____

   _____

3. What happens to children if nobody reports child maltreatment?

   _____

   _____

   _____

4. Under what circumstances do I have to file a report?

   _____

   _____

   _____

5. What will happen to me if I don't report?

   _____

   _____

   _____

6. What if I'm wrong and the parents sue me?

   _____

   _____

   _____

Compare your answers to those at the end of the module and discuss them with your trainer.

Summarizing Your Progress

You have now completed all of the learning activities for this module. Whether you are an experienced teacher or a new one, this module has probably helped you develop new skills for promoting good health and nutrition for preschoolers. Compare your answers to the sample responses on the completed chart at the end of the module.

- Turn back to Learning Activity I, Using Your Knowledge of Child Development to Promote Good Health and Nutrition, and add to the chart specific examples of what you learned about promoting good health and nutrition during the time you were working on this module. Compare your answers to the sample responses on the completed chart at the end of the module.

- Next, review your responses to the pre-training assessment for this module. Write a summary of what you learned, and list the skills you developed or improved.

_____

_____

_____

_____

_____

_____

_____

_____

_____

If there are topics you would like to know more about, you will find recommended readings listed in the orientation.

Your final step in this module is to complete the knowledge and competency assessments. Let your trainer know when you are ready to schedule the assessments. After you have successfully completed these assessments, you will be ready to start a new module. Congratulations on your progress so far, and good luck with your next module.

Answer Sheet

Promoting Good Health and Nutrition

Providing Healthy Indoor and Outdoor Environments

1. **What are three things Ms. Williams did to maintain a healthy room?**

    a. She opened the windows to let in fresh air.

    b. She opened the windows only a few inches so that the room would stay warm.

    c. She checked the paper towel and soap supply.

    d. She put out more paper towels.

    e. She conducted a health check on the children.

    f. She placed the tissues where the children could reach them.

2. **What did Ms. Williams do to keep germs from spreading?**

    a. She helped a child blow his nose and threw away the used tissue.

    b. She washed her hands and helped the child wash his.

Helping Children Develop Good Health Habits

1. **What three healthy things did Mr. Lopez do with the children?**

    a. He ate apples, a healthy food.

    b. He let the children help him clear off the table.

    c. He helped the children brush their teeth after lunch.

2. **How did Mr. Lopez teach the children ways to keep themselves healthy?**

    a. He talked to them about their health routines.

    b. He ate apples, helped clear the table, and brushed his teeth. By doing the things he wanted to teach, he was a model for the children.

Recognizing and Reporting Child Abuse and Neglect

1. **What are the clues to possible child abuse in this situation?**

   a. Carolyn has bruises on large areas of her back.

   b. The bruises are loop-shaped.

   c. Some of the bruises seem old, some new.

   d. Carolyn says she was "whipped."

2. **How did Ms. Lee support Ms. Kim?**

   a. Ms. Lee tells Ms. Kim she's glad she came to her.

   b. She encourages Ms. Kim to discuss her concerns and to maintain confidentiality.

   c. She helps her make a note for the file.

   d. She calls Child Protective Services and makes a report.

Using Your Knowledge of Child Development to Promote Good Health and Nutrition

WHAT PRESCHOOL CHILDREN ARE LIKE	HOW TEACHERS CAN USE THIS INFORMATION TO PROMOTE GOOD HEALTH AND NUTRITION
They can run, jump, hop, kick, climb, throw, and use indoor and outdoor large muscle equipment.	Provide opportunities for children to use large muscles so they receive plenty of exercise.
They can dress themselves.	Provide opportunities for children to dress themselves. Remind them to wear jackets outdoors when it is cold so that they stay healthy.
They understand relationships expressed by "if...then" or "because" clauses.	Tell children what they can do to keep themselves and others healthy by using examples: "If you use a tissue when you sneeze, then you won't spread germs."
They ask questions for information.	Answer children's questions about health and nutrition with simple, concrete answers so that they have the information they need to stay healthy.
They can learn by observing and imitating adults.	Show children you care about being healthy and eating good foods so that they will learn by imitating you.
They are beginning to blow their own noses.	Place tissue boxes where children can reach them. Remind them to throw away used tissues so that germs are not transmitted by children touching themselves and others.
They can use the toilet and wash their hands.	Remind children to use the toilet as needed. Be sure there is always a supply of soap, paper towels, and toilet paper in the bathroom so they can take care of their own physical needs.

HEALTHY

WHAT PRESCHOOL CHILDREN ARE LIKE	HOW TEACHERS CAN USE THIS INFORMATION TO PROMOTE GOOD HEALTH AND NUTRITION
They can pour from small pitchers and use utensils properly.	Serve family-style meals, encouraging children to serve themselves so that they will learn how to select proper foods.
They can use knives with assistance.	Plan and conduct supervised food-preparation activities so that children can learn to use knives safely.
They develop feelings of self-esteem, good or poor, related to how people respond to and treat them.	Listen attentively to children and give them respect and consideration.

Reporting Child Abuse and Neglect

1. Why do child maltreatment laws exist?

To provide protection for children who cannot protect themselves.

2. Why do child maltreatment laws exist?

These laws exist to protect children. If a child is a victim of maltreatment, the only way that the child and family will receive help is if a report is filed.

3. What happens to children if nobody reports child maltreatment?

If the maltreatment goes unnoticed and unreported, it is likely that it will continue and perhaps escalate.

4. Under what circumstances do I have to file a report?

If your knowledge of the child and his or her family and your professional training and experience lead you to suspect child maltreatment, then you must file a report.

5. What will happen to me if I don't report?

If you fail to report, under your state's laws you might be subject to fines or even a jail sentence.

6. What if I'm wrong and the parents sue me?

When you make a report in good faith, the law protects you. You cannot be sued for reporting child maltreatment because as an early childhood professional, you are mandated to do so.

Glossary

Abstract	Existing in someone's mind—ideas or thoughts rather than real items.
Body fluids	Liquids and semi-liquids eliminated by or present in the body, such as feces, urine, mucus, and saliva.
Concrete	Relating to real objects or pictures.
Diet	The kind and amount of food and drink regularly consumed.
Disinfectant	A cleaning solution that destroys the causes of infection.
Emotional abuse	Acts of commission or omission on a child by a parent or parent substitute that result in emotional harm to the child.
Hygiene	Practices that preserve good health and eliminate disease-producing germs.
Infection	Invasion of the body by tiny organisms that cause disease.
Neglect	Failure to provide a child with food, clothing, medical attention, or supervision.
Nurturance	Behavior that is warm and caring and that leads to a feeling of comfort and love.
Nutrient	A component of food that offers nourishment to the body.
Nutritious	Having large amounts of vitamins, minerals, complex carbohydrates, or protein, and being low in fats, salt, and sugar.
Physical abuse	Bodily injury that was inflicted or was allowed to be inflicted, other than by accident.
Sexual abuse	Any form of sexual activity between a child and an adult, for the sexual pleasure or profit of the adult. It includes fondling, intercourse, and sexual exploitation (prostitution, pornography).
Sodium	A mineral normally found in seafood, poultry, and some vegetables; one of the components of table salt.
Starch	A carbohydrate food such as cereal, potatoes, pasta, and bread.

Module 3
Learning Environment

What Is the Learning Environment and Why Is It Important?

The learning environment is the physical space in which you care for young children. It includes both the outdoor and indoor play spaces. Features such as the size of the room, the colors, the type of flooring, the amount of light, and the number of windows all influence the quality of the indoor environment. Outdoors, a good environment has soft and hard surfaces, shady and sunny areas, and protected and safe places to run and play.

Perhaps the most important part of the learning environment is the interaction of the children and adults who work, play, and learn together in this space. So that children can learn, you must create an atmosphere of caring and trust.

The furniture in the room and how you arrange it are also part of the learning environment. Materials and equipment you select for preschool children and how you organize these things send important messages to the children. The schedule and routines you follow each day also add to the learning environment.

You spend a major portion of each day in the classroom environment. The quality of this environment is therefore very important. If it is attractive and appealing, you may find you enjoy your work with children much more. If it is well-planned and organized to meet the needs of the children you teach, it can make your job a lot easier. If the schedule and routines are appropriate for the ages of the children in your care, each day will probably go more smoothly.

A good learning environment gives you more time to play with children and to enjoy your job. It meets the needs of both the children and the adults who care for them.

Establishing and maintaining a learning environment involves:

- organizing indoor and outdoor areas that encourage play and exploration;

- selecting and arranging appropriate materials and equipment that foster growth and learning; and

- planning and implementing a schedule and routines appropriate to the ages of the children.

Listed on the following page are examples of how teachers demonstrate their competence in establishing a learning environment.

Organizing Indoor and Outdoor Areas That Encourage Play and Exploration

Here are some examples of what teachers can do.

- Provide soft, cozy areas where children can play alone, read a book, or sit back and watch.

- Organize the outdoor area with room for large-muscle activities such as riding tricycles, climbing, running, and jumping.

- Create well-defined and well-equipped interest areas.

- Define separate spaces outdoors for active and quiet play.

Selecting and Arranging Appropriate Materials and Equipment That Foster Growth and Learning

Here are some examples of what teachers can do.

- Select puzzles with only four or five pieces so that children who can handle only that many pieces will succeed.

- Display learning materials related to current activities (for example, firefighter hats, fire engines, and books on firefighters after a trip to the fire department).

- Use low, open shelves so children can reach materials they need.

- Find dolls, picture books, and toys that reflect different ethnic backgrounds and children with handicapped conditions.

Planning and Implementing a Schedule and Routines Appropriate to the Ages of the Children

Here are some examples of what teachers can do.

- Provide a good balance between active times (such as outdoor play) and quieter activities (such as story time).

- Allow time for children to complete certain daily routines, such as hand washing, on their own.

- Take time to talk and play with each child alone as well as to work with groups of children.

- Plan something for children to do during transitions between activities so that children won't be restless.

Creating and Using an Environment for Learning

The following situations show teachers setting up and using learning environments for preschool children. As you read them, think about what the teachers in each scene are doing and why. Then answer the questions following each episode.

Organizing Indoor and Outdoor Areas That Encourage Play and Exploration

Mr. Lopez looks around the play yard. He sees lots of children acting frustrated. Sarah is in the shed pulling on a tire that is under a tangle of boards, riding toys, and rakes. Benjamin struggles to pull his bike out of the shed. Andy drops the watering can when a child chasing a ball races by the tomato plants he is watering. "This place needs some organizing," Mr. Lopez thinks. Over the next week, he makes changes to encourage children's play and exploration. First, he arranges the tires and boards so that children can get them easily. He hangs their gardening tools within easy reach on the door of the storage shed. He moves the bikes to the path and the balls to the grass away from the garden. He tells the children about the different areas and reminds them where to ride their bikes and throw balls.

1. **What did Mr. Lopez know about the children?**

   _____

   _____

   _____

2. **What are examples of quiet and active materials that children might want to play with and explore in this yard?**

   _____

   _____

3. **How did Mr. Lopez use this information about children and different activities to organize an outdoor area that would encourage play and exploration?**

   _____

   _____

   _____

Selecting and Arranging Appropriate Materials and Equipment That Foster Growth and Learning

It's rest time and Ms. Williams is using the time to plan what materials she will need for the next day. During the morning, all the children made get-well cards to send to a child who is in the hospital. There was a lot of interest in doctors and hospitals, so Ms. Williams brought out two story books on going to the hospital. She is now preparing a hospital prop box to add to the house corner. In it she puts two white lab coats, a stethoscope, ace bandages, and a pad and pencil. She knows that the children will be very interested in this new prop box. Then she decides to set up the water table. It has been been a calming activity for this group of children. She has noticed that several children have seemed anxious during the past few days. She decides to add blue coloring to the water and sets out plastic squeeze bottles, eye droppers, measuring cups, and plastic tubes for the water table.

1. What did Ms. Williams know about the children?

_____

_____

_____

2. What activities and materials was Ms. Williams planning for the children?

_____

_____

_____

3. Why do you think Ms. Williams was planning to include water play as an activity?

_____

_____

_____

Planning and Implementing a Schedule and Routines Appropriate to the Ages of the Children

It is clean-up time in the three-year-old room. Ms. Richards is working with a small group in the block area to help with clean-up. It seems as if every block is out. "We have a big job in the block corner today," she says. "Let's start by finding all the blocks that look like this one. See how many triangles you can find." When all the triangle blocks are on the shelf, Ms. Richards says, "Jamie, what shape should we clean up next?" Jamie holds up a cylinder and everyone collects them next. Ms. Kim realizes that the other children are going to be finished cleaning up before the block builders. She goes around to each interest area and tells the children that they should go to the meeting area when they are finished cleaning up and select a book to look at. "I'll be there to read our story in just a few minutes," she says. When the block builders finish their clean-up, Ms. Kim is ready to read her story.

1. How did Ms. Richards make cleaning up the blocks a learning activity?

   _____

   _____

   _____

2. What did Ms. Kim do to make sure that the children who were finished cleaning up were involved in a meaningful activity?

   _____

   _____

   _____

Compare your answers with those on the answer sheet at the end of this module. If your answers are different, discuss them with your trainer. There can be more than one good answer.

How Your Environment Affects You

We are all affected by our environment. Whether sitting in the living room, shopping in a store, climbing a mountain, or sitting in a staff lounge, we react to the environment. Our surroundings affect:

- how we feel;
- how comfortable we are;
- how we behave; and
- how well we can accomplish what we need to do there.

Think for a moment about how you feel and behave in the following situations.

- Standing in a hot, crowded bus or subway where you are sandwiched in among strangers. (Perhaps you pull your shoulders in, try to avoid any contact with others, and count the minutes until you get off.)

- Eating in a special restaurant with a favorite friend. The lights are low, and the noise level is muffled. The smells are delicious, and attractive pictures hang on the walls. (You are probably relaxed, enjoying a delightful dinner, feeling special and unhurried.)

- Preparing a meal in a strange kitchen when the owner is not there to help you. (This can be very frustrating, especially if you can't figure out how the kitchen is organized. You spend lots of time looking for the things you need. It's inefficient, and you may not cook as well as you usually do.)

It's easy to see in these examples how our environment can affect our actions and our feelings. But the influence of our surroundings is not always so clear. Sometimes we are not aware of how the environment is making us feel and act.

To identify some less obvious factors in the environment that support you or work against you, take time to answer the following questions. Think about a store where you enjoy shopping. It can be a grocery store, clothing store, hardware store, or any other store. As you imagine yourself in this store, think of what makes it a good experience. What makes it easy to accomplish what you want do there?

Type of Store: _____

Why do you enjoy shopping there?

_____

_____

_____

Now think about a store you dislike going to. When you are there, you feel frustrated and angry. You may decide never to return again. What's different about this store?

Type of store: _____

Why do you dislike shopping there?

_____

_____

_____

Look over your answers to these two questions above. Many of the factors you identified that make shopping enjoyable or difficult apply to the classroom environment as well. Your work environment should support you and work for you. It should be organized and planned to support the goals you have for children and to make your job easier and more enjoyable.

Now think of your favorite place to be; it can be indoors or outdoors. Close your eyes for a moment and imagine yourself in that space. How does it feel? Smell? Look? What do you hear? What are you doing? Are you alone, or are other people with you? Describe your favorite place below.

_____

_____

_____

_____

Many times when people describe their favorite space, they identify features such as the following:

- a quiet place to be alone,
- a soft and comfortable place to stretch out,
- a place where music is playing,
- a bright and sunny place, or
- a colorful and attractive place.

There may be many other features that describe your favorite place. Because you like this type of environment, you feel comfortable and relaxed. Keep these features in mind as you examine the learning environment. A comfortable environment for young children and for you makes teaching more satisfying.

When you have finished this overview section, complete the pre-training assessment. Refer to the glossary at the end of this module if you need definitions of the terms that are used.

Pre-Training Assessment

Listed below are the skills that teachers use to create and use an environment for learning. Think about whether you do these things regularly, sometimes, or not enough. Place a check in one of the columns on the right for each skill listed. Then discuss your answers with your trainer.

SKILL	I DO THIS REGULARLY	I DO THIS SOMETIMES	I DON'T DO THIS ENOUGH
ORGANIZING INDOOR AND OUTDOOR AREAS THAT ENCOURAGE PLAY AND EXPLORATION 1. Setting up interest areas indoors and outside so children can choose their own activities.			
2. Making sure there are private, soft, and cozy areas in the indoor and outdoor space where children can be alone.			
3. Arranging indoor and outdoor areas for children to use large muscles.			
4. Locating interest areas so that quiet and noisy activities are separate.			
5. Creating inviting and workable interest areas.			
SELECTING AND ARRANGING APPROPRIATE MATERIALS AND EQUIPMENT THAT FOSTER GROWTH AND LEARNING 6. Selecting materials and equipment that challenge children and allow them to experience success.			

SKILL	I DO THIS REGULARLY	I DO THIS SOMETIMES	I DON'T DO THIS ENOUGH
7. Organizing materials and displaying them with labels to help children make choices and take care of materials.			
8. Selecting materials based on the interests and growing abilities of children.			
9. Conveying positive messages (e.g., this is a safe place; you belong here; you can find what you need) by how you organize your environment.			
10. Making sure that toys and decorations reflect the family backgrounds of the children in the room.			
11. Providing a wide variety of materials to encourage dramatic play, construction, small muscle development, and thinking skills.			
PLANNING AND IMPLEMENTING A SCHEDULE AND ROUTINES APPROPRIATE TO THE AGES OF THE CHILDREN 12. Planning a balanced daily schedule of lively and quiet activities and small group and individual activities.			
13. Using daily routines to help children learn new skills and concepts.			

SKILL	I DO THIS REGULARLY	I DO THIS SOMETIMES	I DON'T DO THIS ENOUGH
14. Planning different kinds of activities to make transition times go smoothly.			
15. Planning different kinds of outdoor experiences for children every day.			

Review your responses, then list three to five skills you would like to improve or topics you would like to learn more about. When you finish this module, you will list examples of your new or improved knowledge and skills.

_____

_____

_____

_____

_____

_____

_____

_____

_____

_____

_____

_____

Now begin the learning activities for Module 3, Learning Environment.

I. Using Your Knowledge of Child Development to Create a Learning Environment

In this activity you will learn:

- to recognize some typical behaviors of preschool children; and

- to use what you know about preschool children to create a good environment for learning.

A good learning environment for preschool children will invite them to explore, keep them involved, and make it easier for them to share, to live cooperatively with others, and to take responsibility for helping to maintain the environment. Preschool children have many skills and interests as well as needs that should be considered in planning the learning environment. They enjoy new challenges and will eagerly explore interesting and new materials you put out in the room.

Preschool children are increasingly social. They are learning how to share and to take turns, and increasingly they realize the advantages of working together. They learn these skills by having many opportunities to work with one or two other children. A good learning environment is therefore divided into several interest areas where children can work together undisturbed.

Preschool children can express their ideas and feelings in many ways. Using crayons, markers, and paints, they learn to represent these ideas in symbols. Playing with blocks or in the house corner, they create scenes from their own experiences and learn more about the world around them. Planning a learning environment for preschool children means creating a setting and providing appropriate materials that enable them to expand their skills and understandings and to grow in all areas of development.

You know from your own experience that preschool children have lots of energy. They are acquiring all kinds of large and small muscle skills, and they want to practice these skills, over and over again. A good learning environment offers children ample opportunities to practice newly found skills.

The chart on the next page identifies some typical behaviors of preschool children. Included are behaviors relevant to creating and using an appropriate learning environment. The right column asks you to identify ways that teachers can use this information about child development to create a learning environment. As you work through the module you will learn new strategies for creating and using a learning environment, and you can add them to the chart. You are not expected to think of all the examples at one time. If you need help getting started, turn to the completed chart at the end of this module. By the time you complete all the learning activities, you will find that you have learned many ways to create a good learning environment for preschool children.

Using Your Knowledge of Child Development to Create a Learning Environment

WHAT PRESCHOOL CHILDREN ARE LIKE	HOW TEACHERS CAN USE THIS INFORMATION TO CREATE A LEARNING ENVIRONMENT
They need to exercise their large muscles in activities such as running, jumping, climbing, and riding tricycles.	
They develop small muscle control to hold or use pencils, cut with scissors, and fit together toys with small pieces.	
They are learning to share and to wait for a turn.	
They become very social and like to play with one or two others. They can play cooperatively. Often they have "best friends."	
They sometimes need to get away from the group and be by themselves.	

WHAT PRESCHOOL CHILDREN ARE LIKE	HOW TEACHERS CAN USE THIS INFORMATION TO CREATE A LEARNING ENVIRONMENT
They draw pictures and create objects that represent real things.	
They like to help out and have responsibilities.	
They understand that everything has a place, and they learn where things go.	
They love to make-believe. Their dramatic play goes from family roles to people in the community and super-heroes.	
They can do many things and have lots of interests.	

When you have completed as much as you can do on the chart, discuss your responses with your trainer. As you proceed with the rest of the learning activities, you can refer back to the chart and add more examples of how teachers create a learning environment for preschool children.

II. Establishing Interest Areas

In this activity you will learn:

- to identify what kinds of interest areas are appropriate for preschool children; and

- to locate and define interest areas in your room.

Good classroom learning environments for preschool children are divided into interest areas. This is done for several reasons. First, young children work best in small groups. By dividing your space into smaller areas, you can limit the number of children who can play together in any one area.

Another reason for creating interest areas is to offer children clear choices. Sometimes children want to work quietly alone or with one other child. An area set aside for books, art activities, or table toys allows several choices for quiet activities. Areas set aside for dramatic play, block building, woodworking, or large muscle activities give children several options to choose from.

Indoor Space

In deciding how many interest areas to create in your room, the size of your group must be considered. Areas for certain interests should be consistently available to children each day. These areas include:

- blocks
- table toys
- art

- sand and water
- house corner
- books

If space is limited, areas for other activities can be made available on a rotating basis. These can include:

- woodworking
- music
- science

- cooking
- large muscle equipment

Arranging Interest Areas

Once you have identified the areas you want to set up, the next step is deciding the best place for each area. Some suggestions for locating interest areas are listed below.

- Quiet areas (such as books, art, table toys, and private spaces) should be separated from noisier areas (such as blocks, house corner, and woodworking).

- Materials used together should be grouped together (e.g., crayons near drawing paper, block props near the blocks).

- Shelves, furniture, and different floor coverings should be used to define the boundaries of each area.

- The art area should be uncarpeted and located near water if available.

- Blocks need clearly marked floor space and protection from traffic. Flat carpeting is best for this area.

- The library corner needs good light.

Outdoor Space

Your center's outdoor play space can also be divided into areas. A variety of surfaces and equipment invite different activities. Open space and sturdy climbing equipment are good for large muscle play, but outdoor space is ideal for other types of activities as well. Almost anything you do indoors can be done outdoors, weather permitting.

The more carefully you plan your outdoor space, the more opportunities you offer children to learn and to grow. Here are some ways to use the outdoor environment creatively.

- A low table in warm weather can be used for water play, finger painting, or play with clay or playdough.

- A large tractor tire, hung by three strong ropes or chains, can make a great swing for three children.

- Cable spools from the telephone company are great for climbing.

- Boxes and planks can be moved around and made into many different constructions.

- A wire cage for a rabbit allows children to care for a pet and play with it outdoors.

- A garden that children can plant and water provides many good learning experiences.

- Buckets of water and large paint brushes can offer children just as much fun as painting at an easel.

In this learning activity, you will review two different arrangements of a preschool classroom and identify strengths and weaknesses of each plan. Then you will draw a plan of your own indoor or outdoor area and decide on what changes you want to make to improve the learning environment.

Classroom Arrangements[1]

Using the guidelines for arranging indoor space, identify the strengths and weaknesses of Floor Plan A.

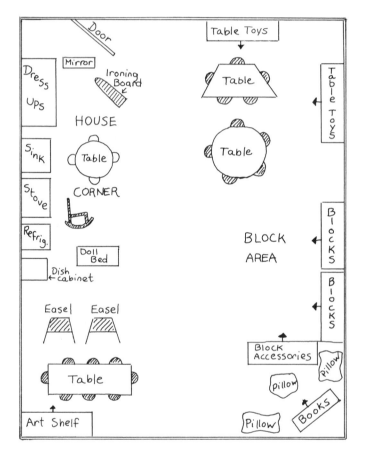

Strengths:

_____

_____

_____

_____

_____

[1]From Diane Trister Dodge, *A Guide for Supervisors and Trainers on Implementing the Creative Curriculum* (Washington, DC: Teaching Strategies, Inc., 1988).

Weaknesses:

_____
_____
_____
_____
_____

Now look at Floor Plan B, which shows the same room rearranged. What is different? In what ways is this arrangement better?

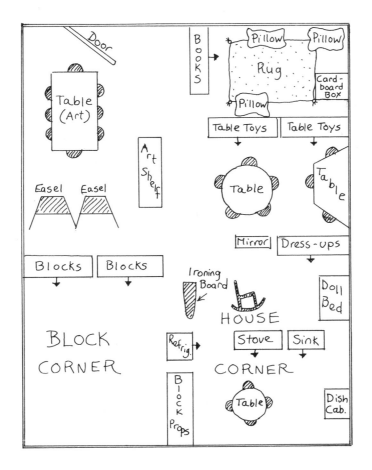

Differences in Floor Plan B:

_____

_____

_____

_____

_____

_____

_____

How is Plan B better?

_____

_____

_____

_____

_____

Compare your answers to those on the answer sheet at the end of this module.

Now use the space below to draw a plan of your indoor or outdoor space as it is now.

On the basis of what you have learned, what changes do you want to make? (If you choose the outdoor area, there may not be as many things you can change. However, you can bring indoor materials and equipment outside to create new activity areas.) Redraw your plan, showing how you want to rearrange your learning environment.

Discuss your floor plans with your trainer and other teachers who use the same space. Decide what changes you will make.

III. Selecting and Organizing Materials

In this activity you will learn:

- to select materials that are developmentally and culturally appropriate for each interest area; and

- to organize and display these materials in ways that invite children to play and care for them.

Defining interest areas is the first step in creating an environment for learning. Now you are ready to make those areas work. Interest areas work when the following things occur:

- The interest areas invite children to use them.
- Children know how to use the materials once they enter an area.
- Children are involved.
- Children are successful when they use the materials in an area.
- Children respect materials and help care for them.

For interest areas to work, teachers have to select materials that are appropriate and organize and display these materials properly. When interest areas are organized in this way, children are more likely to make good use of them and to take care of the materials.

Selecting Appropriate Materials

Selecting the right materials for each interest area depends partly on what materials are available in your center. In an established center, each room already has a supply of materials and toys appropriate for the age group of the children. However, there are ways to expand this supply. You can rotate toys, using them for a few weeks and then putting them away for a while. Children will find matching games or props for the block area just as interesting in March as they were in September if they have been out of sight for several months in between.

Sometimes it is possible to share materials with another room, especially if the children are similar in age. Many good materials for preschool children can be collected and brought from home. For example, you can bring in dress-up clothes, props for the house corner, plastic bottles and measuring cups for the water table, bottle caps to sort and match, and collections for the science table. Finally, many excellent materials and games can be made.

In selecting materials, ask yourself these questions.

- Will it interest the children? Your daily observations of the children will help you identify special interests.

- Do the children have the skills to handle it? For example, are they ready for ten-piece puzzles or only for puzzles with five pieces?

- Will it challenge children to think and explore? Assorted buttons or bottle caps will be just as interesting as colored shapes for sorting.

- Does it reflect the cultural backgrounds of the children and show people with handicapping conditions engaged in meaningful tasks? Pictures in children's books, wooden figures for the block area, and dolls in the house corner should reflect the diversity of our society and help children accept and respect these differences.

- Is it in good condition? This means no broken parts and no missing pieces. Materials should be clean and free of splinters or any jagged edges.

- Does it help achieve your goals for children? For example, will it help children develop creativity? Learn to think? Develop language skills? Develop small and large muscle control?

This last question can be answered best after you have completed Modules 4 through 10. In these modules you will find many ideas for selecting materials that will promote children's physical, cognitive, social, and language development.

Organizing and Displaying Materials

The organization and display of materials in the classroom is the next thing to consider. Activity areas will work much better if the materials are well-organized and inviting to children.

- There should be a specific place for each of the materials in the room. Picture labels taped on the shelves can help children find and return the materials they use.

- Materials used together should be grouped together.

- Toys with small parts or pieces should be stored in containers such as boxes or dish pans.

In this learning activity you will use two checklists to identify materials and equipment you have in each interest area. One checklist is for the indoor learning environment; the second is for the outdoor learning environment. After completing the survey, use the chart that follows to list what materials you want to add to each area and how you plan to organize and display these materials to make the interest area a good place for children to learn.

Checklist for Indoor Interest Areas

The checklist below describes nine interest areas and lists suggested materials and equipment for each area. Read the list and make a check beside each item you now have in your room. There are spaces for you to add items to the list.

A **dramatic-play** or house corner can be defined by shelves and furniture. It should be well-equipped with props and materials that encourage make-believe play. Because a child's family life is so important, you will see a lot of dramatic play if this area is filled with objects that the child knows.

Equipment and Furniture

__ Stove	__ Sturdy bed that holds a child
__ Sink	__ High chair
__ Cabinet	__ Mirror—full length
__ Refrigerator	__ A place to hang dress-up clothes
__ Small table and two to three chairs	

Props and Materials

__ Dishes and silverware	__ Tablecloth
__ Pots and pans	__ Dress-up clothes for men and women
__ Cooking utensils	__ Telephones (at least two)
__ Aprons	__ Jewelry
__ Pot holders	__ Suitcases and pocketbooks
__ Toasters	__ Hats
__ Dolls (reflecting children's ethnicity)	__ Shoes
__ _____	__ _____
__ _____	__ _____

A **table-toy area** provides a place for the small games and toys that children often use at tables or on the floor. Toys should be rotated weekly so children always have something new. Good table toys help children appreciate likenesses and differences, a skill that is important for reading, and they develop small muscle control, which is crucial for writing.

__ A low shelf to display toys	__ Attribute blocks
__ A low table with four to five chairs	__ Nesting cups or rings
__ A puzzle rack	__ Cuisenaire Rods
__ A selection of puzzles (about five)	__ Homemade games

__ Pegs and pegboards

__ Beads and laces

__ Parquetry blocks

__ Colored inch cube blocks

__ Items for sorting and classifying
(bottle caps, keys, buttons)

__ Bristle Blocks

__ Tinker Toys

__ Stacking rings

__ Sewing cards

__ _____

__ _____

__ _____

__ _____

The **block area** should be well protected and out of the line of indoor traffic. Shelves can define the building area. A flat carpet is nice for building. Block building allows children to think, play, and solve problems. They learn about sizes and shapes. Unit blocks help children grasp basic math concepts. Through dramatic play with blocks and props, children learn more about the world around them.

__ Low shelves for storage (preferably two)

__ Colored inch cubes for decorating buildings

__ Unit blocks in a variety of sizes and shapes

__ Wood or rubber animals (zoo and farm)

__ Small cars and trucks

__ Traffic signs

__ Wood or rubber people

__ _____

__ _____

__ _____

__ _____

The **art area** generally includes easels and a table on which to do art activities. Near the table there should be a shelf with art materials organized and on display. Through art, children express ideas and feelings and they develop self-esteem when adults respect their work.

__ A two-sided easel

__ Paint brushes with long and short handles

__ Paint holders

__ Crayons—large and of good quality

__ Water-based paint in a variety of colors

__ Assorted water-based markers

__ Large school pencils

__ Sponges for clean-up

__ Collage items (scraps of paper and fabric, buttons, feathers, yarn, ribbon)

__ Glue

__ Fingerpaint paper

__ Easel paper

__ Drawing paper

__ Construction paper

__ Playdough and utensils

__ Scissors

__ Smocks

__ _____

__ _____

__ _____

__ _____

The **library area** should be located in a quiet corner of the room, preferably near a window with natural light. In this area children can learn to respect and care for books. They can read pictures and look through books you've read to them. This area should be a restful place. The library area can be set up in many different ways.

___ A display shelf for books (one that shows front cover)

___ A small table with two or three chairs

___ Several large pillows

___ Soft carpeting

___ Books in good condition

___ Books on a variety of topics

___ Books showing men and women in different roles

___ Books showing different ethnic groups

___ Books appropriate for the children's ages

___ Decorations (a plant, pictures on walls, a tablecloth)

___ A record player with headphones and records

___ A tape recorder with headphones and cassettes

___ Puppets

___ A flannel board

___ _____

___ _____

___ _____

___ _____

A **large muscle area** is great to have for indoor play. Many centers do not have enough indoor space to include this area; they provide for large muscle activities outdoors. If you do have room indoors for this area, indicate what equipment and materials it contains.

___ A large indoor climber   ___ A set of large hollow blocks

___ A loft with a ladder   ___ Large-wheeled toys

___ Cardboard cartons for children to crawl into   ___ A balance beam

___ _____   ___ _____

___ _____   ___ _____

A **sand and water table** makes a wonderful interest area. Both materials add softness to the environment. Children can spend long periods of time playing in water or sand. They can explore how they feel and what they can do. Sand and water are very calming materials. You don't need more than two inches of sand or water to make this a great activity.

__ A sand and water table

__ Basins to hold sand and water

__ A shelf or box to hold equipment

__ Waterproof aprons

__ A supply of empty plastic squeeze bottles

__ Funnels

__ _____

__ _____

__ Plastic pitchers

__ Plastic basters or eye droppers

__ Plastic hoses

__ Plastic boats

__ Measuring cups

__ Sponges and mops for clean-up

__ _____

__ _____

A **science area** often becomes a place to set up experiments and display collections. It may also be a place to display one very special item such as a nautilus shell or a snake's molted skin. Materials should be changed often. A science area will appeal to children when it includes materials that encourage children to explore and use them.

__ A table or shelf for display

__ Display table (for objects that children and staff bring in)

__ Animal(s) in a cage and food

__ Books related to the displays

__ Fish bowl

__ An old alarm clock with the back removed

__ Balance scales

__ Magnets and an assortment of metal objects

__ Magnifying lenses

__ Seeds growing

__ Tape measure

__ A Slinky

__ _____

__ _____

__ _____

__ _____

The **woodworking area** provides a wonderful variety of activities for preschool children. Sometimes a workbench is kept outdoors, sometimes in the classroom. It should be located near other noisy activity areas. A teacher should supervise the area constantly.

__ A sturdy workbench (or homemade substitute)   __ A vise

__ Soft wood   __ Sandpaper

__ A pegboard or shelf for storing tools   __ Saws

__ Hammers   __ Nails with large heads

__ Screwdriver and screws   __ Hand drills

__ Assorted objects: bottle caps, wooden
   wheels, leather scraps

__ _____   __ _____

__ _____   __ _____

Checklist for Outdoor Interest Areas[2]

The outdoor environment provides a whole new world for children to learn about and to explore. New scenery and a change of pace promote creativity as well as physical, motor, and sensory growth. Playing outdoors is also a good way for children to release pent-up energy. The outdoor area is as important as the inside area, and teachers need to plan outdoor activities as carefully as they plan indoor ones.

Use the checklist below to help you evaluate your center's outdoor area.

Activities and Equipment

A variety of equipment is provided to stimulate different types of physical activity.

__	Balls	__	Climbing equipment
__	Balance beams	__	Jump ropes
__	Wheel toys	__	Slides
__	Swings	__	Punching bag
__	Sacks	__	Hobby horse

Climbing equipment allows children to explore different spaces.

__	Tunnels	__	Barrels
__	Ramps	__	Platforms
__	Knotted rope	__	Packing case
__	Cardboard boxes	__	Sawhorses
__	Seesaws	__	Spools

There are play areas at different levels.

__	Platforms	__	Large rocks
__	Tunnels	__	Ladders

The equipment invites cooperative play.

__	Outdoor blocks	__	Dramatic-play props
__	Rocking boat	__	Telephones

---

[2]Adapted from Penny Lovell and Thelma Harms, "How Can Playgrounds Be Improved?," *Young Children* (Washington, DC: National Association for the Education of Young Children, March 1985), pp. 3-7.

Creative materials are easily available for children.

__	Clay	__	Water
__	Woodworking	__	Sand
__	Paints		

There are special interest areas.

__ Garden plots

__ Fenced areas for animals

__ Nature area with native plants, trees, rocks, and insects

Organization of Play Area

__ The play area is enclosed by a fence that has childproof exits.

__ There are clear pathways and enough space between areas to avoid crowding and accidents.

__ There are small-group interest areas for books, music, arts, and crafts.

__ Different types of interest areas are separated; active play areas are near each other and away from quiet play areas.

__ Space and equipment are organized so that children are clearly visible in all areas of the outdoor space.

__ Open space is available for active or group play.

__ Some space is allocated to encourage quiet, thoughtful play. Examples include grassy areas near trees or a sandbox away from traffic.

__ There is easy access to the outdoors from the indoor playroom.

__ There is easy access to bathrooms.

__ A drinking fountain is available.

__ Adequate storage for outdoor equipment is provided.

__ Drainage is good enough to keep all surfaces usable and to prevent standing mud holes.

__ A comfortable place is provided for adults to observe children.

Variety of Play Surfaces and Materials

___ A paved or hard-surfaced area is available for riding wheel toys, playing group games, and dancing.

___ A grassy or soft-surface play area is provided for tumbling, running, and sitting.

___ There are large play areas for climbing.

___ An adequate amount of the play area is covered for use in wet weather.

___ There are sunny areas in the cold winter months.

___ There are shady areas in the hot summer months.

Materials are available for water play.

___	Hoses	___	Short lengths of rubber hose
___	Pails	___	Measuring cups
___	Shallow pans	___	Corks
___	Squeeze bottles	___	Plastic bottles
___	Cups	___	Funnels
___	Sponges	___	Egg beaters
___	Soap	___	Tea kettle
___	Dolls	___	Sprinkler tops

Materials are available for digging in the sand box.

___	Milk cartons	___	Human and animal figurines
___	Plastic bottles	___	Cottage-cheese cartons
___	Jello molds	___	Nest of painted cans
___	Cookie cutters	___	Muffin tins
___	Spoons	___	Pans
___	Dishes	___	Cups
___	Small blocks	___	Watering cans
___	Ladles	___	Sieves
___	Screens	___	Pitchers
___	Coffee pots	___	Sifters
___	Sprinkler	___	Sugar scoops

Soft material is provided under climbing areas and moving equipment.

__	Sawdust	__	Grass
__	Sand	__	Bark

Play areas are varied to allow children to interact in groups of various sizes.

__ Boxes, tents, or tunnels for one child to "get away"

__ Tires, logs, or bushes that create small areas for one to three children

__ Open spaces for active or group play

Improvements to the Indoor Learning Environment

Use the middle column in the chart below to identify what materials you would like to add to each of the interest areas in your indoor learning environment. In the next column, record your ideas for organizing and displaying the new materials in ways that will invite children to use and care for them.

INTEREST AREA	MATERIALS YOU WANT TO ADD	HOW YOU WILL ORGANIZE AND DISPLAY THEM
Dramatic play (house corner)		
Table toys		
Blocks		
Art		

INTEREST AREA	MATERIALS YOU WANT TO ADD	HOW YOU WILL ORGANIZE AND DISPLAY THEM
Library		
Large muscle		
Sand and water		
Science		
Woodworking		

Improvements to the Outdoor Learning Environment

The chart below will help you identify what areas you have or plan to add to your outdoor learning environment.

INTEREST AREA	MATERIALS YOU WANT TO ADD	HOW YOU WILL ORGANIZE AND DISPLAY THEM

After completing these two charts, discuss your ideas with your trainer. Develop a plan for adding new materials to enhance your indoor and outdoor learning environments.

IV. Shaping the Messages in Your Learning Environment

In this activity you will learn:

- to create a learning environment that encourages independence, security, and a sense of belonging; and

- to arrange your indoor and outdoor space to give children positive and clear messages.

All environments convey messages. Every room in your house says something different. Your living room probably has soft furniture, low tables with magazines, lamps, and perhaps a soft carpet. The message is: "Come sit down. Read. Talk. Relax."

A fast-food restaurant is designed to get you in and out quickly. It is set up so you can select your food, get it immediately, pay, and be seated in a matter of minutes. The message is: "Hurry up."

Many schools have individual desks lined up facing the front of the room. Sometimes the desks are bolted to the floor. The message is: "No talking to other children. Listen to the teacher. The teacher conveys all information."

Your center's indoor and outdoor spaces also convey messages to children. If the environment is attractive, cheerful, orderly, and filled with interesting objects, the message is: "This is a good and interesting place. We care about you. You can have fun here."

If a child entering your room sees a cubby with his picture and name on it, his art work displayed on the wall, and a place for his toothbrush, the message he is likely to receive is: "You belong here. We will help you take care of your things. This is your space, too."

A cozy corner of the room filled with large pillows, bright lights, and a shelf full of attractive books says to a child who likes books: "Come sit here. Choose a book you like. Enjoy yourself."

These examples illustrate positive messages that the environment can send to children. They are messages you can easily build into your own learning environment for children.

What messages do you want children to receive when they come into your room? The following are some important messages your environment can communicate:

- "This is a cheerful and happy place."

- "You belong here, and we like you."

- "This is a place you can trust."

- "You can do many things on your own and be independent."

- "You can get away and be by yourself when you need to."

- "This is a safe place to explore and try out your ideas."

In this learning activity you will read "Messages in the Environment" to discover what your learning environment communicates to the children. You will then list ways in which your learning environment conveys messages and write down any changes you want to make in those messages. After completing the reading, review the example and then complete the learning activity.

Messages in the Environment[3]

Here are some suggestions of how a classroom environment might convey positive messages to children.

"This is a cheerful and happy place."

- Walls are painted neutral colors (light gray, off-white, beige), and bright colors are used selectively—for shelves, for highlights, or certain activity areas.

- Furniture is clean and well-maintained. Wood or plastic furniture is better than metal furniture.

- Storage shelves are low, so children can reach things, and are kept neat with picture labels, so children know where things are stored. Toys with small parts are kept in boxes, ice cream containers, plastic dish pans, or baskets.

- Children's art work is attractively displayed where they can easily see it. Care is taken to avoid putting so much on the walls that children become confused.

- The room exhibits other decorative touches, including plants, displays of collections (such as shells, leaves, and stones), pretty fabrics to cover pillows or to use as tablecloths, and a well-lit fish tank.

- Areas of the room contain soft places for children (including carpets, large pillows, and stuffed chairs), soft materials (water, playdough) for children to play with, and soft pets (guinea pigs, rabbits).

"You belong here, and we like you."

- There is a cubby for each child, with the child's name or picture inside.

- There is a place to keep a special blanket and a stuffed animal for nap time.

- There is a labeled place for each child's toothbrush.

- Each child's art work is displayed and protected.

- Pictures on the walls, in books, and in learning materials show people of different ethnic backgrounds.

---

[3] Adapted from Diane Trister Dodge, *The Creative Curriculum for Early Childhood* (Washington, DC: Teaching Strategies, Inc., 1988), pp. 18-21.

- There are toys and materials that will interest specific children.

- There is child-sized furniture.

"This is a place you can trust."

- Furniture and materials are arranged consistently so children know where to find the things they need.

- Shelves are neat and uncluttered so children can see what choices are available.

- A well-defined schedule is provided so children learn the order of events during the day.

- Consistency is provided in routines such as toileting, eating, and nap times.

- Pictures illustrate the schedule so children can "read" it.

"You can do many things on your own and be independent."

- Materials are stored on low shelves where children can easily get the things they want.

- Materials are located in the areas where they will be used (for example, table toys are kept on a shelf near low tables; blocks and block props, in the block area).

- Materials that will be used together are stored together.

- Picture labels on the shelves tell children where each toy or object belongs.

- A job chart shows how each child helps keep the room neat.

- Open spaces outdoors encourage children to run.

"You can get away and be by yourself when you need to."

- There are small, quiet areas of the room that accommodate one to two children.

- There is a large pillow or a stuffed chair off in a corner.

- There is a large cardboard carton to crawl in.

- There are headphones for a phonograph or tape recorder.

CARING FOR PRESCHOOL CHILDREN

"This is a safe place to explore and try out your ideas."

- There are protected and defined quiet areas for small group activities (for example, a table with three or four chairs enclosed by low shelves containing table toys).

- There is protected floor space to build with blocks without fear of room traffic.

- The yard is fenced and well-protected.

- Attractive displays of materials invite children to use them.

- Some toys are rotated so each week there is something new to interest the children.

Read the example below. Then use the blank chart to list ways in which your learning environment communicates each message. Add any new ideas you may want to try to enhance your environment.

Messages in the Environment
(Example)

"This is a cheerful and happy place."	
How the Environment Says This Now	**New Ideas To Try**
Walls are painted off-white; shelves are bright blue.	*Put in a fish tank with a light and soft pillows nearby.*
Plants are in each window; carpets are in the book area and block area.	*Add large stuffed pillows in the book area.*
Children's art work on the walls is hung at their eye level.	*Put a colorful tablecloth in the house corner.*

"This is a cheerful and happy place."	
How the Environment Says This Now	**New Ideas To Try**

"You belong here, and we like you."	
How the Environment Says This Now	**New Ideas To Try**

"This is a place you can trust."	
How the Environment Says This Now	**New Ideas To Try**

"You can do many things on your own and be independent."	
How the Environment Says This Now	**New Ideas To Try**

"You can get away and be by yourself when you need to."	
How the Environment Says This Now	**New Ideas To Try**

"This is a safe place to explore and try out your ideas."	
How the Environment Says This Now	**New Ideas To Try**

After you have completed the chart, discuss your ideas with your trainer and colleagues. Agree on the changes you will make. Use the space below to note what changes you make.

_____

_____

_____

_____

_____

_____

_____

_____

_____

Over the next few weeks, write down how children react to the changes you have made in the learning environment.

CHANGES	EFFECT ON CHILDREN'S BEHAVIOR

V. Planning Your Daily Routines and Schedule

In this activity you will learn:

- to plan routines and a daily schedule that meet children's needs; and

- to use transition periods as learning times.

The daily program consists of routines and learning activities with transitions in between. Routines are the daily events that must take place:

- arriving and leaving;
- eating;
- sleeping or resting;
- toileting;
- dressing and undressing to go outdoors (in cool weather); and
- cleaning up.

The period of time between one activity and the next is called a transition. Teachers need to plan for these times of the day as carefully as they do for activity periods.

The schedule defines the events of the day. It shows how you expect the day's activities to flow, in what order, and for how long. The younger the child, the more flexible the schedule must be. Preschool children will see many routines as things that must be done quickly so they can get on to what they really want to do. Even so, it's important not to rush them.

Preschool children can follow regular routines and a consistent order of activities. What is a good schedule for preschool children? No one schedule will work for all groups and all teachers, but there are some guidelines to follow in planning your schedule. A good schedule should provide the following:

- a balance between active periods and quiet times;

- sufficient time for routines and transitions between activities;

- time outdoors as well as indoors;

- times when children can make their own choices as well as times for adult-led activities;

- chances for children to be together in small groups, to be part of the whole group, and to be alone if they want to; and

- time for clean-up and other housekeeping chores.

The amount of time you allow for each part of the schedule conveys a message. It tells the children and their parents what you value. For example, preschool children enjoy having several activities to choose from. These children can spend long periods of time at one activity—building a block structure, making a collage, or playing in the house corner, for example. If you allow only 30 minutes a day for free play, you are saying that you do not value play as being important in children's growth and development.

In this learning activity, you will look at a sample daily schedule for preschool children. Then you will examine your own daily schedule. Finally, you will learn some ways to make transitions occur smoothly.

SAMPLE DAILY SCHEDULE

7:30 - 8:15   **Children Arrive**: Children participate in   **Early Morning**
quiet activities and prepare for breakfast.   **Schedule**

8:15 - 9:00   **Breakfast and Clean-Up**: As children
finish breakfast, they read books or listen to
music until all are ready for the next activity.

===

9:00 - 10:00   **Self-Selected Activities**: Children   **Morning**
choose activities in the following areas: **Schedule**

- art   • blocks
- books   • table toys
- house corner   • sand and water

10:00 - 10:15   **Clean-Up**: Children put away toys and materials;
as each child finishes, he or she selects a book to read
until all are ready for the next activity.

10:15 - 10:30   **Circle Time**: Teacher plans one or more of the
following activities:

- conversation and   • stories
sharing time   • flannel board
- music and movement   • finger plays

10:30 - 10:45   **Snack**

10:45 - 11:45   **Outdoor Play**: Children select from a variety of outdoor
activities such as sand play; using balls, jump ropes, and
large wheeled toys; gardening; painting; caring for pets;
swinging; climbing; and so on.

11:45 - 12:00   **Quiet Time and Preparing to Go Home**: (for morning
programs): Children select books or table toys that are
easy to put away, or listen to records, while small groups
put coats on and prepare to leave.

===

12:00 - 1:00   **Prepare for Lunch, Eat, Clean-Up**: As children   **Lunch**
finish lunch, they go to the bathroom in small
groups and read books on their cots in preparation
for nap time.

1:00 - 1:10   **Quiet Activity Prior to Nap**: Children hear a
                     story or song by a teacher, classical music, or a story
                     record.

===

1:10 - 3:00   **Nap Time**: As children wake, they read books or   **Nap Time**
                     play quiet games, such as puzzles or Lotto, on their
                     cots; children who do not sleep or who awaken early are
                     taken into another section of the room or into another
                     room to look at books, play with table toys, and engage
                     in other quiet activities.

===

3:00 - 3:30   **Snack and Preparation to Go Outdoors**   **Afternoon
                                                                                 Schedule**

3:30 - 4:30   **Outdoor Play**: Children select from a variety of outdoor
                     activities such as sand play; using balls, jump ropes, and
                     large wheeled toys; gardening; painting; caring for pets;
                     swinging; climbing; and so on.

4:30 - 5:15   **Selected Activities**: Children select from activities or
                     materials as identified in morning period.

5:15 - 6:00   **Clean-Up and Small Group Quiet Time**:
                     After the snack and until children leave, teachers plan
                     quiet activities, including the following:

- table toys   - songs, finger plays,
- stories   or music
- coloring

Why is this schedule appropriate for preschool children?

_____
_____
_____
_____
_____
_____

Daily Schedule

How does your schedule measure up to the guidelines? In the space below, write down the daily schedule you now follow. Use the checklist that follows to assess your schedule. Then note any changes you would like to try.

TIME	ACTIVITY
_____	_____
_____	_____
_____	_____
_____	_____
_____	_____
_____	_____
_____	_____

Daily Schedule Checklist

1. The schedule has sufficient time for routines. _____

2. There is a balance between active and quiet times. _____

3. There are times for children to play alone. _____

4. There are times for children to play together. _____

5. There are times for children to play with teachers. _____

6. There are teacher-directed activities. _____

7. There are times for free play. _____

8. Outdoor activities are scheduled twice a day. _____

9. The major events of the day occur in the same order each day. _____

10. Sufficient time is allowed for transitions from one activity to the next. _____

Revised Daily Schedule

TIME	ACTIVITY
_____	_____
_____	_____
_____	_____
_____	_____
_____	_____
_____	_____
_____	_____

Discuss your ideas with the teachers who work with you and decide what changes you will try.

Transitions

Transitions can be problem times. If children have nothing to do between activities, they can become restless. They sometimes act in ways that teachers don't like—wrestling with one another or running around the room. This is because they are bored.

During a transition, there are always some children who are still busy completing an activity and some just waiting for the next one. If one teacher is helping the children who are finishing an activity and the other teacher plans something for the rest of the group, transitions usually run more smoothly.

Here are some other tips for making transitions go better:

- Give children a warning that a transition is coming: "In five minutes it will be time to clean up."

- Involve children in transition activities such as setting up for meals, collecting the trash, washing the paint brushes.

- Provide clear directions to children during transition times and keep expectations age-appropriate: "Please find your mat and sit in the listening area and I'll be right there to read a story."

- Be flexible whenever possible. Allow children extra time to complete special projects or activities when they seem very interested and involved. "We're going to let the block builders finish their building while the rest of us start to clean up. Then we can all hear about what happened in the block corner today."

- Allow time for children to share what they have worked on during free play before asking them to clean it up. For example, you could plan a meeting time in between and let children share what they did. Then you might ask for volunteers to clean up different areas of the room and assign tasks.

- Give children something to do if they are finished with an activity or task. For example, those who are finished eating or cleaning up could take a book to look at while they wait for the others, or start getting their coats on and go outside with one teacher.

- Establish a signal to let children know you need quiet or that it's time to clean up (e.g., a bell or blinking the lights).

Transition times can be used to teach new concepts, to practice skills, and to enhance creativity. Here are some suggestions for making transitions important learning times.

- Play a game of follow the leader. You can lead the children in picking up toys, going to the bathroom, making funny gestures, etc.

- Call out different categories as you move children from one activity time to another. ("If you're wearing red today, you can get your coat on." "Everyone wearing sneakers with laces can go quietly to the juice table.")

- Ask children to try out unusual ways to move. ("Let's go to our meeting place like big, slow, heavy elephants.")

- When you want to quiet children down so they can listen to you, play a clapping game—clap out different beats, loud and soft, and get children to follow.

- Learn finger plays that you can teach the children or special songs you can sing.

In this learning activity you will try out three different ideas to use during transitions. After trying them with the children in your class, record the results.

1. **Transition Activity**

   _____

   _____

   _____

   Results

   _____

   _____

   _____

2. **Transition Activity**

   _____

   _____

   _____

   Results

   _____

   _____

   _____

3. **Transition Activity**

   _____

   _____

   _____

   Results

   _____

   _____

   _____

Discuss these transition activities with your trainer. If any of the transition activities you tried did not work, discuss what may have gotten in the way.

Summarizing Your Progress

You have now completed all of the learning activities for this module. Whether you are an experienced teacher or a new one, this module has probably helped you develop new skills in creating a learning environment for preschoolers. Before you go on, take a few minutes to summarize what you've learned.

- Turn back to Learning Activity I, Using Your Knowledge of Child Development to Create a Learning Environment, and add to the chart specific examples of what you learned about creating a good learning environment during the time you were working on this module. Compare your ideas to those in the completed chart at the end of the module.

- Next, review your responses to the pre-training assessment for this module. Write a summary of what you learned, and list the skills you developed or improved.

_____

_____

_____

_____

_____

_____

_____

_____

_____

_____

If there are areas you would like to know more about, you will find recommended readings listed in the orientation.

Your final step in this module is to complete the knowledge and competency assessments. Let your trainer know when you are ready to schedule the assessments. After you have successfully completed these assessments, you will be ready to start a new module. Congratulations on your progress so far, and good luck with your next module.

Answer Sheets

Creating and Using an Environment for Learning

Organizing Indoor and Outdoor Areas That Encourage Play and Exploration

1. **What did Mr. Lopez know about the children?**

   a.   The children were frustrated when they could not get equipment they wanted.

   b.   Some children's play and work was being interrupted by other children playing ball.

2. **What are examples of quiet and active materials that children might have wanted to play with or explore in this play yard?**

   a.   Quiet things would include sand and plants.

   b.   Active things would include bikes and balls.

3. **How did Mr. Lopez use this information about children and different activities to organize an outdoor area that would encourage play and exploration?**

   a.   He organized toys and equipment so things were easy to see and within children's reach.

   b.   He designated certain areas for certain activities to protect quiet play and to give children space for active play.

Selecting and Arranging Appropriate Materials and Equipment That Foster Growth and Learning

1. **What did Ms. Williams know about the children?**

   a.   They were concerned about the classmate who was in the hospital.

   b.   Some children were especially active and anxious.

   c.   The children would be very interested in the hospital prop box.

2. **What activities and materials was Ms. Williams planning for the children?**

    a.   She brought out materials about hospitals—a hospital prop box, books on going to the hospital—so children could talk about hospitals and play hospital.

    b.   She picked out two new table toys and planned a water-play activity so there would be other interesting choices in addition to the prop box.

3. **Why do you think Ms. Williams was planning to include water play as an activity?**

    a.   She had noticed that several children had been unusually anxious.

    b.   She felt that water play would be a calming activity for this group.

    c.   She added materials to the water-play activity that might encourage children to play hospital in this area as well as in other areas.

Planning and Implementing Schedules and Routines Appropriate to the Ages of the Children

1. **How did Ms. Richards make cleaning up the blocks a learning activity?**

    a.   She helped the children by participating in the clean-up.

    b.   She made up a game of finding different shapes to clean up, thus teaching children the names of the block shapes.

    c.   She gave the children a chance to identify blocks they wanted to clean up.

2. **What did Ms. Kim do to make sure that the children who were finished cleaning up were involved in a meaningful activity?**

    a.   She spoke to each group of children and told them to select a book to look at in the meeting area.

    b.   She made sure that the children knew what to do and where to go when they were finished.

    c.   She followed through on her promise to read a story.

Classroom Arrangements

Strengths of Floor Plan A

- The shelves holding table toys are located near the tables where they will be used.

- The book area is in a protected corner.

- The art shelf is near a table and easels.

- House corner equipment and furniture is all together.

Weaknesses of Floor Plan A

- All the shelves are against the walls.

- The open spaces invite children to run.

- The block area is open to the rest of the room and in the way of traffic.

- There are no enclosed areas.

- The book corner (a quiet area) is right near the block area, which tends to be quite noisy.

Differences in Floor Plan B

- Shelves are used to define different activity areas.

- Tables are moved to activity areas.

- Table toys are enclosed by shelves and away from the line of traffic.

- Easels are in a protected area.

- The block area is protected and near other active areas.

- The book area is far from noisy interest areas and looks secluded and cozy.

How Is Plan B Better?

- Children can work in small activity areas and feel more protected.

- The block area is more protected so block buildings are not as likely to be knocked down.

- Quiet interest areas (for example, art, table toys, and books) are grouped together.

- Materials are stored on shelves in the areas where they are to be used.

- During dramatic play, the house corner can spill over into the block corner.

Using Your Knowledge of Child Development
to Create a Learning Environment

WHAT PRESCHOOL CHILDREN ARE LIKE	HOW TEACHERS CAN USE THIS INFORMATION TO CREATE A LEARNING ENVIRONMENT
They need to exercise their large muscles in activities such as running, jumping, climbing, and riding tricycles.	Set aside an indoor area for large play equipment. Plan some activities that use large muscles (for example, pounding clay or dough, woodworking). Make sure the outdoor area is safe for running and climbing.
They develop small muscle control to hold or use pencils, cut with scissors, and fit together toys with small pieces.	Set out toys with small pieces (for example, pegs and pegboards, laces and beads, Legos). Give children daily chances to use playdough, clay, and other art materials to develop small muscle control.
They are learning to share and to wait for a turn.	Provide duplicates of some popular toys and materials. Show children how long they have to wait—using a clock or a timer, or writing their names on a list to help them learn to share.
They become very social and like to play with one or two others. They can play cooperatively. Often they have "best friends."	Plan lots of small group activities. Define small areas for activities where several children can work together. Put out props for dramatic play and encourage children to play together.
They sometimes need to get away from the group and be by themselves.	Set up areas where children can be alone—a large stuffed chair, a loft, or a big cardboard box to hide in, and a listening area with headphones. Give them opportunities to be alone.
They draw pictures and create objects that represent real things.	Give children a good supply of unit blocks and props (for example, farm and zoo animals, people, cars). Keep crayons, markers, and large pencils on low shelves for use every day. Talk with children about what they do.

WHAT PRESCHOOL CHILDREN ARE LIKE	HOW TEACHERS CAN USE THIS INFORMATION TO CREATE A LEARNING ENVIRONMENT
They like to help out and have responsibilities.	Decide on jobs that children can do, and make a job chart. Have cards with children's names on them to show who has each job (for example, feeding pets, watering plants, setting tables, passing out snacks).
They understand that everything has a place, and they learn where things go.	Carefully organize materials. Put things together that are used together (for example, put crayons and markers near drawing paper). Make picture labels to put on shelves to show where items belong, to help children see that everything has a place.
They love to make-believe. Their dramatic play goes from family roles to people in the community and super-heroes.	Set up a dramatic play area that looks like a home. Put out dress-up clothes, kitchen utensils, and so on. Gradually add different kinds of props—for example, for playing hospital, fire-fighter, grocery store, or shoe store—to encourage dramatic play.
They can do many things and have lots of interests.	Give lots of choices. Add new materials and new toys so children often find something new to do.

Glossary

Daily schedule

How you anticipate and plan for the day's activities. The schedule includes the times of day and the order in which activities will occur.

Learning environment

The complete makeup of each room in a child development center. The learning environment includes the space and how it is arranged and furnished, routines, materials and equipment, planned and unplanned activities, and the people in the room.

Routines

Scheduled activities that occur every day, including meals, naps, toileting, washing hands, and going outdoors, which can all offer opportunities for children to learn.

Transitions

The in-between times in a daily schedule when children have completed an activity period and are moving to the next one.

Module 4
Physical

What Is Physical Development and Why Is It Important?

Physical development refers to the gradual gaining of control over large and small muscles. It includes acquiring gross motor skills such as crawling, walking, running, and throwing, and fine motor skills such as holding, pinching, and flexing fingers and toes. Coordinating movement is also an important part of physical development. We use our senses—especially sight, sound, and touch—to coordinate the movement of our large and small muscles.

Adults use a wide range of physical skills every day. We walk and run, often several miles a day, in our homes and at our work sites. We lift and manipulate large and small objects. We grasp pencils, pens, cups, and other small items. Because we regularly use our large and small muscles, we often don't think about the skills involved. But in fact, we developed these skills through many years of practice.

A tremendous amount of physical development takes place during a child's first five years of life. During this time children learn to control their body muscles and to practice the physical skills they will use for the rest of their lives. These skills may be refined during adolescence and adulthood. Therefore, it is crucial for young children to have many opportunities to learn and practice basic physical skills.

Young children do not have to be reminded to practice these skills. Most infants will gleefully kick their legs and reach for objects. Toddlers often push, pull, and turn over anything they can get their hands or feet on. And most preschool children delight in running and climbing as well as in building and knocking down. Young children use their large and small muscles, along with all their senses, to discover their world and the effects they can have on it.

Physical development is also important for developing self-esteem. We develop views of ourselves and attitudes about attempting new tasks on the basis of how we feel about our bodies and what we think we can or cannot do physically. Young children who have had many successful experiences using their fine and gross motor skills tend to feel that they are competent. They are likely to continue to attempt new tasks without worrying about failure.

Adults play an important role in promoting children's physical development. They provide safe spaces indoors and outdoors for children to move their bodies. As a teacher, you schedule time for active play each day, and you encourage children to use their bodies and all their senses as they play. You reinforce fine and gross motor skills by letting children know that you are aware of their physical activity and by praising them for their accomplishments.

You also set the stage for children to experience success as they use their large and small muscles. As in other areas of development, children attain and use physical skills gradually. By selecting materials and equipment matched with each child's developmental level, you help children learn. You also help them use their muscles safely. In this way children can practice skills such as drawing, climbing, or riding a tricycle without being hurt or frustrated.

Promoting children's physical development involves:

- reinforcing and encouraging physical development;

- providing equipment and activities for gross motor development; and

- providing equipment and activities for fine motor development.

Listed below are examples of how teachers demonstrate their competence in promoting children's physical development.

Reinforcing and Encouraging Physical Development

Here are some examples of what teachers can do.

- Schedule time for active play every day. "It's raining hard today, Shawn, so help me move this table and we'll set up the jungle gym over here."

- Help and encourage children as they learn new skills. "You're learning to pour your own juice, Margo. I'll turn the pitcher around so you can reach the handle."

- Encourage children to use their large and small muscles in coordinated ways. "Do you want to play with the playdough, Sean? You can take some from the bowl in front of Susan and then get a rolling pin from the other end of the table."

- Help children develop an awareness of rhythm so they can coordinate their body parts. "How else can we dance to *Peanut Butter?*"

- Encourage children to use all their senses to explore size, shape, volume, and other characteristics of objects. "Chaundra, tell me what you know about the clay. How does it feel? What does it smell like? What kind of a sound will it make if we drop some on the table?"

Providing Equipment and Activities for Gross Motor Development

Here are some examples of what teachers can do.

- Use a variety of materials and equipment that require children to use their large muscles. "Felipe and Tamila certainly enjoy carrying the chairs outside. What else could they safely move?"

- Play indoor and outdoor noncompetitive games with children. "In this game we'll all take turns going from here to the tree in a different way. Crystal, how are you going to move to the tree?"

- Encourage the development of self-help skills using large muscles. "How can you reach the sink, Jan? That's right, if you can get the hollow block and stand on it, you will be able to reach the sink."

- Plan and implement increasingly difficult activities in which large muscles are used. "Let's arrange the tires in a new way for the children to jump in and out."

Providing Equipment and Activities for Fine Motor Development

Here are some examples of what teachers can do.

- Use a variety of art materials that require children to use their small muscles. "Lloyd and Maddie, would you like to try weaving with the tag board and yarn today?"

- Encourage the development of self-help skills using small muscles. "Theresa, you zipped your jacket today. Good for you!"

- Plan and implement increasingly difficult activities in which small muscles are used. "This finger play is about catching a bee. I'll teach you the words and what to do with your fingers and hands."

- Select table toys such as pegs and pegboards, beads and laces, construction toys that fit together, and colored inch cubes that allow children to practice their fine motor skills.

Promoting Children's Physical Development

In the following situations, teachers are promoting children's physical development. As you read each one, think about what the teachers are doing and why. Then answer the questions that follow.

Reinforcing and Encouraging Physical Development

"Here's the pitcher," says Ms. Kim to Robert. "Hold your cup with one hand when you pour so the cup won't move away from you." Robert holds his cup and pours the milk very quickly so that it overflows. "Oops, that milk came out too fast, didn't it?" smiles Ms. Kim. "There's a sponge on the sink you can use to clean it up." While Robert gets the sponge, Shannon picks up the pitcher. "I can make it go slow, Ms. Kim. Watch me." Shannon holds the pitcher and pours the milk very slowly, stopping before it gets to the top of her cup. "Good job, Shannon," says Ms. Kim. "Your hand and arm muscles were working well. I know that Robert is going to go slower next time too." Robert nods his head and smiles as he wipes up the spilled milk. "My peas keep falling off my fork," explains Patrick. "Use your spoon, silly," says Robert. "That would help, wouldn't it?" says Ms. Kim. "What else could you do?" Shannon looks up and says, "You could stick your peas on your fork like this," and spears four peas on her fork. Several other children at the table begin spearing their peas. "Well, we certainly did solve that problem," says Ms. Kim.

1. **How did Ms. Kim encourage the children to use their small muscles?**

   _____

   _____

   _____

2. **What did Ms. Kim then say to reinforce the children's efforts and build self-esteem?**

   _____

   _____

   _____

Providing Equipment and Activities for Gross Motor Development

"It must be something about the rain!" Ms. Williams says to Mrs. Frilles. Free play had been very noisy today as the four-year-olds tested the block area's limits for throwing and the house corner's limits for banging pots and pans. "I think we need to move around a lot," she tells the children. "But we can't go out," Mark moans. "It's raining!" "No, but after we clean up we'll try some new ways to move our bodies," Ms. Williams answers. As the last blocks are put away, several children and Ms. Williams push the bookcases against the wall. "We'll need this space for moving," she tells them. Ms. Williams uses a long rope to make a large circle in the center of the area. "I want three of you to move inside this circle. Dora, Sam, and Joe, how can you move without bumping into each other?" The three children walk inside the circle, avoiding each other. "Can you move in different ways now?" she asks. As they move about, Ms. Williams says, "Dora is jumping! Sam is galloping! Joe looks like he's floating!" Ms. Williams then makes several other rope circles around the room and asks children to move in them in any safe way they want. The children walk, hop, leap, skip, slide, sway, and crawl, as Ms. Williams asks them to call out the names for their movements. "What terrific movers!" she exclaims. "Maybe we can go out for a few minutes. Let's get on our raincoats, hats, and boots, and run once around the playground in between the rain drops." The children quickly get dressed and walk out the door.

1. **How did the children let Ms. Williams know they were ready for gross motor activities?**

2. **What gross motor activities did Ms. Williams provide?**

Providing Equipment and Activities for Fine Motor Development

Mr. Lopez and Ms. Green planned to expand the variety of fine motor activities in their room. This week they introduced several new experiences. "Becky, I see what you've done with the shaving cream! You've made some wiggly lines and some round circles, and you've put some on your cheeks. "How does the shaving cream feel?" asks Ms. Green. "Cold, and wet and smooth," answers Becky. As Ms. Green watches, Becky continues to use her finger to draw shapes in the shaving cream. She brings her left hand up to the table top and uses all her fingers to trace straight and curved lines through the shaving cream. Then she uses her whole hand to smooth out the shaving cream so she can start again. Nearby, Mr. Lopez sits in the block area with several children. "Vroom," Andy says, as he pushes a car between two walls of blocks. Some of the blocks begin to tumble, and Sarah and Jerome move their wooden people out of the way. "The blocks are falling!" Sarah says. She, Jerome, and Andy push their cars and people on the floor to move them around the fallen blocks. "Your cars are riding and your people are walking around a lot of obstacles. Good work, kids," Mr. Lopez says.

1. **What activities did Ms. Green and Mr. Lopez provide for fine motor development?**

   _____

   _____

   _____

2. **How did they reinforce the children's small muscle play?**

   _____

   _____

   _____

Compare your answers with those on the answer sheet at the end of this module. If your answers are different, discuss them with your trainer. There can be more than one good answer.

Taking Care of Your Own Body[1]

As a teacher, you are concerned about children's physical development. Yet to work well, it is essential that you take care of yourself, too. How many times a day do you:

- pick up a child?

- lean over a step-stool in front of a sink to wash your hands?

- sit on the floor and bend forward to play with a child?

- sit on a child-sized chair?

These are normal activities for teachers of young children. They are also activities that can produce sore backs and limbs. There are ways to maintain good posture and flexibility and to avoid physical pain as you care for children. Here are some suggested practices:

- Keep your lower back as straight as possible and avoid slouching when sitting or standing.

- Put one foot up on a stool or step when standing for a long time.

- Bend your knees, not your back, when you are leaning forward.

- Wear low-heeled, soft-soled, comfortable shoes to maintain proper posture.

- Bend your knees, tuck in your buttocks, and pull in your abdominal muscles when lifting a child or a heavy object.

- Avoid twisting when lifting or lowering a child or a heavy object. Hold the child or object close to you.

- Avoid standing for long periods with a child on your hip.

- Use adult-sized tables and chairs, if possible, when meeting with other adults or when participating in training.

- Talk with your supervisor and colleagues about staff coverage for short morning and afternoon breaks. Relax during these breaks! (Doing some stretching exercises is also a good way to spend breaks.)

Teaching is a physically demanding job. For you to help children grow and develop in appropriate ways, you need to be in good physical shape. Think about your daily movements and your environment, and answer the questions below.

---

[1]Based on Susan S. Aronson, M.D., "Coping with the Physical Requirements of Caregiving," *Child Care Information Exchange* (Redmond, WA: Exchange Press, Inc., May 1987), pp. 39-40.

How can you improve your posture and movements throughout the day?

_____

_____

_____

_____

What changes to the environment or the schedule can you suggest so that you and your colleagues can avoid sore backs and limbs?

_____

_____

_____

_____

The suggestions you have just read and the ones you noted, along with regular exercise and good health and nutrition practices, can help you promote your own physical development as you promote the physical development of young children.

When you have finished this overview section, you should complete the pre-training assessment. Refer to the glossary at the end of this module if you need definitions of the terms that are used.

Pre-Training Assessment

Listed below are the skills that teachers use to promote children's physical development. Think about whether you do these things regularly, sometimes, or not enough. Place a check in one of the columns on the right for each skill listed. Then discuss your answers with your trainer.

SKILL	I DO THIS REGULARLY	I DO THIS SOMETIMES	I DON'T DO THIS ENOUGH
REINFORCING AND ENCOURAGING PHYSICAL DEVELOPMENT 1. Scheduling time for active play every day.			
2. Helping and encouraging children when they are learning new skills.			
3. Encouraging children to coordinate movements of their large and small muscles.			
4. Providing safe and interesting objects for children to listen to, taste, smell, look at, pick up, and put down.			
5. Observing and recording information about each child's physical strengths, interests, and needs.			
6. Helping children become aware of rhythm through music and movement activities.			
PROVIDING EQUIPMENT AND ACTIVITIES FOR GROSS MOTOR DEVELOPMENT 7. Arranging the room with a variety of textures and heights for children to climb over, under, around, and through.			

SKILL	I DO THIS REGULARLY	I DO THIS SOMETIMES	I DON'T DO THIS ENOUGH
8. Using a variety of materials and equipment to promote gross motor development.			
9. Playing indoor and outdoor noncompetitive games with children.			
10. Encouraging the development of self-help skills that use large muscles.			
11. Planning and implementing increasingly difficult activities in which large muscles are used.			
12. Making good decisions about when to intervene directly and when to let a child work out a problem.			
PROVIDING EQUIPMENT AND ACTIVITIES FOR FINE MOTOR DEVELOPMENT 13. Using a variety of materials that require children to use their small muscles.			
14. Providing opportunities to develop small muscles by grasping, throwing, catching, rolling, squeezing, dropping, pounding, pulling, zipping, buttoning, and so on.			
15. Encouraging the development of self-help skills that require small muscle use.			

SKILL	I DO THIS REGULARLY	I DO THIS SOMETIMES	I DON'T DO THIS ENOUGH
16. Planning and implementing increasingly difficult activities in which small muscles are used.			
17. Allowing children to set tables for meals, wipe spills, sweep up sand, and so on.			

Review your responses, then list three to five skills you would like to improve or topics you would like to learn more about. When you finish this module, you will list examples of your new or improved knowledge and skills.

_____

_____

_____

_____

_____

_____

_____

_____

Now begin the learning activities for Module 4, Physical.

I. Using Your Knowledge of Child Development to Promote Physical Development

In this activity you will learn:

- to recognize some typical behaviors of preschool children; and

- to use what you know about children to promote their physical development.

Children grow and develop rapidly during the preschool years. Although they grow at different rates and have different capabilities, they develop according to the same pattern. Most children are able to control their head movements first. Next they develop control of their torsos and arms, and finally their legs. Most children gain control of their torsos before they can move their hands and feet in highly skilled ways. Gross motor skills usually appear before those involving small muscle use. Movement normally begins to take place with muscles close to the body center and moves outward as the child matures. Each child learns and uses physical skills according to his or her own "body clock." For example, some children stand on their own at 7 months; some do not stand alone until 11 months. While the age when children accomplish a skill varies from child to child, the pattern rarely does. To understand preschool children's physical development, teachers need to be aware of the sequencing and range of motor skills of children ages three to five.

Three-Year-Olds

Three-year-olds are usually sure and nimble on their feet. They walk and can turn sharp corners with ease. They can walk up stairs using alternate feet. Often they will jump from the bottom stair and land on both feet. They enjoy pushing and riding tricycles, using swings, and throwing, catching, and kicking large balls.

Three-year-olds usually enjoy large muscle activities over those which use their small muscles. However, they are beginning to develop control of their fingers, hands, and wrists. They can use large and small pegs and pegboards. They enjoy playing with puzzles that have a few large pieces and sometimes prefer things with knobs for easier grasping. They can pour from pitchers, unbutton large buttons, and feed themselves with forks. With experience they learn to hold crayons with their fists and then finally with their thumbs and fingers. They scribble in a controlled fashion, using vertical, horizontal, and circular strokes.

Four-Year-Olds

Four-year-olds have all the energy of three-year-olds but more control. Their running and walking movements tend to have sudden starts and stops. They usually can walk up and down stairs smoothly with an alternating forward foot. Hopping is a favorite action of these children, and they can normally hop in a sequence of two or three hops. This leads to a beginning skip; they learn to skip with one foot and take a walking step forward with the other. Balancing on a walking board also becomes a favorite activity for four-year-olds. They can often walk for several feet without touching the ground or do so only once for balance. They can climb with assurance and fearlessness.

Four-year-olds have more refined small muscle movements and eye-hand coordination than three-year-olds. They can cut with scissors and make recognizable shapes with crayons. They can lace shoes; zip, unzip, and unsnap most clothing; serve and eat with a fork and spoon; and use knives for spreading and some cutting. Finger, hand, and wrist control allows them to build detailed structures with unit blocks, Bristle Blocks, Ring-a-Majigs, and other construction materials.

Five-Year-Olds

By age five most children are refining the skills they have acquired during the last several years. They can run faster and climb higher and more freely. They can walk up and down stairs with alternating feet. They can hop on one foot for a long distance and usually master skipping with alternating feet. They can also walk the full length of a balance beam without stepping off. Games involving kicking and throwing balls become a favorite activity, as fives can usually succeed in getting the ball where they want it.

Fine motor skills are well-developed in most five-year-olds. Their drawings and paintings tend to represent real objects; much detail is included. They can cut shapes with scissors. Serving food and eating are handled well, with all utensils usually used properly. Five-year-olds have little difficulty dressing and undressing themselves and can handle most buttons, snaps, zippers, and buckles. Printing ability is present in most five-year-olds. They will print over and over the words and numerals that are "important," such as their names and the numerals 1 to 5.

The chart on the next page lists some typical behaviors of preschool children. Included are behaviors relevant to physical development. The right column asks you to identify ways that teachers can use this information about child development to promote children's physical development. Try to think of as many examples as you can. As you work through the module you will learn new strategies for promoting children's physical development, and you can add them to the child development chart. You are not expected to think of all the examples at one time. If you need help getting started, turn to the completed chart at the end of the module. By the time you complete all the learning activities, you will find that you have learned many ways to promote children's physical development.

Using Your Knowledge of Child Development to Promote Physical Development

WHAT PRESCHOOL CHILDREN ARE LIKE	HOW TEACHERS CAN USE THIS INFORMATION TO PROMOTE PHYSICAL DEVELOPMENT
They walk easily and can balance themselves on one foot for several seconds at a time.	
They run, jump, and hop.	
They throw balls overhead and catch bounced balls.	
They climb.	
They dance to music.	

WHAT PRESCHOOL CHILDREN ARE LIKE	HOW TEACHERS CAN USE THIS INFORMATION TO PROMOTE PHYSICAL DEVELOPMENT
They manipulate objects with their hands and fingers to see how objects fit together and work.	
They create large and small objects with clay and play dough.	
They fingerpaint, draw, and paint with large brushes on an easel.	
They cut with scissors.	
They string beads, lace, zip, and weave.	

When you have completed as much as you can do on the chart, discuss your answers with your trainer. As you proceed with the rest of the learning activities, you can refer back to the chart and add more examples of how teachers promote children's physical development.

II. Observing and Planning for Children's Gross Motor Development

In this activity you will learn:

- to identify children's developing gross motor skills; and

- to plan activities that help children practice gross motor skills.

Most preschool children love activities that involve the use of their large muscles. In an environment designed for young children, gross motor development can take place throughout the day. Given a variety of equipment and materials, children with different abilities can all experience success.

Teachers should provide various spontaneous or pre-planned adult-directed activities to help preschool children develop their gross motor skills. As in other areas of growth and development, these activities should be based on each child's interests, strengths, and needs. Activities can be planned for one child, a small group, and the whole group. Moving to music is a particularly successful activity to get children to use their large muscle and coordination skills.

The sequencing of gross motor development is usually the same for all children. However, each child has his or her own pace for growth and learning. As you play with children and observe their indoor and outdoor activities, you learn a lot about the physical skills they have acquired and the rate at which they learn new skills.

The skills listed on the following chart are normally evident in preschool children. The ages noted are the average ages at which children successfully master each skill. Most children will perform a skill with success before achieving the next one on the list. However, you will probably notice that each child in your group is working on developing several skills at one time.

Gross Motor Skills

BEHAVIOR	AGE
Balances on one foot for a few seconds	3 years
Walks on a line	3-4 years
Jumps from a low height	3-4 years
Climbs stairs using alternate feet	3-4 years
Squats in place	3-4 years
Runs	3-4 years
Throws ball purposely overhead	3-4 years
Catches 12-inch ball that is thrown	3-4 years
Skips on one foot	3-4 years
Hops on one foot for four hops	3-4 years
Climbs up objects such as ladders and other equipment	4-5 years
Broad-jumps 2 to 3 feet	4-5 years
Catches 12-inch ball that is bounced	5-6 years

BEHAVIOR	AGE
Skips on alternate feet in continuous movement	5-6 years
Jumps rope	5-6 years
Uses overhead ladder	5-6 years
Walks on a balance beam	5-6 years

Once you know the skills children have acquired and the ones they are trying to learn, you can plan activities to help them practice gross motor skills. Outdoor activities are an excellent way to promote gross motor skills, as are music and movement.

Outdoor Play

In the outdoors, children are free to move and use their bodies in space. The outdoor environment is a world for children to explore and learn about, as well as a place where they can release pent-up energy.

The selection and placement of large fixed equipment is not usually a responsibility of teachers. Frequently, the outdoor area comes equipped with wheel toys and stationary swings, slides, climbers, and a sandbox. To stimulate different types of physical activity, you can provide additional materials for games with preschool children. These may include:

- soft balls and soft bats
- jump ropes
- bean bags and targets
- rocking boats

- tunnels and balance beams
- cardboard boxes
- woodworking tools

As you play outdoors with children and encourage their gross motor skills, you should keep the following suggestions in mind.

- **Interact with small groups and individuals often.** Avoid chatting with teachers from other rooms or participating as the "coach" in large group activities only.

- **Do things on the child's level as much as possible.** Kneel or crouch, and toss balls and bean bags at a speed young children can handle.

- **Stress cooperation over competition.** Encourage children to concentrate on enjoying the things they can do with their bodies, refining the skills they have, and learning new skills. They also can learn to value playing physical games with other individuals who have differing gross motor abilities.

- **Accept children's real fears of heights, moving fast on wheel toys, and so on.** Offer to hold their hands, climb with them, or provide other types of physical assistance when appropriate. Try not to challenge them to go beyond what they think is safe.

- **Circulate around the outdoor area when not involved in an activity.** Invite individual children to play with you, or encourage those who are wandering to play together. Often children become withdrawn outdoors when they think that their involvement will cause them embarrassment.

Music and Movement Activities

Many opportunities for gross motor development are present during music and movement activities, indoors and outdoors. Children enjoy dancing, marching, and creatively using their bodies in different ways, with and without musical accompaniment. Music and movement activities should take place throughout each day. They work well as the major component of circle times. Children can interact with each other and teachers as they move in space and watch others do creative things with their bodies. These activities also allow children to move from one activity to another during transitions. When children have participated in group movement experiences, they often will initiate these activities in open areas during free play.

Movement activities can take many forms. With small and large groups you could ask preschoolers to do the following:

- use their bodies to become animals, buildings, or vehicles;

- move from one place to another, slowly like a snail, jumping like a kangaroo, or slithering like a snake;

- stretch high or make themselves big or small; and

- move their heads in different ways: move their arms, hips, and ribs.

For music and movement activities to take place effectively in the preschool environment, several important factors should be considered, including:

- **Space.** A large open area such as the block area or a separate circle-time area is needed for large groups. A wood or carpeted floor is best to prevent injuries. There should be no obstacles such as furniture, equipment, or toys on the floor. Adequate ventilation and heating are important. An interest area might be set aside for spontaneous movement activities during free play. Some centers use a portion of the book/listening area for music and movement. For outdoor experiences, a large, open, grassy area away from equipment and wheel toy paths is appropriate.

- **Props.** Record players and records, or tape recorders and cassettes, can be used for musical accompaniment. Some teachers can master notes and chords on guitars, recorders, or other string or wind instruments. Drums are useful for establishing a beat or as a signal for the group to gather or freeze in a shape. Children's marching band instruments can be incorporated into many activities, both teacher-directed and child-initiated.

Teachers use a number of techniques to promote creative movements. You communicate enthusiasm not only in words but also by joining in the fun. When you plan and conduct movement activities, keep the following points in mind.

- **Allow for creativity.** Let the children know that all movements are acceptable as long as they are safe and do not ridicule others. You can ask them to:

  - "Move the way a lazy elephant might move."

  - "Show us how a tired body moves."

  - "Use your body to solve this problem: You're inside a large paper bag and you want to get out."

  Teachers may suggest shapes or emotions for children to act out, but the way this is done should be left to the children.

- **Provide support.** Let the children know that you are aware of their movements. Praise their efforts while avoiding judgmental or sexist statements. You could say:

  - "Vanessa's lazy elephant was slow and graceful" instead of "Vanessa was a pretty elephant."

  - "Tony burst through the side of his paper bag to get out. Good work!" instead of "Just like a big boy! Tony used his super powers to get out of the bag."

- **Get involved.** Movement activities call for involvement by teachers. Your participation gives children clues for what they could be doing. Also, by joining in you let them know that movement is as important as building with blocks, reading stories, and other activities you normally take part in. You could model the way you think a lazy elephant might move or the way you think a happy body jumps in the air. Some preschoolers may imitate your movement at first. As others go beyond what you model, you can point out the different ways individuals are moving.

- **Maintain a good pace.** Children need time to discover things they can do with their bodies. Begin slowly. Enjoy the pace created by a movement activity. Be sure there is a balance of active and not-so-active experiences. After the children have walked heavily and noisily as elephants, you could ask them to be quiet snowflakes. Then they could be snowflakes in a raging blizzard. If the group gets out of control, it is time to move on to another activity.

In this learning activity you will observe two children in your group and identify the gross motor skills they are using. Then you will plan movement activities and outdoor activities to give these children opportunities to practice and refine their skills. Begin by reviewing the example that follows.

Gross Motor Skills
(Example)

Child: _Alex_   **Age:** _3 years 8 months_   **Date:** _June 5_

Gross motor skills this child has mastered:

Climbs stairs alternating feet

Jumps in place

Jumps from a low height

Throws ball overhead

Runs

Gross motor skills this child is learning:

Catching a ball that is thrown

Skipping on one foot

Movement activities that are appropriate for this child:

Moving across the room like a rabbit or a frog to practice hopping and jumping

Outdoor activities that are appropriate for this child:

Hopscotch to practice hopping on one foot

A bean bag game to practice throwing and catching

Take balls out to practice throwing and catching

Gross Motor Skills

Child: _____   Age: _____   Date: _____

Gross motor skills this child has mastered:

_____

_____

_____

_____

_____

_____

Gross motor skills this child is learning:

_____

_____

_____

_____

_____

_____

Movement activities that are appropriate for this child:

_____

_____

_____

_____

_____

Outdoor activities that are appropriate for this child:

_____

_____

_____

_____

_____

_____

Gross Motor Skills

Child: _____   **Age:** _____   **Date:** _____

Gross motor skills this child has mastered:

_____

_____

_____

_____

_____

_____

Gross motor skills this child is learning:

_____

_____

_____

_____

_____

_____

_____

Movement activities that are appropriate for this child:

_____

_____

_____

_____

_____

_____

_____

Outdoor activities that are appropriate for this child:

_____

_____

_____

_____

_____

_____

Discuss your observations and plans with your trainer.

III. Observing and Planning for Children's Fine Motor Development

In this activity you will learn:

- to identify children's developing fine motor skills; and

- to plan activities that help children practice fine motor skills.

Young children need to develop their small muscles for many tasks. Coordinating hands, fingers, and wrists is necessary for writing and drawing. Strength in the small muscles is needed for cutting with scissors and using other tools. Control is required for buttoning, zipping, holding utensils, and other tasks. These skills are an important part of the early years, and they are refined, adapted, and used for tasks later in life, such as writing, typing, driving, cooking, and playing musical instruments.

Preschool children often select things to do that involve the use of small muscles. As children develop control and coordination of their fingers, hands, and wrists, they delight in stringing beads, completing puzzles, and placing pegs in pegboards.

Throughout the day, most preschool children will initiate activities that help them develop their fine motor skills. Children put together Legos and Unifix cubes in the table toy area. They build roads with unit blocks and push cars along their highways. They use tongs and egg beaters in the house corner, and paint brushes and playdough in the art area. Collections of shells, rocks, beans, and so forth on the science table provide children with opportunities to pick up and move small objects. Turning a jump rope outdoors allows them to coordinate wrist and hand motions. With an appropriate indoor and outdoor environment, the chances for children to use their small muscles are almost endless.

Each child has his or her own pace for successfully learning to use fingers, hands, and wrists. Although children may attempt tasks using a wide range of small muscle skills, they usually master these skills in a sequence. The fine motor skills listed on the following chart are typically demonstrated by preschool children. The average age at which children develop these fine motor skills is also identified.

Fine Motor Skills

BEHAVIOR	AGE
Uses scissors to cut paper	3 years
Puts on shoes	3-4 years
Dresses him/herself	3-4 years
Drives nails and pegs	3-4 years
Builds towers with cubes and other small objects	3-4 years
Holds writing and drawing utensils	3-4 years
Strings beads	3-4 years
Puts round pegs in round holes on pegboard	3-4 years
Builds bridges with cubes	3-4 years
Builds tall towers with cubes	4-5 years
Begins to draw pictures that represent real things	4-5 years
Prints some recognizable letters	4-5 years
Learns to lace shoes	5-6 years

Your role in promoting preschool children's fine motor development begins with setting up and maintaining a rich environment. It also includes planning and conducting a variety of activities in which children use their small muscles, and providing encouragement and guidance for children as they play. As children use their hands and fingers during activities, you will observe that most of them have developed a preference for using their right or left hand. Most children establish a preferred hand by the time they are three years old. Some do not. It is important for adults not to make a fuss over this issue. Teachers should encourage children to use whichever hand they prefer, placing objects in their preferred hand and specifically describing their actions (for example, "Tommy is drawing with his left hand!"). They will then become more skillful in using their preferred hand. It is frustrating for children—and also a waste of time—to force them to become right-handed if their preference is for their left hand.

Sensory awareness—using sight, sound, touch, taste, and smell to get information—is a large part of fine motor development. Activities in which children use their senses as they manipulate objects help them coordinate movements. Teachers can provide experiences in which children:

- serve food;

- tear, peel, slice, and scrape vegetables and fruits for food-preparation activities;

- squeeze and identify objects hidden inside "feely" bags;

- hold and pass around small canisters with various scents in them; and

- listen to small items rattle and bounce in "sound" canisters.

While a variety of cognitive concepts are being learned with these types of activities, fine motor skills are also being developed as children get information from their senses.

In this learning activity you will observe two preschool children in your group over a five-day period and identify the fine motor skills they are using. You will then plan activities to give the children opportunities to practice and refine their skills.

Fine Motor Skills
(Example)

Child: _Emma_ **Age:** _3 years, 8 months_ **Date:** _April 29_

Fine motor skills that this child has mastered:

Tearing paper

Stringing beads

Holding a paint brush

Using a fork

Fine motor skills that this child is learning:

Cutting with scissors

Using tongs at water play table

Activities that would be appropriate for this child's skills:

Using pegs and pegboards of a variety of sizes

Using playdough with various utensils

Playing with the Bristle Blocks

Fine Motor Skills

Child: _____   Age: _____   Date: _____

Fine motor skills that this child has mastered:

_____

_____

_____

_____

_____

_____

_____

_____

Fine motor skills that this child is learning:

_____

_____

_____

_____

_____

_____

_____

_____

Activities that would be appropriate for this child's skills:

_____

_____

_____

_____

_____

_____

_____

Fine Motor Skills

Child: _____   Age: _____   Date: _____

Fine motor skills that this child has mastered:

_____

_____

_____

_____

_____

_____

_____

_____

Fine motor skills that this child is learning:

_____

_____

_____

_____

_____

_____

_____

_____

Activities that would be appropriate for this child's skills:

_____

_____

_____

_____

_____

_____

Discuss your observations and plans with your trainer.

IV. Creating an Environment That Promotes Physical Development

In this activity you will learn:

- to select materials and equipment that help children develop gross and fine motor skills; and

- to use the environment in ways that encourage development of gross and fine motor skills.

When teachers know the range of physical skills that children can learn at a given age and stage of development, they can set up an environment that encourages further development of these skills.

The preschool environment should be one in which children feel confident and reassured as they climb, balance, draw, hop, dance, serve themselves, and eat. Teachers help children achieve feelings of confidence by maintaining an environment that conveys positive messages to children. As discussed in Module 3, Creating an Environment for Learning, these messages include the following:

- *"This is a cheerful and happy place."*
- *"You belong here, and we like you."*
- *"This is a place you can trust."*
- *"You can do many things on your own and be independent."*
- *"You can get away and be by yourself when you need to."*
- *"This is a safe place to explore and try out your ideas."*

You can convey these messages in your room and outdoor area in many ways. A cheerful and happy place contains soft materials, such as playdough, to stretch and roll. A room that says "you belong here" has child-sized equipment for climbing. A place each child can trust uses a consistent schedule so children know that the opportunity to run fast and jump happens each day during outdoor play time. A place to do many things on one's own has low shelves for children to select pegs and pegboards, crayons and paper, and other materials for small muscle use. A place where a child can get away and be alone has a cozy corner where the child can relax. And a safe place to explore has an enclosed block area so each child can safely pile blocks and build structures.

Most preschool children will practice skills they have already perfected as well as those that offer them a challenge. The environment you set up should provide many opportunities for children to use their large and small muscles in every interest area. The chart on the following pages lists examples of fine and gross motor play that preschool children enjoy in the room and outdoors.

INTEREST AREA/ACTIVITY	FINE AND GROSS MOTOR PLAY
House corner	Lifting dolls, cooking and eating utensils, and pots and pans. Opening and closing cabinet doors. Setting the table and passing serving bowls. Using zippers, buttons, buckles, and snaps as they put on and take off dress-up clothes.
Table toys	Taking out and putting in puzzle pieces. Snapping Bristle Blocks and Legos together. Stringing beads. Picking up and dropping sorting items (buttons, bottle caps) into trays.
Blocks	Lifting unit blocks and hollow blocks. Placing one block on top of another. Moving wooden people, cars, and trucks.
Art	Painting large strokes at the easel. Drawing lines and shapes with crayons. Running fingers through finger paint or shaving cream. Pasting and gluing paper, fabric, feathers, and so on to make collages and assemblages. Molding and stretching playdough and clay.
Library	Turning the pages of a book. Placing headsets on their ears. Pressing buttons on a tape recorder. Moving felt pieces on a flannel board.
Large muscle and music (indoors)	Climbing the rungs of an indoor climber. Balancing in a rocking boat. Stepping up and down stairs on an upside-down rocking boat. Crawling in a cardboard box. Walking on a balance beam. Creating movements to music. Following directions for movement to music.

INTEREST AREA/ACTIVITY	FINE AND GROSS MOTOR PLAY
Sand/water table	Pouring from a pitcher. Squeezing sponges and turkey basters. Directing the spray from a squeeze bottle. Feeling the textures of wet and dry sand. Rotating wrist or forearm to use eggbeaters or screw-on jar lids.
Science and nature	Sprinkling food into a fish bowl. Picking up rocks, shells, and other collections. Lifting small objects while looking through a magnifying glass. Carrying a pitcher to water plants.

Woodworking	Holding a nail in one hand and using a hammer
	    with the other.
	Turning the rod on a vise.
	Placing tools on pegboard hooks.
	Making back-and-forth arm motions with saws
	    and sandpaper.

Outdoors	Throwing, catching, and kicking balls. Climbing ladders. Swinging from rungs on a climber. Crawling through tunnels. Pedaling a tricycle.

The types of materials you use in your environment will vary according to the ages of the children in your group and their strengths, needs, and interests. Older preschool children who have had many opportunities to use their large and small muscles can usually have success with more challenging learning materials and equipment than can three-year-olds and children with limited experiences.

In this learning activity you will identify fine and gross motor skills for the preschool children in your group, select interest areas where children can learn these skills, and list the appropriate materials. First read the example. Then complete the blank form that follows.

Creating Learning Environments for
Fine and Gross Motor Development
(Example)

Date: _March 15_   Ages: _3's and early 4's_

SKILL	INTEREST AREA	MATERIALS
Eye-hand coordination	Table toys	Large beads and shoe laces for stringing. Paper plates and yarn for lacing.
Throwing underhand	Outdoors	Bean bags and large cardboard box with holes for bean bag tossing. Large and medium balls for throwing.
Buttoning and unbuttoning	House corner	Doll clothes with large buttons and buttonholes.

Creating Learning Environments for
Fine and Gross Motor Development

Date: _____   Ages: _____

SKILL	INTEREST AREA	MATERIALS

Discuss this exercise with your colleagues and your trainer. Make changes to your environment as the children's interests, strengths, and needs change.

V. Helping Children Develop Positive Self-Concepts Through Physical Development

In this activity you will learn:

- to recognize how physical development helps children develop socially and emotionally; and

- to interact with children in ways that encourage a positive self-concept.

Early childhood educators have long recognized the important role that physical development plays in helping children feel good about themselves. When a child learns to throw a ball, to jump a distance, or to cut with a pair of scissors, the sense of accomplishment is enormous. The pride that comes from successfully mastering physical skills makes children feel good about themselves. This sense of confidence and competence leads to emotional security and a willingness to risk learning difficult cognitive tasks. Thus, by including physical development in the early childhood curriculum, you are promoting the child's growth in all areas and contexts.

Encouraging Positive Self-Concepts Through Interactions with Children

Although most children will eventually develop physical skills on their own, not all children will feel proud of their accomplishments if they receive no encouragement or support for their efforts. This is especially true if children are slow in development or feel pressure from adults. Your encouragement is therefore crucial to ensuring a sense of success. Here are some ways that teachers can provide encouragement.

- **Review for children how to do an activity right before they try it:** "John's ready to throw the ball to you. Follow the ball with your eyes, and keep your arms stretched out."

- **Suggest how a child can overcome an obstacle:** "I'll give you a push on the swing. Then you can use your legs to keep going."

- **Verbally reassure a child who is reluctant or frightened:** "I know this can be scary. Let me hold your hand while you start walking."

- **Praise a child for trying something new:** "I watched you go down the slide all by yourself. That was terrific, Renee."

- **Praise a child for progress, without making comparisons to other children:** "You ran a lot further around the yard today than you did last month, Lamont. Did you know that?"

When encouraging children, be sure to let them know that you are praising them for their efforts—not how they stack up next to other children or standards. Children need to be made to feel important in their own right, not for meeting set measures of success. As always, it's important to be genuine in your praise. If praise comes too often and is vague, it loses its value. On the other hand, sincere praise can make a child feel good and try harder.

Encouraging Positive Self-Concepts Through Materials and Activities

Children learn to succeed when they are placed in an environment that challenges them to try harder. If materials and activities are too easy, children become bored and uninterested. Children need their minds and bodies to be challenged. At the same time, if the environment is too challenging, children will become frustrated and give up.

For teachers, the key to success is to create an environment that interests the children and is appropriate for their capabilities. In the example below, the teacher selected materials and planned an activity to help Sharon practice fine motor skills. While the activity was a good one for developing these skills, it was not appropriate for this child because it was beyond what she could do.

Sharon, Age 3

Sharon loves to tear pieces of paper during art. She is accomplished at this but needs practice in other fine motor skills, as evidenced by the difficulty she has in pouring liquids.

Materials/activity selected:

Cutting with scissors.

Reasons for choice:

Sharon likes making collages and has never tired of tearing paper. Scissors will give her an opportunity to advance, while developing new fine motor skills.

What was observed:

Sharon could hold the scissors properly and make cutting motions in the air. However, she could not apply the skill to paper. She kept trying to cut paper, which would fall from her left hand or crumple into a mass. She refused assistance and became very agitated. Following this experience, she has refused to do art activities for several days now.

Recommendations:

Sharon needs to be given materials that will not frustrate her and with which she can experience success. Her experience with the scissors needs to be offset with positive ones. The scissors were a poor choice; they are too advanced for Sharon at this stage in her development.

In this activity, you will read several sample situations and decide what activities you could plan and what you would say to help each child feel successful and competent.

WHAT THE CHILD IS DOING	WHAT ACTIVITIES/ MATERIALS WOULD HELP THIS CHILD	WHAT YOU COULD SAY TO ENCOURAGE THE CHILD
Jason can kick objects forward with ease but is having difficulty kicking objects backward.		
All the children except Eduardo had fun walking on coffee can stilts. Eduardo can't seem to stay up on the "stilts."		
Every time the ball is thrown at Maria she ducks or, more frequently, runs out of its path.		
Lucy enjoys stringing large beads. One time she tried to make a necklace of smaller beads. She got frustrated and spilled the entire box of beads on the floor.		
Matthew likes to help pour juice for snacks. However, every time he takes a turn at helping, he spills a large amount of juice. Still, he loves to help out.		

Review your responses with your trainer.

Summarizing Your Progress

You have now completed all of the learning activities for this module. Whether you are an experienced teacher or a new one, this module has probably helped you develop new skills for promoting the physical development of preschool children. Before you go on, take a few minutes to summarize what you've learned.

- Turn back to Learning Activity I, Using Your Knowledge of Child Development to Promote Physical Development, and add to the chart specific examples of what you learned about promoting children's physical development during the time you were working on this module. Compare your ideas to those in the completed chart at the end of the module.

- Next, review your responses to the pre-training assessment for this module. Write a summary of what you learned and list the skills you developed or improved.

_____

_____

_____

_____

_____

_____

_____

_____

If there are topics you would like to know more about, you will find recommended readings listed in the orientation.

Your final step in this module is to complete the knowledge and competency assessments. Let your trainer know when you are ready to schedule the assessments. After you have successfully completed these assessments, you will be ready to start a new module. Congratulations on your progress so far, and good luck with your next module.

Answer Sheets

Promoting Children's Physical Development

Reinforcing and Encouraging Physical Development

1. **How did Ms. Kim encourage the children to use their small muscles at lunch time?**

   a. She allowed them to pour the milk themselves.

   b. She told them how to do it so the cup wouldn't move.

   c. She had Robert use a sponge to wipe up his spilled milk.

   d. She asked them to think of a way to pick up peas so the peas wouldn't fall off the fork.

   e. She allowed them to spear peas with the fork, which develops finger muscles and eye-hand coordination.

2. **What did Ms. Kim say to reinforce the children's efforts and build self-esteem?**

   a. She told Robert the milk came out too fast and asked him to wipe it up instead of making him feel bad that he spilled the milk.

   b. She told Shannon that her hand and arm muscles were working well.

   c. She reassured Robert that his hand and arm muscles would make the milk go more slowly next time.

   d. She told the children how well they solved the problem of peas falling off the fork.

Providing Equipment and Activities for Gross Motor Development

1. **How did the children let Ms. Williams know they were ready for gross motor activities?**

   a. They began testing limits in the block area and house corner.

   b. Mark wanted to go outside.

2. **What gross motor activities did Ms. Williams provide?**

   a. She set up rope rings for movement.

   b. She let the children run around the playground briefly in their rain gear.

Providing Equipment and Activities for Fine Motor Development

1. What activities did Ms. Green and Mr. Lopez provide for fine motor development?

Shaving cream, cars, wooden people, blocks.

2. How did they reinforce the children's small muscle play?

    a. They described children's actions and asked questions to let the children know they were aware of what they were doing.

    b. They praised the children's work.

Using Your Knowledge of Child Development to Promote Physical Development

WHAT PRESCHOOL CHILDREN ARE LIKE	HOW TEACHERS CAN USE THIS INFORMATION TO PROMOTE PHYSICAL DEVELOPMENT
They walk easily and can balance themselves on one foot for several seconds at a time.	Use a balance beam or tape a strip of wide adhesive to a floor or mat to give children practice in walking. Children can move across the beam in various positions (arms in front, behind them; sideways; backward) and obstacles can be placed on the beam for children to step over. A tape path (or unit blocks) can be laid out as a walking course. Turns, curves, and obstacles can be added to the course to increase skills. To increase balance skills further, children can be given practice walking on tin can stilts. For more challenge, children can progress from tuna fish can stilts to juice can stilts. With practice children can learn to turn, jump, and even walk an obstacle course on their stilts.
They run, jump, and hop.	Plan and conduct noncompetitive games for children to practice movement skills. Arrange indoor and outdoor environments with furniture and equipment for children to jump, hop, and skip around and over.
They throw balls overhead and catch bounced balls.	Provide bean bags and balls of various sizes for children to throw and catch.
They climb.	Allow adequate time for children to use indoor and outdoor climbing equipment. Encourage children who are learning to climb so they feel competent and are not frustrated or fearful.
They dance to music.	Provide large and small group music activities in which children can move to different rhythms. Use a variety of music experiences that provide directions for children's movement as well as those which allow children to create their own movements so they can develop a sense of rhythm.
They manipulate objects with their hands and fingers to see how objects fit together and work.	Provide a variety of puzzles, table toys, house corner props, and art materials for children to practice picking up and placing small objects to help them develop eye-hand coordination.

WHAT PRESCHOOL CHILDREN ARE LIKE	HOW TEACHERS CAN USE THIS INFORMATION TO PROMOTE PHYSICAL DEVELOPMENT
They create large and small objects with clay and play dough.	Have clay and playdough available often in the art area. Encourage children to roll, pinch, squeeze, pound, and pull so they can refine movements made with their fingers.
They finger paint, draw, and paint with large brushes on an easel.	Have easels, paints, paper, crayons, and other drawing materials available every day in the art area. Encourage children's coordination of arm, wrist, and hand movements.
They cut with scissors.	Provide tongs, clothespins, and child-sized left- and right-hand scissors for children to practice cutting skills.
They string beads, lace, zip, and weave.	Provide fabric with zippers, yarn, string, laces, beads, spools, and other materials for children to practice stringing, lacing, weaving, and self-help skills.

Glossary

Eye-hand coordination The ability to direct finger, hand, and wrist movements to accomplish a fine motor task—for example, fitting a peg in a hole or piling blocks.

Fine motor skills Movements that involve the use of small muscles of the body, hands, and wrists—for example, picking up puzzle pieces or cutting with a pair of scissors.

Gross motor skills Movements that involve the use of large muscles of the body, the entire body, or large parts of the body—for example, running, hopping, or climbing.

Physical development The gradual gaining of control over large and small muscles.

Sensory awareness The gaining of information through sight, sound, touch, taste, and smell—for example, smelling spices or turning in the direction of a voice.

Spatial awareness The knowledge that the body takes up space and can move in space—for example, crawling inside a box.

Module 5
Cognitive

What Is Cognitive Development and Why Is It Important?

Cognitive development is the process of learning to think and to reason. We have learned a great deal about children's cognitive development from the work of Jean Piaget, who carefully observed young children to find out how they think at different ages and how they learn. He defined a series of stages that all children progress through from birth to maturity. Through his research, he noticed that children think differently from adults. For example, young children believe that water in a short, wide glass increases in amount if it is poured into a tall, thin glass. This is because children think it looks like there is more water in the tall glass; they can't remember that the same amount of water has been poured into a different glass. Eventually, they understand that the amount of water remains the same. This understanding comes when children are old enough to be able to think more abstractly and after they have had many experiences playing with water. It is through their play with real objects and materials that children come to understand the world around them.

Children develop their cognitive skills in everything they do. They are continually exploring and investigating everything around them. You have undoubtedly experienced how many things young children notice. They see the smallest caterpillar that you walk right by. And for them it's not enough to see the caterpillar; they have to touch it, pick it up, examine it closely, even smell it. By using all their senses, young children develop a real understanding of caterpillars. When they hear the word caterpillar, they learn a label for this object they have explored. And on another day, when they see a worm, the same children may say, "Look at the caterpillar!" This is because they have noticed that a worm and a caterpillar have some characteristics in common. Although they are not actually correct, they are using their cognitive skills.

A child's cognitive development is not measured only by what information the child knows. A very important factor is whether a child has the self-confidence and skills to explore, to try out ideas, to solve problems, and to take on new challenges. Helping children develop and use their cognitive skills is a crucial part of being a teacher. If you can help children begin to see themselves as good learners, you will prepare them for school and for life.

Teachers have a special opportunity to promote children's cognitive development. Most young children are eager to explore the world around them, to find out how things work. They want to learn what they can do with things they see in the world. Teachers can build on this natural curiosity to promote cognitive development. First, they can provide opportunities for children to use all their senses to explore their environment. Second, teachers can help children feel good about expressing their ideas and solving problems on their own. And finally, teachers can help children develop new concepts and acquire thinking and reasoning skills appropriate for their age and stage of development.

*ɔ*ting children's cognitive development involves:

- providing opportunities for children to use all their senses to explore their environment;

- interacting with children in ways that help them develop confidence and curiosity; and

- providing opportunities for children to develop new concepts and skills.

Listed below are examples of how teachers demonstrate their competence in promoting children's cognitive development.

Providing Opportunities for Children to Use All Their Senses to Explore Their Environment

Here are some examples of what teachers can do.

- Include children in simple food-preparation activities, letting them see, touch, taste, and smell a variety of foods.

- Call attention to sensory experiences in the course of daily routines with children. "Doesn't the finger paint feel smooth?" "The snap on your jacket goes pop when it opens." "The orange smells delicious."

- Take a "listening walk" with a small group of children to discover different sounds.

- Make "sound boxes" for the science table so children can put them in order from loudest to quietest and match the ones that sound the same.

- Provide matching games in the table toy area. "You put the two circles together! Can you find a shape that looks like this one?"

Interacting with Children in Ways That Help Them Develop Confidence and Curiosity

Here are some examples of what teachers can do.

- Comment on a child's ideas. "You made a train out of those blocks. What a good idea!"

- Ask children questions to help them learn to recall events and to understand how past events relate to what is happening now. "Remember what we saw last time we came to this park? How can we make sure that no one gets hurt on the swing this time?"

- Extend children's thinking by asking questions. "Yes, you are right, ducks can fly. What other things can fly?"

- Extend dramatic play. "I see your baby is sick today. What do you think we should do about a sick baby?"

- Ask a group of children, "What do you think we need to do to make this playdough less sticky?" and try out the ideas they suggest.

- Encourage children to ask questions by answering the many questions they ask.

Providing Opportunities for Children to Develop New Concepts and Skills

Here are some examples of what teachers can do.

- Offer children simple, clear choices when the decision should be theirs. "Do you want to paint at the easel or use the finger paints?"

- Collect a variety of materials (e.g., plastic bottle caps, beans, buttons, etc.) and encourage children to sort them in different ways. "Can anyone find another cap that is like this one in some way? Good, Jake. Tell us why you picked this one. How are they the same?"

- Provide basins of water and objects so children can discover what sinks and what floats.

- Point out patterns that children have created and repeated. "You have a special way of stringing these beads. You are putting on a red, yellow, and green bead; then another red, yellow, and green. Now you have red and yellow. What color bead will you use next?"

- Talk with children about changes they see as the seasons change and help them make a group mural to show what they see.

Promoting Children's Cognitive Development

In the following situations, teachers are promoting children's cognitive development. As you read each one, think about what the teachers are doing and why. Then answer the questions that follow.

Providing Opportunities for Children to Use All Their Senses to Explore the World

Ms. Richards is sitting with a group of three children at the science table. She has just introduced them to the balance scale she made out of wood scraps, margarine tubs, and string. "Can you make your hands into a balance scale?" she asks, showing them what she means. "Now, suppose I put one of these blocks in your right hand. What would happen to your scale?" She places a block in each child's right hand and they discuss how it pushes that hand down. "Now, let's see which is heavier, the block or these four marbles." Ms. Richards places four marbles in each child's left hand. The children "weigh" each hand and discuss which feels heavier. There are different opinions. "How could we find out for sure which is heavier?" she asks. "We could weigh them on the scale," suggests Emily. "Let's try it," says Ms. Richards. Emily places her block in one margarine tub and the four marbles in the other tub. The tub with the block sinks down. "I was right," says David. "The block is heavier."

1. How did Ms. Richards teach the children about balance scales by letting them use their senses?

_____

_____

_____

2. What skills and concepts were the children learning in this activity?

_____

_____

_____

Interacting with Children in Ways That Help Them Develop Confidence and Curiosity

Ms. Williams is watching three children building a tall tower in the block area. She can see that if they add any more blocks, the building is likely to fall. She knows that even if it falls, no one is going to get hurt. When the building comes crashing down, Ms. Williams goes quietly into the block area and kneels down near the children. "I see your building fell down," she says calmly. "What do you think happened?" Terry says, "We made the building too tall." Ms. Williams asks, "Do all tall buildings fall down?" "No," says Heather, "this one was too skinny." Ms. Williams then asks, "How could you build a tall building so it will be stronger and won't fall down?" After thinking a minute, Sam responds, "We could make it fatter on the bottom so it would be stronger." "Why don't you try that," says Ms. Williams, "and see what happens?"

1. **Why did Ms. Williams not interfere with the three block builders when she could see their building might fall down?**

_____

_____

_____

2. **How did Ms. Williams encourage the children to think through and solve the problem on their own?**

_____

_____

_____

Providing Opportunities for Children to Develop New Concepts and Skills

Jerome, a new child at the center, is sobbing. His daddy has just said good-bye. Mr. Lopez kneels down next to Jerome. "Your daddy went to work. I know it makes you sad to say good-bye. Would you like to look at a picture of your daddy?" he asks. Jerome nods through his tears. They walk over to the wall where pictures of children and their families are hanging at a child's level. "Daddy," says Jerome pointing to his father's picture. Jerome picks up the toy telephone and hands the receiver to Mr. Lopez, who says into the phone, "Jerome was sorry to see you leave this morning. We've been looking at your picture." He hands Jerome the phone. Jerome holds it to his ear and smiles. Later in the day, Mr. Lopez sees Jerome playing in the house corner. Jerome says to his doll, "I have to go to work now. I'll see you later." Although it is snack time, he doesn't interrupt the game. He knows dramatic play gives Jerome a chance to feel in control of someone's leaving and coming back.

1. **How is Jerome's sadness about separating from his daddy related to his cognitive development?**

_____

_____

_____

2. **What things in the environment helped Jerome deal with separation?**

_____

_____

_____

3. Why didn't Mr. Lopez interrupt Jerome when he was playing in the house corner?

_____

_____

_____

Compare your answers with those on the answer sheet at the end of this module. If your answers are different, discuss them with your trainer. There can be more than one good answer.

Your Own Experiences with Learning

Cognitive development continues throughout life. People don't stop learning when they leave school. They continue to develop their ability to think and to reason. You probably know people you feel are good learners and thinkers. In many situations you no doubt consider yourself a good learner. People who have confidence in their ability to learn generally have some of the following characteristics.

- They are not afraid to accept a challenge. "I don't know the answer but I'll find out."

- When they confront a problem, they don't give up if they can't resolve it right away. They try to figure out what to do. If a child's behavior is continually annoying them, they try to find out what is causing the behavior and what they can do to improve the situation.

- They are curious and interested in learning new things. "I hear that book is really interesting. I'd like to read it when you are finished."

- They are creative thinkers—they can look at something and see lots of possibilities. "I think the children would use the house corner more if we reorganized it and moved it closer to the block area."

- They speak up and say what they think. "I'm not sure I agree with you. Here's what I see happening."

It's not just how much information people have but how they use their thinking abilities that is important. We don't all know the same things, nor do we need to. A car mechanic knows a lot about the parts of a car, what makes it go, and how to fix it. When there's a problem, the mechanic tries to figure out the cause. If you know very little about how a car operates, this doesn't make you less smart. You know other things the car mechanic doesn't know. What's important is whether you each have the confidence and skills to learn what you need in your own lives.

Many factors affect our ability to learn something new. Most important is whether the new information is useful to us. If we can see a way to use what we are learning, we are likely to be more interested in putting forth the effort. It helps if the new information is related to something we already know about, or know how to do—or to something we've wanted to know for some time.

Each of us has a different style or way of learning that works best for us. Some of us need to read over directions and think about them for a while. Some of us need to watch someone else demonstrate a task. Some of us need to hear directions explained a couple of times.

As an adult you are aware of what helps you learn a new skill or new idea. Think of a time recently when you were in a learning situation—for instance, learning to swim, taking an adult education course, or going through these modules. List four factors that made it easier for you to learn in that situation.

1. _____
   _____

2. _____
   _____

3. _____
   _____

4. _____
   _____

Some factors that affect our ability to learn relate to the teacher or to the material itself: how the information is presented, how it is organized, and whether it is on our level. Our readiness to learn is also affected by how we feel at the time. If we are tired, distracted, uncomfortable, or unsure of what is expected of us, we are less likely to learn.

This training program is designed to help you learn new concepts and skills and feel good about yourself as a learner. The training program design includes a number of strategies to make it a positive learning experience:

- The information is organized into individual modules so you won't be overwhelmed with too much information at once.

- All the modules relate to your work and should be immediately useful.

- You may use the modules in whatever order you prefer.

- There are many examples within each module to help you understand the content.

- Answer sheets, a colleague, or your trainer can give you feedback.

- You receive your own set of materials to keep as an ongoing reference on the job.

- You complete many of the learning activities with the children you teach.

As you enhance your skills and knowledge in ways that make you feel confident, you will be able to do the same thing for children. Like you, young children learn best when they are interested in and ready to receive new information. They like to try out new ideas and discover what works and what doesn't on their own. As you go through these modules, you will try out many ideas and discover for yourself what approaches work best for you and for the children in your care.

When you have finished this overview section, you should complete the pre-training assessment. Refer to the glossary at the end of this module if you need definitions of the terms that are used.

Pre-Training Assessment

Listed below are the skills that teachers use to promote children's cognitive development. Think about whether you do these things regularly, sometimes, or not enough. Place a check in one of the columns on the right for each skill listed. Then discuss your answers with your trainer.

SKILL	I DO THIS REGULARLY	I DO THIS SOMETIMES	I DON'T DO THIS ENOUGH
PROVIDING OPPORTUNITIES FOR CHILDREN TO USE ALL THEIR SENSES TO EXPLORE THEIR ENVIRONMENT 1. Planning activities that allow children to safely use and refine their senses of smell, taste, sight, hearing, and touch.			
2. Talking to children about what they are learning through their senses.			
3. Selecting materials that encourage children to use all their senses to learn.			
INTERACTING WITH CHILDREN IN WAYS THAT HELP THEM DEVELOP CONFIDENCE AND CURIOSITY 4. Providing experiences that challenge children and also allow them to experience success.			
5. Providing opportunities for children to learn about cause and effect.			
6. Asking questions that encourage children to think and reason.			

SKILL	I DO THIS REGULARLY	I DO THIS SOMETIMES	I DON'T DO THIS ENOUGH
7. Respecting children's questions and knowing how to respond in ways that promote their thinking.			
8. Knowing when to intervene and when to allow children to solve problems on their own.			
PROVIDING OPPORTUNITIES FOR CHILDREN TO DEVELOP NEW CONCEPTS AND SKILLS 9. Creating an environment that helps children learn concepts and skills.			
10. Selecting materials and activities that help children learn to classify and sequence.			
11. Selecting materials and activities that help children understand what numbers are.			
12. Planning experiences that help children expand their understanding of the world around them.			
13. Helping children learn to identify likenesses and differences.			
14. Helping children understand cause and effect through their own experiences.			

Review your responses, then list three to five skills you would like to improve or topics you would like to learn more about. When you finish this module, you will list examples of your new or improved knowledge and skills.

_____

_____

_____

_____

Now begin the learning activities for Module 5, Cognitive.

I. Using Your Knowledge of Child Development to Promote Cognitive Development

In this activity you will learn:

- to recognize some typical behaviors of preschoolers; and

- to use what you know about preschool children to promote their cognitive development.

Preschool children learn by exploring, pretending, and experimenting. Through play, they come to know the world around them.

The play of preschool children tends to have a purpose. They can tell you what they want to do and why. "The baby is sick and I'm the doctor. You drive the ambulance." They can talk about their discoveries. "Look, I made pink! I mixed red and white, and it came out pink." And they ask lots of questions and can keep you very busy supplying answers. "Why is the grass green?" "What do birds do when it rains?"

Because preschool children are able to use words to express their ideas, adults sometimes expect them to know more than they really do. For example, a four-year-old may be able to count perfectly to 20, but the same child may give you three blocks when you ask for five. He or she has memorized the names of numbers but doesn't really understand the concept of five objects.

Teachers of preschool children have to be good listeners and observers in order to know what children really understand and what they are ready to do. Preschool children still need lots of time to play and explore with all their senses. These experiences help them develop their thinking skills and gain a genuine understanding of new concepts.

The chart on the next page lists some typical behaviors of preschool children. Included are behaviors relevant to promoting children's cognitive development. The right column asks you to identify ways that teachers can use this information about child development to promote cognitive development. Try to think of as many examples as you can. As you work through the module you will learn new strategies for promoting children's cognitive development, and you can add them to the child development chart. You are not expected to think of all the examples at one time. If you need help getting started, turn to the completed chart at the end of the module. By the time you complete all the learning activities, you will find that you have learned many ways to promote children's learning.

Using Your Knowledge of Child Development
to Promote Cognitive Development

WHAT PRESCHOOL CHILDREN ARE LIKE	HOW TEACHERS CAN USE THIS INFORMATION TO PROMOTE COGNITIVE DEVELOPMENT
They learn by using all their senses—smelling, tasting, touching, hearing, and seeing.	
They use their imaginations continually—they love to role play, imitate, and engage in in dramatic play.	
They are interested in cause and effect—what makes things happen.	
Their vocabulary is expanding rapidly—they know the names of many things and can explain their ideas.	
They are curious and want to explore many things.	

WHAT PRESCHOOL CHILDREN ARE LIKE	HOW TEACHERS CAN USE THIS INFORMATION TO PROMOTE COGNITIVE DEVELOPMENT
They believe there is a purpose for everything and ask lots of questions: "Why?" "How?" "What?"	
They can reason and think logically sometimes, but often they are not accurate in their thinking.	
They are developing an understanding of number concepts but need lots of experiences with real objects.	
They learn concepts and skills such as matching, classification, and identification of shapes and colors by playing with toys and objects.	

WHAT PRESCHOOL CHILDREN ARE LIKE	HOW TEACHERS CAN USE THIS INFORMATION TO PROMOTE COGNITIVE DEVELOPMENT
They have lots of ideas of their own and like to gather information about the world.	
They are developing the ability to understand how picture, letter, word, and numeric symbols can stand for real objects and ideas.	

When you have completed as much as you can do on the chart, discuss your answers with your trainer. As you proceed with the rest of the learning activities, you can refer back to the chart and add more examples of how teachers can promote children's cognitive development.

II. Helping Children Learn to Make Sense of the World

In this activity you will learn:

- to observe how preschool children make sense of the world around them; and

- to listen to and understand children's thinking.

Adults learn by doing, reading, and listening. Your ideas about preschool children are tested and reinforced when you try out certain activities with them and observe the results. As you read the words on this page, you take meaning from them because you understand the concepts they represent, and you can add this information to what you already know. You are also able to learn by listening to a speaker talking about a particular subject. If the topic is of interest to you, you are likely to gain new information.

Preschool children learn differently. Written words have little or no meaning for them. They might be able to recognize some letters and numbers and even some words—especially their names. But they are certainly not ready to learn from printed pages. Nor do young children learn best by sitting and listening. They learn best by doing. They have to try things out, act on objects, and see for themselves what happens. They have to develop knowledge from their own experiences.

You may have heard people say that young children have their own way of thinking. As a teacher working with children every day, you have probably enjoyed the "funny" things they sometimes say. You may have been surprised at a misunderstanding a child expressed. Knowing why children say and do these "funny" things will help you understand how preschool children think. It will also help you appreciate how hard they try to understand the world around them.

Preschool Children Think Very Concretely

Preschool children are still developing an understanding of words, and sometimes they get confused. Words don't always have the same meaning for young children that they have for adults.

- A three-year-old told her mother: "We went on a walk at school today. We were looking for signs of winter, but all I saw was one STOP sign."

- A teacher put on a record and told the children to "move to the music," meaning "move your bodies as the music makes you feel." The children got up and moved over to the record player.

These children took the words they heard very literally. They had a different understanding of the adults' words than the adults intended, and they acted on what they thought was meant.

Preschool Children Are Beginning to Understand Cause and Effect

It's hard work figuring out what makes things happen. Preschool children use their own experiences and put things together that sometimes are not related.

- "Today we are having fish for lunch because the teacher is late. Whenever the teacher is late, we have fish."

- A four-year-old noticed that a friend didn't want ice cream for dessert. Later that night, the friend got sick. The next day, when offered ice cream, the child said, "Yes, I want some, because if I don't have ice cream, I'll get sick like Laurie did."

Even though these children were not correct in their conclusions, they were still using good thinking skills.

Preschool Children Judge Things by How They Look

If something looks bigger, they believe it must be bigger, even if logical thinking indicates that it is the same size or amount.

- If you put some sand in a low, long tray and then let a child watch you put the same amount of sand into a flower-pot, he or she might say there is more sand in the pot than in the tray because the sand seems "deeper" in the smaller area.

- Young children often break up their crackers at snack time because to them, lots of small pieces seem like more than one large piece.

Preschool Children Ask Lots of Questions

By questioning, children acquire new information. They want to know the purpose of everything, so they ask **why** questions.

- "Why does the alarm clock go off in the morning?"

- "Why does the car need gas?"

They ask **what** questions to learn what things are called.

- "What is the thing that covers the light bulb?"

- "What color is this?"

They ask **how** questions to better understand processes and relationships.

- "How does the water get hard into ice cubes?"

- "How did he get home when the bus broke down?"

Answering the many questions young children ask can be tiring for both teachers and parents. Sometimes a simple answer is all that is required: "That color is green." Sometimes you can use the question to help a child think: "What are some ways you think he might have gotten home when the bus broke down?"

In this learning activity you will observe and listen to the children in your group over a one-week period. Look for examples of how they are trying to make sense of the world. Try to find examples of the following:

- concrete use of words;

- cause-and-effect thinking;

- judging things by how they look; and

- typical questions preschoolers ask.

First read the example that follows. Then use the chart on the following page to record your observations.

Observing Children's Thinking
(Example)

WHAT CHILDREN SAID OR DID	THIS WAS AN EXAMPLE OF
Tim was sure his piece of clay was bigger than Vanessa's because his was taller and hers was flatter. (They were the same.)	*Judging by how things look.*
When I told Delores she had "sharp eyes," she put her hands to her eyes and said, They're not sharp."	*Concrete use of words.*
After a storm Susan said, "Thunder makes the rain."	*Cause-and-effect thinking.*

Observing Children's Thinking

WHAT CHILDREN SAID OR DID	THIS WAS AN EXAMPLE OF

When you have at least five examples, share them with your trainer.

III. Promoting Children's Thinking Skills

In this activity you will learn:

- to recognize the skills children use in learning; and

- to promote children's thinking skills.

There is an endless amount of information that preschool children can learn. As important as what they learn, however, is whether they are learning how to learn and whether they feel good about their ability to learn.

Teachers can help preschool children develop the skills they need to understand the world. Some thinking skills that children can develop and use throughout their lives are described below.

Noticing Characteristics of Things

Through their senses—touching, seeing, hearing, smelling, tasting—preschool children can identify the characteristics or details of things around them. They can learn to label these characteristics: hard/soft, red/green, loud/quiet, sour/sweet. Here are some questions you can ask to help children become aware of the characteristics of things around them:

"How does it feel?"

"What does this smell remind you of?"

"What makes this one different from the other?"

Identifying Likenesses and Differences

Preschool children can identify things that are the same and different. This is an important skill in learning to read. To understand the symbols used in reading, children must be able to tell the difference between q and p, d and b. Before they can do this, they need lots of opportunities to compare, to match, and to identify how things are the same and how they are different. Here are some questions you can ask to guide children in identifying likenesses and differences:

- "Are these two the same or are they different?"

- "Can you find another shape that looks like this one?"

- "How are these two buttons the same? How are they different?"

Classifying

Classification is an important skill that children use in making sense of the world. When a small boy says to a female teacher, "You can't be a Mommy, you're a teacher," he is classifying. He has put this woman in a group of people called "teachers," and he thinks she can't also be a mother because that's another group. This is typical thinking for young children.

When preschool children classify, they sort objects, people, events, and ideas into groups on the basis of traits that these things have in common. Here are some questions you can ask to help children develop their classifying skills:

- "What different groups could we make with these bottle caps?"

- "How else can we group these buttons?"

- "How are all the shapes in this group alike?"

- "If you are wearing something red today, you may get your coats on to go outside."

Preschool children are usually quite interested in comparing what they are wearing, playing with, or eating, and this interest also helps them learn to classify. You can encourage children to compare in a friendly, nonjudgmental way so that they learn to appreciate sameness and difference without forming prejudices.

Sequencing

Sequencing is the ability to put things in a certain order. A time sequence would be first, next, last; a sequence of sizes would be small, medium, and large. There can be sequences in sounds from loudest to quietest, and there can be sequences in color shades from darkest to lightest.

The ability to identify and order sequences is important for an understanding of number concepts. First, children need to be able to count in order correctly. You may have heard a child count proudly, "1, 2, 7, 5, 8, 9, 10." Children need lots of real-life opportunities to practice counting in the proper sequence.

Another basic aspect of sequencing is understanding that numbers stand for a quantity of things. Five has real meaning to a child only if he or she understands that a group of five objects has one more than four and one less than six. Here are some questions you can ask to help children develop their sequencing skills:

- "What happened first in the story? Then what happened? What happened last?"

- "You made a pattern with your beads—red, yellow, blue, red, yellow, blue, and red again. What color is going to come next?"

- "You made a long worm with the playdough. Can you make another one bigger than this one? Now can you make one that is smaller?"

Understanding Cause and Effect

Preschool children are constantly trying to figure out why something happened or what is going to happen next. For example, a five-year-old child noticed that the water level in the fish tank had gone down. He said to his teacher, "Look, the fish are drinking the water!" Rather than explaining to the child about evaporation, the teacher asked questions and suggested a way for the child to learn what really caused the water to go down.

- "What makes you think the fish are drinking the water?"

- "You mean if we put out a bowl of water without any fish, the water wouldn't get lower? Let's try it and see what happens."

The children in this class soon discovered that even without fish the water level got lower. The teacher then planned some activities to enable the children to learn more about evaporation: painting with water on a chalkboard and taking a walk after a rain shower when the sun was out.

This learning activity will help you become more aware of the skills that preschool children use in learning to think. Keep in mind the different thinking skills just described. Observe the children as they work in different interest areas and note examples of how they are using their thinking skills. Then record what you said to promote their learning. Begin by reading the example on the next page. Then complete the chart that follows these readings by writing your own observations of what your preschool children are doing and how you are helping them learn to think.

Promoting Children's Thinking
(Example)

THINKING SKILL	INTEREST AREA	WHAT THE CHILDREN DID	WHAT YOU SAID TO PROMOTE THINKING AND LEARNING
Noticing characteristics of things	*Science table*	*Emilio picked up and examined shells in a collection we put out.*	*"How does that shell feel?" "Which one is your favorite?" "What do you like about it?"*
Identifying likenesses and differences	*Table toys*	*Cheryl took out a Lotto game and spread out all the small cards of zoo and farm animals. She picked up a card with a zebra and matched it to a horse.*	*"Those pictures really look a lot alike, don't they? How are these two animals the same?" "Can you see any ways in which they are different?" "Yes, this one has black and white stripes and the other is all brown. Can you find another picture of an animal with black and white stripes?" "Good for you! You found one that matches."*
Classifying	*Table toys*	*Three children sat at a table and played with a button collection. Tony collected all the red buttons. Marguerite especially liked a large, shiny, brass button.*	*"I see you put these buttons together. How did you decide they belong together?" "That's a nice shiny one, isn't it? Can you find any other buttons that look like that one?"*

THINKING SKILL	INTEREST AREA	WHAT THE CHILDREN DID	WHAT YOU SAID TO PROMOTE THINKING AND LEARNING
Sequencing	*Outdoors*	*Dean and Chaundra collected leaves from the playground. They spread them out on a table to examine them.*	*"It looks like you found all sorts of leaves today. Some are big and some are little. Which is the biggest? What's the next biggest? Which one comes next?" "Can you find the smallest one?"*
Understanding cause and effect	*Blocks*	*Maddie built a road with a ramp for her car. She made the ramp so steep that the car went down too fast and fell off the road. She grew frustrated.*	*"Looks like that car is going too fast. What could you do to make it go slower?" When she couldn't think of an idea, I said, "Suppose this block wasn't so high. I'll hold it down lower so you can see what happens to the car now.*

Promoting Children's Thinking

THINKING SKILL	INTEREST AREA	WHAT THE CHILDREN DID	WHAT YOU SAID TO PROMOTE THINKING AND LEARNING
Noticing character-istics of things			
Identifying likenesses and differences			

THINKING SKILL	INTEREST AREA	WHAT THE CHILDREN DID	WHAT YOU SAID TO PROMOTE THINKING AND LEARNING
Classifying			
Sequencing			
Understanding cause and effect			

Discuss your observations with your trainer.

IV. Creating an Environment that Promotes Cognitive Development

In this activity you will learn:

- to use the environment to help children learn new concepts and skills; and

- to select materials that invite children to explore and question.

Because the physical environment of the center is such a large part of the children's world, it is important for teachers to plan that environment carefully so that it supports cognitive development. In Learning Activity III, Promoting Children's Thinking Skills, you learned how to help children develop the following skills:

- noticing the characteristics of things;
- identifying likenesses and differences;
- classifying;
- sequencing; and
- understanding cause and effect.

If the materials in your center are carefully organized and displayed, children will be helped to learn these skills as they select materials, use them, and return them. In a way, you can look at the physical environment as the textbook for the curriculum. Most of the concepts and relationships you want to help children learn are present in the environment. Some concepts in the environment are colors, shapes, and sizes. Some relationships in the environment are graded sizes; what plants need to grow; what happens when you put a round object on a ramp (such as a car on a block); and how adding water to solids (such as clay) changes them.

Because the environment contains so many different concepts and relationships that children can observe and explore, it is important for you to think carefully about what materials you select for the children to use. The more varied the environment, the more preschool children can learn. An interesting environment invites children to wonder:

- What would that feel like?
- How does it smell?
- What would happen if I put these two colors together?
- How can I make this bigger?
- How does this seed become a plant?
- What happens to the snow when we bring it inside?

In this learning activity you will examine ways you can organize your room to help preschool children develop concepts and skills. Then you will read a list of sample materials that teachers can use to promote children's cognitive development. You will select one new set of materials to display in your room and observe how children use these materials.

Organizing the Environment to Teach Children Concepts and Skills[1]

The chart below shows how concepts and skills can be reinforced by the arrangement of the classroom environment. After you have reviewed the chart, think about how you have arranged materials in your room. Think of some ways in which you have set up your room (or might set it up) so that it helps children develop concepts and skills. List your ideas in the last column.

CONCEPTS/SKILLS	IDEAS FOR ORGANIZING THE ENVIRONMENT	WHAT CAN YOU DO IN YOUR ROOM?
Identification/ Matching	Small variety of basic materials in beginning of year. Two of each object (for instance, block accessories). Labels for each object so children match the object with a picture.	
Classification	Different labels for blocks and for accessories. Separate dishpans for zoo animals and farm animals with photos of each as a label. Separate labels in the house corner to show the different types of materials: yellow for cooking utensils, red for cleaning utensils, blue for eating utensils. Large and small items in the house corner.	

[1]Based on the slide/videotape *The New Room Arrangement as a Teaching Strategy* (Washington, DC: Teaching Strategies, Inc., 1991).

CONCEPTS/SKILLS	IDEAS FOR ORGANIZING THE ENVIRONMENT	WHAT CAN YOU DO IN YOUR ROOM?
Sequencing	Materials for washing brushes and hands placed from left to right in order of the steps to follow: soapy water for dirty brushes, rinse buckets for washing hands, paper towels and waste basket. Pictures to show the steps in brushing teeth.	
Color	A display table with different objects and pictures that are yellow.	

Discuss your ideas with your trainer. Decide on what you can do in your room arrangement to help children develop skills and concepts. Try out some of your ideas. Use the space below to note how children react to the changes you made.

_____

_____

_____

_____

_____

_____

_____

_____

_____

Materials That Promote Cognitive Development

The materials you select for children to use and explore also help promote their cognitive development. There are many fine materials you can purchase for your room. But don't overlook the wonderful "junk" you can collect and use to promote cognitive development. Some examples of materials you can provide are given below.

- **Collections:**

  - keys
  - buttons
  - seeds and pits
  - beans
  - rocks
  - shells
  - leaves

- **Objects to explore and to use in exploring:**

  - a magnifying glass and containers with different kinds of sand and dirt
  - magnets and objects to test
  - an old clock to take apart
  - an ant farm
  - a balance scale and objects to weigh
  - nuts and bolts to fit together
  - scent jars filled with different things to smell
  - measuring implements: rulers, cups, spoons, tapes, yardsticks

- **Table toys to manipulate:**

  - attribute blocks or beads
  - seriation games and toys (e.g., nesting cups, sound cannisters, texture games, color chips)
  - puzzles
  - colored cubes
  - Cuisenaire rods
  - shape-sorting boxes
  - purchased games such as Lotto games, number games, and card games
  - parquetry blocks
  - beads for stringing
  - pegboard and pegs

Identify items from this list that you have available but have not yet used with the children in your room. When you have the materials ready, put them out in the room and observe what children do with them. Record what you see. First read the example on the next page.

Children's Use of New Materials
(Example)

Materials selected:

Assorted plastic bottle caps (e.g., from milk cartons, shampoo and liquid detergent bottles)

Why did you select these materials?

The caps are colorful and appealing. I thought the children would enjoy playing with them. I thought of lots of ways they might classify them—on the basis of color, size, those with writing, those with movable parts (spouts), and so on.

How did you display the materials?

I put all the caps on a large tray and put it on a table during free play.

What did you observe children doing?

Several children came over and picked up the caps, examining them. Two children started "building" with them—piling them on top of each other. Another child tested which ones he could roll on the floor.

What did you say or do to promote children's thinking?

I asked a small group, "What can you tell me about these caps?" They said things like "some are red," "these are big ones," "this one has a spout that moves up and down," and "this one has numbers on it." I picked up one cap and asked the children if they could find any more like it. They showed me which ones matched and told me why.

Now record what happens when you add new materials to your room to promote the children's cognitive development.

Children's Use of New Materials

Materials selected:

_____

_____

_____

_____

_____

Why did you select these materials?

_____

_____

_____

_____

_____

How did you select these materials?

_____

_____

_____

_____

_____

What did you observe children doing?

_____

_____

_____

_____

_____

What did you say or do to promote children's thinking?

_____

_____

_____

_____

Discuss your experiences with your trainer.

V. Helping Children Learn to Solve Problems

In this activity you will learn:

* why it is important for preschool children to develop problem-solving skills; and

* to ask questions that encourage children to think and solve problems.

Problem-solving is the process of thinking of and trying out solutions to problems. Preschool children develop problem-solving skills when they have many opportunities to think for themselves. When teachers provide an environment that encourages safe exploration, children are able to solve real problems in their play.

Teachers also promote problem-solving by talking to children and asking them the kinds of questions that lead children to think of their own solutions. Teachers don't need to have all the answers. They do need to ask open-ended questions that encourage children to think. Open-ended questions have many possible answers. For example, if you ask "what do you think we should feed the guinea pig?" you will get many different answers. If you ask "do guinea pigs eat lettuce?"—a closed question—the children will answer either yes or no. They will not have to stretch their thinking.

Open-ended questions help children build on the things they already know. Because they don't have "right" or "wrong" answers, these questions encourage curiosity and imagination. Young children like to copy adults, and when asked many open-ended questions they begin posing such questions themselves, which further encourages their curiosity and learning.

The following situation shows how Ms. Williams helped Joey learn to solve a problem. She used a lot of open-ended questions to help Joey be a problem-solver.[2]

> Joey was playing with some toy cars on the floor, when one of them rolled under the shelf. "Oh, no," said Joey as he heard it bang against the wall. "Ms. Williams," he said, "my car's under the shelf!" Ms. Williams came over to Joey. "Well, how can you get it out?" He stretched his arm under the shelf as far as it could go, but he couldn't feel the car. "You try," he said. Ms. Williams got down and felt around under the shelf. "That was a good idea you had, but I guess my arm isn't long enough either. Now what?" Joey had another idea. He would try with his foot. When his leg wouldn't fit in the space under the shelf, he tried the other leg, then gave the shelf an angry kick. "I know you feel angry, but kicking the shelf won't help," Ms. Williams said. "Think about why it didn't work." Joey said, "My leg is too big." Ms. Williams smiled. "Right. What could we use that would fit?" Joey thought for a minute and said, "Hey, a stick."

---

[2]Adapted from Bess-Gene Holt et al., *Getting Involved: Your Child and Problem-Solving* (Washington, DC: Government Printing Office, 1981), p. 3.

"Good idea, Joey." She went to the closet and came back with a broom, which she put down beside him. It didn't take Joey long to figure out that he could use the broom. He poked the broom handle under the shelf and out rolled the car. Joey smiled and crawled after it.

Together, Joey and Ms. Williams solved the problem. The next time his car or another toy goes under a piece of furniture, he will know that he can use a stick to get it out. Joey also learned that he is capable of solving his own problem. His confidence in his ability to solve problems will help him next time.

Why Problem-Solving Skills Are Important

Young children are learning how to learn: how to get information, how to make sense of the world, and how to solve problems. Their experiences affect how they view learning. Children who see themselves as problem-solvers are more likely to feel both curious and capable when they get older. They will probably be successful in school because they will feel good about their ability to learn.

When children participate actively in problem-solving activities, they learn more than when they are just told the answer. Most children can learn to memorize facts, but learning to make sense of the world is a far more useful skill.

What Teachers Can Do to Encourage Problem-Solving

One of the best ways for you to encourage problem-solving is to show your own interest in learning about the world and your excitement about what's going on in the room. Children will soon pick up on your enthusiasm and become more inquisitive learners themselves. Your attitude is very important and is the basis for the other techniques you can use to encourage problem-solving. Some suggestions follow.

- Offer plenty of practice in problem-solving: puzzles and games, riddles, and so on. Make solving problems fun; encourage a positive attitude toward it.

- Be patient. Don't rush in with an answer. Children may need many opportunities to try and try again. You can help them by saying "I can see how hard you are trying" or by asking questions that may prompt a solution that will work. When Ms. Williams asked Joey, "What could we use that would fit?" she helped him try again.

- Accept and respect whatever responses children give. They think in different ways than adults do. Children will continue to solve problems when they feel that all their ideas are accepted and valued. Praise their creative thinking.

- Allow plenty of time for children to talk. Young children may have trouble putting their thoughts into words. It may take some time for them to express their ideas.

- Give children a chance to work out their own problems. If you do step in, offer help a little at a time. Ms. Williams didn't simply use the broom to get the car out herself. She helped Joey think of this solution by himself. When a child's solution to a problem doesn't work, help him or her try other possibilities. Let the child know that a solution that doesn't work isn't a failure; it's a step in the process of problem-solving.

- Respond to children's simple questions by asking them questions that stimulate their thinking: "Yes, Renee, we're having orange juice for snack. Where do you think our orange juice comes from?" This gives Renee a chance to use her thinking skills as well as get an answer to her question.

- Explain your own problem-solving to children by telling them why you are doing what you do to deal with a problem—say, a broken record-player needle or a leaky faucet in the center. Think out loud as you solve everyday problems so children will see that this activity is a normal part of daily living, not a threatening or "testing" activity.

- Let children know that you are watching them solve problems. Your presence and attention as they work is an important source of support to young children.

- Encourage multiple solutions to keep children thinking about new possibilities and options.

Teachers can also promote problem-solving skills by asking open-ended questions throughout the day and listening to children's answers. Some examples follow.

- When reading a story, stop and ask, "What do you think will happen next?" This gives children a chance to predict what will happen.

- When doing a finger play, ask, "What new ways can we move our fingers?" This gives children the chance to use their own ideas instead of just memorizing the finger play.

- When outside on a walk, ask, "Where do you think those clouds are going?" This helps children think about the world without worrying about right or wrong answers.

- When out in the playground, ask, "What games can four children play with one ball?" This helps children think of ways to play and cooperate with each other.

- When passing by the house corner, ask, "What are you cooking today? How do you make that?" This helps children expand their play and stretch their imaginations.

- When playing in the block corner, ask, "How did you know to put the car at the top of the ramp to make it roll?" This helps children think about what they have learned from their experiences.

- When talking about yesterday's walk in the woods, ask, "What are some things you remember about the woods?" This helps children recall their experiences.

- When looking at a picture book about cars, ask, "What would happen if all the cars stopped working?" This helps children use their imagination in new ways.

- Any time during the day, ask, "What might happen if...?" This helps children learn to predict consequences.

In this learning activity you will select an indoor or outdoor area to focus on for one day. Then you will record the interactions you have with children and the open-ended questions you use to help them develop problem-solving skills. After reviewing your notes, repeat the activity, this time trying to ask even more open-ended questions. Begin by reading the example that follows; then complete the blank chart.

Asking Open-Ended Questions
(Example)

Area: _Playground—swings and climber_   **Date:** _July 14_

INTERACTION	OPEN-ENDED QUESTIONS ASKED
Pushing Bonita on the swing. She likes the way the wind blows her hair back.	_"Bonita, why do you think the wind blows your hair back?"_
Catching children at the bottom of the slide. Vanessa wants to go down on her stomach.	_"Vanessa, I know you would like to slide down on your tummy. What do you think might happen to you if you did?"_
Talking to Lloyd and David on the climber. They like being at the top.	_"How do you feel when you're on top of the climber? What can you see when you're so high up? What do you do when you want to get back down again?"_
Getting the children together to go back inside. Susan asks what we're going to do this afternoon.	_"What do you think we should do first when we get inside? What should we do next?"_

Asking Open-Ended Questions

Area: _____   **Date:** _____

INTERACTION	OPEN-ENDED QUESTIONS ASKED

Discuss this activity with your trainer.

After your discussion with your trainer, repeat the activity. You may want to review the learning activity to get more ideas of open-ended questions that can extend children's thinking.

Area: _____ **Date:** _____

INTERACTION	OPEN-ENDED QUESTIONS ASKED

Discuss this activity once again with your trainer.

VI. Planning Activities That Promote Cognitive Development

In this activity you will learn:

- to select and try out appropriate activities that promote children's cognitive development; and

- to reinforce the concepts and skills that children are learning in the activity.

Why should teachers plan special activities to promote cognitive development? Almost anything that happens during the day can be used to help children learn to think. When a teacher sees a child enjoying finger painting and says, "I can see you like that finger paint. How does it feel to you?" the teacher is encouraging the child to think about how the paint feels and to describe the experience in words. When a child says, "My playdough is too sticky," a teacher can promote the child's cognitive development by asking, "What do you think we could try to make it less sticky?"

It's true that skilled teachers can use any opportunity to promote cognitive development. But planning special activities to help children learn a new concept or skill can be enjoyable for the children as well as for the teacher.

Learning takes time. Children need lots of practice before they learn a new concept or skill. You may plan a very successful activity designed to teach children to put objects in order from largest to smallest. But not every child who does the activity will learn the concept; children need lots of opportunities to practice their ability to order objects and to be able to tell you which one is smallest, which is biggest, which goes in the middle.

In planning activities appropriate for preschool children, keep the following guidelines in mind.

- The activity must use real objects and materials.

- The materials must be appropriate for the developmental stage of the children in your group.

- You should have a definite idea of the thinking skills children can acquire by doing the activity.

- You should be open to what children are gaining from the experience. It may be different from what you had planned for them to learn.

This last point is very important. Many teachers have been disappointed because they had a particular result in mind for an activity, and the children reacted in an unexpected way. For example, suppose you plan a walk to gather different kinds of leaves and seeds in the fall. On the walk you pass a crew fixing the road. The children become interested in the road repairs.

Noticing that they are more interested in the repairs than in leaves and seeds, you might decide to change the purpose of the walk and focus on that activity. The fall walk can take place on another day.

In this learning activity you will look through different resource books and select an activity you want to plan for your group. Ask your trainer to help you find appropriate books. After you collect the materials you need, try out the activity with your group. You will find yourself thinking of other ways you can reinforce the concepts and skills that children are learning from the activity. First read the example on the next page; then fill out the form that follows, after you have completed your chosen activity.

A Planned Activity
(Example)

Activity:

Ordering color bottles

Objectives:

To help preschoolers learn to put bottles in order from light to dark

Materials needed:

I used twelve small, clear plastic bottles with caps and green, red, and blue food coloring. There were four bottles for each color. I filled each with water and then added different amounts of food coloring from dark to light. I glued the tops on with contact cement so the children couldn't take them off.

Introducing the activity:

I put the bottles out on a tray and invited three or four preschoolers to sit with me. I asked them what they noticed about the bottles, which ones were the same in some way, and what they could do with them.

How children reacted:

Three children were interested. They examined the bottles and shook them. They tried to take off the tops until I told them they couldn't. Then one child put all the red bottles together, another took all the blue bottles, and a third took the green bottles.

What you said:

I asked, "What can you tell me about these bottles?" Then I asked each child to find the lightest color in the group, the next-to-lightest, and so on. Everyone could order the bottles.

Observations over the next week:

During free play, children came by the science table where the bottles were kept and grouped them by color or put them in order. After about a week, they were less interested. I added two more shades to each color; the children liked that challenge.

How the learning was reinforced:

While preparing to go outside, we talked about who was ready first, then next, and so on. I brought in a key collection and we ordered the keys from smallest to largest. We used the Cuisenaire Rods and put them in order from longest to shortest.

A Planned Activity

Activity:

_____

_____

_____

_____

Objectives:

_____

_____

_____

_____

Materials needed:

_____

_____

_____

_____

Introducing the activity:

_____

_____

_____

_____

How children reacted:

_____

_____

_____

_____

What you said:

_____
_____
_____
_____
_____
_____

Observations over the next week:

_____
_____
_____
_____
_____
_____
_____
_____
_____

How the learning was reinforced:

_____
_____
_____
_____
_____
_____

Discuss your activity with your trainer.

Summarizing Your Progress

You have now completed all of the learning activities for this module. Whether you are an experienced teacher or a new one, this module has probably helped you develop new skills for promoting children's cognitive development. Before you go on, take a few minutes to summarize what you've learned.

- Turn back to Learning Activity I, Using Your Knowledge of Child Development to Promote Cognitive Development, and add to the chart specific examples of what you learned about promoting children's cognitive development during the time you were working on this module. Compare your ideas to those in the completed chart at the end of the module.

- Next, review your responses to the pre-training assessment for this module. Write a summary of what you learned and list the skills you developed or improved.

If there are topics you would like to know more about, you will find recommended readings listed in the orientation.

Your final step in this module is to complete the knowledge and competency assessments. Let your trainer know when you are ready to schedule the assessments. After you have successfully completed these assessments, you will be ready to start a new module. Congratulations on your progress so far, and good luck with your next module.

Answer Sheets

Promoting Children's Cognitive Development

Providing Opportunities for Children to Use All Their Senses to Explore Their Environment

1. **How did Ms. Richards teach the children about balance scales by letting them use their senses?**

   a. She had the children use their bodies to create a balance scale.

   b. She let the children weigh two sets of objects in their hands and let them feel the differences in the weights by using their arm muscles.

2. **What skills and concepts were the children learning in this activity?**

   a. They were learning to estimate how much objects weighed.

   b. They were learning to compare the weight of two objects.

   c. They were gaining firsthand experience with how balance scales work.

   d. They were learning that four objects could weigh less than one.

Interacting with Children in Ways That Help Them Develop Confidence and Curiosity

1. **Why did Ms. Williams not interfere with the three block builders when she could see that their building might fall down?**

   a. She knew that no one would get hurt when the blocks fell.

   b. She wanted to let the children find out for themselves what would happen.

2. **How did Ms. Williams encourage the children to think through and solve the problem on their own?**

   a. She was calm when she entered the block area so the children knew she was not upset that the building fell.

   b. She asked questions that helped the children think about what made the building fall.

   c. She didn't give them any solutions but helped them think of their own ideas.

   d. She encouraged them to try out their ideas.

Providing Opportunities for Children to Develop New Concepts and Skills Appropriate to Their Age and Stage of Development

1. **How was Jerome's sadness about separating from his daddy related to his cognitive development?**

    a. He was still learning (and wasn't completely sure) that when people go away, they are going to come back.

    b. It was hard for him to imagine where his father was. It was hard for him to understand and remember when he would come back.

    c. When his father left he felt so sad that he had trouble remembering that he had a good time in the center and that the teachers were also special people in his life.

2. **What things in the environment helped Jerome deal with separation?**

    a. The teacher, Mr. Lopez, respected Jerome's feelings and talked with him about them.

    b. Pictures of his family on the wall, where he could easily see them, helped Jerome cope with his feelings.

    c. Using a toy telephone helped Jerome accept being apart from his father.

3. **Why didn't Mr. Lopez interrupt Jerome when he was playing in the house corner?**

    a. He knew that dramatic play was helping Jerome by letting him feel in control of someone's leaving and coming back.

    b. What Jerome was learning was more important than his coming to the table immediately for a snack.

Using Your Knowledge of Child Development to Promote Cognitive Development

WHAT PRESCHOOL CHILDREN ARE LIKE	HOW TEACHERS CAN USE THIS INFORMATION TO PROMOTE COGNITIVE DEVELOPMENT
They learn by using all their senses—smelling, tasting, touching, hearing, and seeing.	Provide lots of activities and opportunities for children to use different senses so they can refine their abilities to smell, taste, feel, hear, and see.
They use their imaginations continually—they love to imitate, role play, and engage in dramatic play.	Put props in the house corner and block area to encourage children to play. Add new props to help them extend their play so they learn more about the world. Talk to them about their role plays and play with them to build on what they are doing and saying.
They are interested in cause and effect—what makes things happen.	Give children objects to explore and plan activities to enable them to try out ideas and discover for themselves what makes things happen (e.g., what happens if you don't water a plant). Talk to them about what happens and why.
Their vocabulary is expanding rapidly—they know the names of many things and can explain their ideas.	Talk to children about what things are called. Help them learn new words so they can continue to expand their vocabularies.
They are curious and want to explore many things.	Put out new and interesting materials regularly for children to play with to encourage their curiosity and to help them enjoy learning.
They believe there is a purpose for everything and ask lots of questions: "Why?" "How?" "What?"	Take children's questions seriously. Find out what they want to know. Give answers they can understand and ask more questions to stretch their thinking.
They can reason and think logically sometimes, but often they are not accurate in their thinking.	Ask questions and help children think through so they develop confidence in their ability to think and solve problems.

WHAT PRESCHOOL CHILDREN ARE LIKE	HOW TEACHERS CAN USE THIS INFORMATION TO PROMOTE COGNITIVE DEVELOPMENT
They are developing an understanding of number concepts but need lots of experiences with real objects.	Give children many opportunities to sort, group, match, count, and sequence by playing with real objects. Help them practice counting and matching one to one in real-life situations such as setting the table, counting the number of turns, and sorting out the blocks, so they learn how numbers are used and what they mean.
They learn concepts and skills such as matching, classification, and identification of shapes and colors by playing with toys and objects.	Provide appealing table toys and collect objects that will interest children. Talk to them about what they are doing: "You made a row of red pegs." "I see you put all the circles in one pile and the triangles in another. How else could you group these blocks?"
They have lots of ideas of their own and like to gather information about the world.	Take children on short trips to expand their understanding of the world around them. Set out collections of interesting objects on the science table so children can explore and learn new information. Listen to children's ideas and encourage them to share what they think by showing respect for their ideas.
They are developing the ability to understand how picture, letter, word, and numeric symbols can stand for real objects and ideas.	Label objects with pictures, words, and numerals so children can associate the symbols with the objects. Write children's stories on language experience charts and in homemade books for children to see their words recorded.

Glossary

Classify	To put things or events in groups on the basis of what they have in common.
Closed question	A question for which there is only one right answer.
Cognitive development	Development of the expanding ability to think and reason.
Concept	An idea that combines details or several other ideas in an organized way.
Concrete	Relating to real objects.
Discriminate	To notice the differences among things.
Object permanence	Referring to the beginning of abstract thought, when a mental image is maintained of an object that is not within sight.
Open-ended question	A question that can be answered in many ways.
Problem-solving	The process of thinking through a problem and coming up with one or several possible solutions.
Sensory-motor development	The use of one's senses and motor abilities: an essential part of children's cognitive development.
Sequencing	Putting things or events in order.

Module 6
Communication

What Is Communication and Why Is It Important?

Communication means expressing and sharing ideas, desires, and feelings with other people. Our drive to communicate is very strong. Infants communicate their needs by crying. In a very short time, they can communicate joy by smiling and cooing when they see a familiar face. As adults, we convey clear messages through nonverbal communication. Gestures such as a wave or a shrug are readily understood by everyone. Facial expressions such as a smile or a frown communicate feelings as clearly as a pat on the back. We also communicate through images and pictures, which can represent ideas and feelings.

Although all forms of communication—gestures, facial expressions, body language, touch, pictures—are important, communication with language is the most critical. Language allows us to communicate an endless range of feelings and ideas. It enables us to interpret what others say to us. Without language, our ability to express ourselves is limited.

The use of language is crucial to cognitive development. Learning depends on a child's ever-growing ability to understand words and eventually to read and write them. Social development, too, depends on language. The child who has difficulty expressing himself or herself well is often less able to develop friendships. And language is an important factor in emotional development. Children's self-esteem is enhanced by their growing ability to put into words how they feel—to communicate their feelings accurately to others.

The development of language is one of a child's major accomplishments during early childhood. In a few years a child moves from being nonverbal and able to communicate needs only through crying, to developing the ability to speak and understand language. Children learn thousands of words, their meanings, and the rules for using them simply by being around caring adults who talk to them and respond to their efforts to communicate. They are born with the urge to communicate. If we respond to their signals and show encouragement, their interest in expanding their communication skills is virtually limitless.

Teachers can promote communication in several ways. They can interact with children in ways that encourage them to communicate their thoughts and feelings. Teachers can also provide materials and activities that promote communication skills. And finally, teachers can help children develop listening and speaking skills through the use of storytelling, books, poems, finger plays, songs, and records.

Promoting children's communication skills involves:

- interacting with children in ways that encourage them to communicate their thoughts and feelings;

- providing materials and activities that promote communication skills; and

- helping children develop listening and speaking skills.

Listed below are examples of how teachers demonstrate this competence in promoting communication.

Interacting with Children in Ways That Encourage Them to Communicate Their Thoughts and Feelings

Here are some examples of what teachers can do.

- Encourage children to talk to each other. "It looks like Sarah's baby is sick. Why don't you ask her what's the matter?"

- Look for opportunities to involve a quiet child in conversations. "What are you playing with, Marie? Can I sit with you and watch?"

- Accept a child's way of speaking while at the same time modeling correct speech. If a child says "me threw the ball," the teacher might respond by saying, "yes, you threw the ball very well."

- Help children talk about their thoughts and concerns. "How do you feel about what Nicky said? I can see that really made you angry."

- Listen attentively to what children are saying and help them express their ideas. "I think you are saying that you want to play with the playdough now. Is that right?"

Providing Materials and Activities That Promote Communication Skills

Here are some examples of what teachers can do.

- Use puppets to help a shy child talk. "And how are you today, Mr. Rabbit?"

- Set out a water table that will accommodate just a few children so they can talk to each other.

- Comment on what children are doing and experiencing. "This bus ride is so bumpy." "The finger paint feels so cool and smooth."

- Pose questions at snack or meal times to encourage children to talk. "These are really crunchy carrots. What else do we eat that is crunchy like a carrot?"

- Put out interesting props that encourage make-believe and dramatic play.

- Make picture labels for toys and materials that are taped to the shelves where they are displayed.

- Write stories dictated by the children and label their drawings. "I'm going to write what you said about your picture. *This is a bus bringing my mommy home.*"

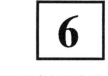

Helping Children Develop Listening and Speaking Skills

Here are some examples of what teachers can do.

- Record favorite stories on a tape cassette so that children can listen to them in a quiet area.

- Encourage children to retell a story they know. "Who remembers what happened in the story when nobody listened to Andrew?"

- Make books about topics that are important to children. "I made a book about all the new things you are learning to do for yourselves. Listen and you will hear all your names in the story."

- Teach children short poems and finger plays during transition times or as part of activities. "This is the way we clean the brushes, clean the brushes, clean the brushes!"

- Select books that will appeal to children and keep them attractively displayed in a quiet area of the room.

- Read to individual or small groups of children using techniques that maintain interest. "Laura can't see the pictures, so I'm going to hold the book up higher."

- Recognize possible delays and impairments that affect hearing or speaking and recommend that the child be assessed.

Promoting Children's Communication

The following situations show teachers promoting the communication skills of preschool children. As you read them, think about what the teachers in each scene are doing and why. Then answer the questions following each episode.

Interacting with Children in Ways That Encourage Them to Communicate Their Thoughts and Feelings

Jerry, who just turned three, is tapping Ms. Kim on her shoulder. When she turns around, Jerry looks at her and then points toward the block corner. "Do you want me to see something in the block corner, Jerry?" asks Ms. Kim. Jerry nods his head and pulls Ms. Kim toward the block area. He points at David, who is making an enclosure for the red truck. "Mine," says Jerry picking up the red truck. "I need it," says David, grabbing it back. "Were you playing with the red truck, Jerry?" asks Ms. Kim. Jerry nods his head and holds the truck closely against his body. "Then tell David you're playing with the truck now. Say, *David, I'm playing with the truck.*" Jerry looks at David and repeats Ms. Kim's words: "I play with truck."

Ms. Kim then asks David what he is making with the blocks. "A garage," says David. "Maybe Jerry could help you and you can make it big enough for the truck and all these cars. Can you help him, Jerry?" Jerry looks at David and says, "Make my own." "Oh," says Ms. Kim, "you want to make your own garage. I have an idea. Why don't we have two garages with a road in between. Then your cars and trucks can go back and forth." The boys agree. "It's nice to see you can work together," says Ms. Kim. "Next time, Jerry, you can use your words to tell David what you want. I'll come back soon to see how you're doing."

1. How did Ms. Kim know what Jerry wanted?

_____

_____

_____

2. How did Ms. Kim help Jerry to communicate his feelings and thoughts using words?

_____

_____

_____

308

Providing Materials and Activities That Promote Communication Skills

"Welcome back!" says Mr. Lopez as Kara, Grace, and Ms. Green come back from their walk to the park across the street from the center. "What did you see on your walk?" "We saw a big bird!" Grace tells him. "And a bird's nest," Kara adds. "The bird was flying around and then it sat on its nest," Grace explains. "That's exciting," says Mr. Lopez, smiling at the girls. "Why don't you two write a story about the bird you saw with Ms. Green?" Kara and Grace get some paper and markers from the shelf and begin scribbling on their paper. "What does your story say?" Ms. Green asks. "That's a picture of the bird," Kara says. "It says *bird*." "Tell me more about the bird you saw," says Ms. Green, and I'll write down what you say. "We saw a big bird," Kara dictates. "It sat on its nest in a tree," Grace adds. Ms. Green writes their words and reads them aloud.

1. **How did Mr. Lopez use a walk to promote communication skills?**

    _____

    _____

    _____

2. **How did Ms. Green promote communication skills as she helped Kara and Grace write a story?**

    _____

    _____

    _____

Helping Children Develop Listening and Speaking Skills

Ms. Williams is about to read a story to a small group of children. It's one she has read before, *Caps for Sale,* so she knows the children will want to take part in the story. She begins by saying, "Today I'm going to read the story about a peddler who sells caps. He has a funny way to carry his caps. Does anyone remember where he carries them?" Several children respond, "On his head." "Right, and here he is," says Ms. Williams, showing the children the cover of the book. "He also has a special order for wearing the caps. First his own checkered cap, then the..." Ms. Williams lets the children tell her which color comes first and then in what order the caps are arranged. She reads the story with lots of expression. She pauses at key passages to let the children fill in with familiar phrases. After reading the story, Ms. Williams brings out some caps so the children can act out the story.

1. What did Ms. Williams do to interest the children in hearing the story?

   _____

   _____

   _____

2. How did Ms. Williams use story time to promote listening and speaking skills?

   _____

   _____

   _____

Compare your answers with those on the answer sheet at the end of this module. If your answers are different, discuss them with your trainer. There may be more than one good answer.

Your Own Experiences with Communication

Communication skills are central to our ability to relate to others. Our relationships with colleagues, friends, and family members depend in large part on how well we can understand and respond to what they have to say and how well they understand us.

In understanding what others have to say, we need to do three things:

- receive the message;

- interpret the message; and

- send back an appropriate response.

Many factors influence how well we understand the communications we receive from others. These factors include how we are feeling at that moment, how well we know the persons communicating with us, and how carefully we listen. For example, suppose you've had a bad morning before coming to work. You are feeling overwhelmed. Your co-worker greets you with the following statement:

"This storeroom is a mess! I can't find anything in it!"

You may interpret this message as a criticism and respond defensively: "When am I supposed to find the time to deal with the storeroom? I can hardly keep up with the classroom!" Your co-worker may be surprised by your response. She might herself react defensively: "Don't you think I'm just as busy as you are?"

On another day, when you are feeling more on top of things, you might interpret the message very differently. Your response might be something like this: "You're absolutely right. We've been so busy with other things, we never seem to get to the storeroom. Maybe we can ask for a parent volunteer to help us out."

Because any message can be easily misinterpreted, it's important to clarify what we think another person really means. Questions that help to clarify the message include the following:

- Are you saying that...?

- Do you mean...?

- Do I understand correctly that...?

- It sounds like you want...?

In conveying our thoughts and feelings to others, we rely on our communication skills to get our messages across accurately. We send messages verbally (using words) and nonverbally (using gestures and body language). Verbal messages can be the clearest kind of message if we say what we mean.

- "I'd like to do something about the storeroom. I can never find what I need. What do you think of the idea of asking a parent to help us out?"

- "I'd love to go to a movie tonight. What time is best for you?"

But even verbal messages can be unclear if we fail to say what we really think and want. Using the same examples, we could say:

- "What are we going to do about the storeroom?" (when we know very well what we think needs to be done).

- "What do you feel like doing tonight?" (hoping the other person will want to go to a movie but remaining unclear about our own wishes).

How do you rate your ability to communicate effectively?

COMMUNICATION SKILLS	MOST OF THE TIME	SOMETIMES	RARELY
I am able to state my ideas clearly.			
I am able to express my feelings in words.			
I say what I think.			
If I'm not sure what someone means, I check out what I think was said.			
I try to interpret nonverbal communication to help me better understand what someone is feeling.			

Review your answers to this brief checklist. Are there any areas that you would like to improve? As you go through this module and learn ways of helping children communicate, you may discover some strategies for improving your own communication skills.

When you have finished this overview section, you should complete the pre-training assessment. Refer to the glossary at the end of the module if you need definitions of the terms that are used.

Pre-Training Assessment

Listed below are the skills that teachers use to promote children's communication. Think about whether you do these things regularly, sometimes, or not enough. Place a check in one of the columns on the right for each skill listed. Then discuss your answers with your trainer.

SKILL	I DO THIS REGULARLY	I DO THIS SOMETIMES	I DON'T DO THIS ENOUGH
INTERACTING WITH CHILDREN IN WAYS THAT ENCOURAGE THEM TO COMMUNICATE THEIR THOUGHTS AND FEELINGS 1. Accepting children's ways of speaking and serving as a model.			
2. Helping children use words to express their thoughts and feelings.			
3. Asking open-ended questions to encourage children to think and express their ideas.			
4. Having conversations with children about their feelings, ideas, and the day's events.			
5. Listening attentively to what children have to say and respecting their ideas.			
PROVIDING MATERIALS AND ACTIVITIES THAT PROMOTE COMMUNICATION SKILLS 6. Arranging the environment to enable preschoolers to work together in small groups.			
7. Providing props and supporting children's dramatic play.			

SKILL	I DO THIS REGULARLY	I DO THIS SOMETIMES	I DON'T DO THIS ENOUGH
8. Planning trips and special activities to expand children's knowledge and vocabulary.			
9. Establishing an inviting book area and helping children use it well.			
10. Selecting books appropriate for the ages and interests of the children.			
11. Using everyday experiences to encourage an interest in and understanding of writing.			
HELPING CHILDREN DEVELOP LISTENING AND SPEAKING SKILLS 12. Knowing the stages of language development and using this information to promote communication.			
13. Reading books to individuals, small groups, or the whole group every day.			
14. Using techniques to keep children's attention and interest during story time.			
15. Planning and leading interesting group times and encouraging children to share ideas and experiences.			

Review your responses, then list three to five skills you would like to improve or topics you would like to learn more about. When you finish this module, you will list examples of your new or improved knowledge and skills.

_____

_____

_____

_____

Now begin the learning activities for Module 6, Communication.

I. Using Your Knowledge of Child Development to Promote Communication

In this activity you will learn:

- to recognize some typical behaviors of preschoolers that are related to communication; and

- to use what you know about preschool children to promote their communication skills.

The foundation for a child's ability to communicate is built early in life. During the first few months, infants cry to communicate their needs. Before very long, adults can distinguish between a cry of discomfort and a cry of loneliness. We soon see clear signs that infants are beginning to communicate more than just their immediate needs. When they smile, coo, and babble at a familiar person, they are communicating pleasure—how happy they are to see someone. In a remarkably short time, infants begin to recognize familiar voices. They understand that words have meanings; they can point to their nose when an adult says, "Where's your nose?" They love to hear adults talk and sing to them and to hear the sounds they make repeated back to them.

Just as in all areas of growth, children develop language at their own pace. Some say their first words at age one. Some hardly speak at all before age two. Most children understand a lot of language long before they can use words themselves.

By the time they reach preschool age, most children have developed a wide range of skills in nonverbal and verbal communication. They are learning new words every day. They express their needs and thoughts verbally and can understand what is said to them. They can sit long enough to listen to a story or a record. They engage in verbal exchanges with other children and adults. Their interest in learning about the world around them is evident in the continual questions they ask that start with *what, how*, and *why*.

Preschool children are developing the ability to use language to explore the world around them. They use language in their play to share ideas and work out difficulties. Language is becoming a powerful tool for them. They can communicate many feelings.

Preschool children are increasingly able to use symbols instead of depending on real objects. For example, they can take a block of wood and pretend it's a telephone so they can call the doctor. Older children may draw pictures that are meant to represent real things. These pictures become increasingly realistic. Their block buildings also are becoming realistic, and often children name these structures. Toward the end of their preschool years, children show more and more interest in understanding print and in writing letters and numbers. All these experiences help children prepare for reading and writing.

The chart on the next page lists some typical behaviors of preschool children. Included are behaviors relevant to the development of communication skills. The right column asks you to identify ways that teachers can use this information about child development to promote communication. Try to think of as many examples as you can. As you work through the module you will learn new strategies for promoting communication, and you can add them to the child development chart. You are not expected to think of all the examples at one time. If you need help getting started, turn to the completed chart at the end of the module. By the time you complete all the learning activities, you will find that you have learned many ways to promote children's communication skills.

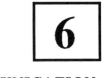

Using Your Knowledge of Child Development to Promote Communication

WHAT PRESCHOOL CHILDREN ARE LIKE	HOW TEACHERS CAN USE THIS INFORMATION TO PROMOTE COMMUNICATION
They sometimes talk to themselves—not for the purpose of communicating with anyone but simply to practice talking and to amuse themselves.	
Then tend to use language freely and creatively in dramatic play.	
They are able to remember stories and retell them, sometimes in correct sequence.	
They like to make up stories of their own.	
They use language, like to make up words and rhymes, and like nonsense words and poems.	

WHAT PRESCHOOL CHILDREN ARE LIKE	HOW TEACHERS CAN USE THIS INFORMATION TO PROMOTE COMMUNICATION
They ask lots of questions.	
They draw pictures and create other representations that look like something. They often name what they make.	
They like to share experiences —things that have happened to them.	
They commonly make mistakes in grammar.	
They enjoy songs, poems, and finger plays and can learn increasingly complex ones.	
They are beginning to understand written symbols— letters, numbers, and some words.	

WHAT PRESCHOOL CHILDREN ARE LIKE	HOW TEACHERS CAN USE THIS INFORMATION TO PROMOTE COMMUNICATION
They are beginning to show interest in writing.	

As you proceed with the rest of the learning activities, you can refer back to the chart and add examples of how teachers promote communication. Discuss your responses with your trainer.

II. Understanding How Children Learn to Communicate

In this activity you will learn:

- to recognize the stages that children go through in learning language; and

- to assess a preschooler's level of language development.

Stages of Language Development[1]

As in all areas of development, children go through predictable stages in learning to communicate verbally. It may be helpful to think of a six-step sequence in language development.

- **Initial responses to language.** Infants listen to the sounds they hear around them. They notice differences in sound, rhythm, and pitch. Infants need to hear lots of speech before they develop their own.

- **Vocalization.** By 3 or 4 months, infants begin to produce their own sounds. They coo and babble. At around 9 to 12 months they start babbling a lot.

- **Word development.** Infants have to separate the different sounds they hear. They begin playing with sounds at around 10 to 15 months. Most infants can understand and respond to a number of words before they can say them. They start using words to name objects and people in their world: "dada," "car." They may say "doggy" for every animal with four legs.

- **Sentences.** Sentences usually begin with two words to describe an action ("me go," "my ball.") They soon learn to add adjectives ("my big ball") and negatives ("No go outside."). By listening to how adults and older children use words, children learn grammar.

- **Elaboration.** Vocabulary increases at an amazing rate. Children's sentences get longer, and they use language to relate to other children and adults. The house corner is a good place to listen to children's expanding use of language.

- **Graphic representation.** By the end of the preschool years, children begin to take an interest in reading and writing. They understand that the written word represents the spoken word, and they try out writing.

---

[1]Based on Ann Miles Gordon and Kathryn Williams Browne, *Beginnings and Beyond: Foundations in Early Childhood Education* (Albany, NY: Delmar Publishers, 1985), pp. 307-308.

What Preschoolers' Language Is Like

Enter any preschool room and you will hear the lively chatter of children talking to one another, to adults, and sometimes to themselves. Preschool children are continually practicing and expanding their communication skills. They do this by talking to one another about taking turns, something that happened to them, or someone they met. They learn how to make themselves heard and understood by another person. Preschool children use language in their dramatic play, which becomes increasingly complex and involved. They talk about what they want to do, who will play what role, and what will happen.

It's not unusual to hear preschool children (especially younger ones) carry on a lively conversation with themselves as they play. This is one way they practice expressing themselves. Sometimes this talking will be a running description of what they are doing. Another time, it may be a chant they repeat over and over. Solitary conversations are normal.

When preschool children converse with one another and in groups, they are learning subtle and complex cues about interaction. They find ways to enter a conversation or change its direction, and they learn how to give and get information from their peers. They also discover what kinds of talk are appropriate in specific situations. Young children teach one another a great deal about the art of conversation—and observant teachers will notice a continual give-and-take as preschoolers converse.

Preschool children enjoy the sound of words. They love chants and songs that involve repetition and words that rhyme:

> "One potato, two potato,
>
> Three potato, four.
>
> Five potato, six potato,
>
> Seven potato, more."

Preschool children sometimes make up their own words, and they use words very creatively. Adults who are good listeners can hear children using language imaginatively.

- "A hopicoper" describes a helicopter.

- "A doesn't-smell bush" describes an azalea bush that doesn't smell.

- "Mess-up paper" is scrap paper.

In one child development center, a five-year-old who had just built a boat out of boxes and blocks in the playground described the "water" around the boat as being "deep as a giant."[2]

---

[2]Used with permission from Claudia Lewis, "Deep as a Giant"—An Experiment in Children's Language, *Childhood Education*, Volume XIV (Wheaton, MD: Association for Childhood Education International, March 1938), pp. 314-316. Copyright © 1938 by the Association.

The teacher picked up on this later and asked a group of children, "What is the deepest thing in the world?" The children responded with many creative ideas:

- "Deep as dirt under the ground."

- "Deep as sand down in the ocean."

- "Deep as from the sky down!"

As preschool children become increasingly skilled in using language to communicate, they are able to convey their feelings in words rather than through actions. The more accurately they can describe what is bothering them, the better they are able to resolve problems.

Common Mistakes in Using Language

It's perfectly natural and normal for preschool children to make mistakes in using language. They try to apply the rules they are learning (such as making the past tense by adding "ed" to a verb), but rules don't always work. Here are some typical mistakes you might hear:

- "I runned all the way."

- "I have two feets."

- "He's badder than anyone."

- "She's my goodest friend."

- "I hurted my knee."

- "I feeled happy."

The best way to respond to such mistakes is simply to restate correctly what the child has said: "Yes, you ran the whole way here." If adults constantly correct what a child says, the child will become discouraged and be less likely to talk.

The preschool years are a good time to notice children who have language difficulties that may require special help. If by age three a child is not speaking, it is important to check for possible hearing or other problems. A child may sometimes continue to use baby talk. Check with the parents and encourage them to work with you to help the child give up his or her baby talk. For example, you might say to a child, "I can understand you better when you don't talk like a baby. Use your big girl voice when you want me to understand you."

Stuttering may also occur when children try to get their words out too fast. The problem often goes away as the child learns to speak more slowly and carefully.

Observing Children's Language Development

In observing a child's language development, it may be helpful to have in mind some specific factors to consider. Here are eight areas you might focus on.[3]

- **Confidence**. The child freely communicates ideas and seems comfortable speaking.

- **Articulation**. The child speaks clearly and can easily be understood.

- **Language production**. The child speaks in sentences and talks with other children and adults.

- **Vocabulary**. The child uses a rich number of words and learns new words.

- **Communication**. The child is able to communicate desires and needs with words and enjoys talking to others.

- **Language understanding**. The child understands words and responds when spoken to.

- **Word play.** The child shows an interest in playing with words, making up rhymes, and singing songs.

- **Listening skills.** The child listens to someone else and can identify words and sounds that are alike and different.

In this learning activity you will observe the language development of two children in your room. Begin by reading "The Speech of Young Children," which starts on the next page. Then use the language checklist that follows to observe the language skills of two children in your class.

[3]Based on Janice J. Beaty, *Skills for Preschool Teachers* (Columbus, OH: Charles E. Merrill Publishing Co., 1984), pp. 113-122.

The Speech of Young Children[4]

"I'm gonna get me a shovel. I'm gonna get me a shovel. I want a shovel. I want a shovel. Here's a shovel. It's my shovel. I'm gonna dig with this shovel. I'm gonna dig a hole with this shovel."

Daniel was playing alone in the sandbox. Who was he talking to? Himself! It isn't strange for young children to talk to themselves. This is the way they practice using words. They say them over and over until their tongues and lips learn how to pronounce the syllables automatically and correctly. Repetition also gives them practice in putting words together. Daniel varied his sentences slightly but stuck to the subject of his shovel.

Inside the child care center, Carrie was pasting leaves to a piece of construction paper. While she worked, she absent-mindedly hummed a rhythm beat to herself: "Tum-tum-de-tum-tum-de-tum..."

Ramon was working out how to put a roof on his garage. "Now I'll put this block on here like this." The block tumbled down. "Why did you do that, you bad block? I know. You're too little. I'll get a bigger one. I'll put it like this, and it'll stay." He succeeds. Talking to himself helped him solve his problem.

In the housekeeping corner four children were talking to a visitor who didn't fit on the child-sized chairs. Their conversation soon turned into a chant:

"Didju ever fit on a little chair?"	"Yes."
"Didju go to school?"	"Yes."
"Didju have a mommy?"	"Yes."
"Didju have a daddy?"	"Yes."
"Didju have a bed?"	"Yes."
"You didn't have no big hands?"	"No."
"You didn't have no glasses?"	"No."
"You didn't have no car?"	"No."
"You didn't have no big shoes?"	"No."
"You couldn't read?"	"No."
"You couldn't write?"	"No."
"You couldn't always button?"	"No."

At this point the teacher joined the group.

"You could learn."	"Yes."
"You could play."	"Yes."
"You could talk."	"Yes."

---

[4]Adapted from Lois B. Murphy and Ethel M. Leeper, *Language Is for Communication* (Washington, DC: U.S. Department of Health, Education and Welfare, 1976), pp. 8-12.

With a listener who obviously was interested, the children were able to make up a game with the words they knew. The visitor caught the spirit of the game and stayed to answer their questions, giving the children an opportunity to practice using words.

Children love to make sounds. The sounds may be words, nonsense syllables, rhythm chants, or the rustling of paper. Often sounds are annoying to adults while giving pleasure to children. "Stop tapping your feet while you eat, Mike," his mother may order. The tapping bothers her, but Mike is not even aware he is doing it.

This is one reason why music and rhythmic exercises are so important in a child care center. A child who responds with enjoyment to sounds is likely to find similar pleasure in words when he or she grows older.

Tommy's teacher usually isn't sure what Tommy is talking about because his conversation never seems to fit the situation at hand. While doing a puzzle, he is likely to come out with statements like this: "We don't want none today."

"What don't you want any of?" his teacher asks.

"Dunno." And with a shrug of his shoulders, Tommy is silent again.

Even in a child with poor speech, there are some signs that a teacher can look for that may indicate healthy speech development in the future.

- Does the child respond with enjoyment to sounds, poetry, dramatic play, stories, and music?

- Does the child call his or her teacher freely by name?

- Is the child able to understand, remember, and respond to the speech of others?

- Does the child seek answers to questions?

When children come to a child care center, they come with all levels of speech development. One child may speak in long sentences with correct grammar and good pronunciation—like Philip, who told the teacher, "I don't have a hammer." Some of Philip's playmates say, "I don't have no hammer." At the other extreme may be the child who answers with grunts and never begins a conversation. In between are all shades of good and poor speech. There's Dorita, who talks so fast that her words tumble out in a torrent of sounds that cannot be understood. And there's Andy, who usually greets everyone with "Punch your nose in." His fierce sentences are a clue to the anger he feels toward his world. Here are some questions to consider:

- Does the child like stories, discussions, and conversation for sharing thoughts as well as for learning facts?

- Does the child try to talk out his or her conflicts and worries?

- Does he or she set limits on other children who are interfering with his or her play?

Teachers can help young children learn to talk. Talk with, not at, the child. Give him or her the courtesy of listening. When children pronounce a word incorrectly or use poor grammar, do not correct them on the spot but repeat their sentences correctly. The teacher did this in responding to Tommy's "we don't want none today." Her answer—"What don't you want any of?"— let Tommy hear his sentence said correctly without being told he was wrong. Children do not like to be embarrassed by constant reminders that they are making errors. Interruptions by adults to correct their speech also disrupt their thoughts. At the same time, most children by the age of three or four want to say words the right way. If they hear good spoken language, eventually they will copy it.

Sometimes children know how to talk but are too bashful to speak in front of strangers. "You should hear her talk at home," Sandra's mother is likely to exclaim when the teacher tells her that Sandra hardly opens her mouth at the center. Sandra probably needs more time alone with the teacher or an aide until she gains her confidence. One teacher made arrangements for an older sister to stay with a two-and-a-half-year-old for a few days to help break the ice. When the younger child relaxed and began to speak, the older child returned to her group.

Teachers have to convince children that they want them to talk. Children who have been told to "shut up" over and over again at home may feel they have nothing to say that is worth listening to. By your actions in listening and responding to a child's talk, you can demonstrate that at least at the child care center, children are not only allowed to talk but are urged to talk. Once children get the idea that being able to talk is a desirable skill, they are likely to continue to improve in speech.

Speech Difficulties

Physical and Mental Defects. Most children are able to use a few words by the time they are two years old, and simple sentences or phrases by the time they are three. However, if a child reaches three-and-a-half without speaking, it is time to find out what is interfering with normal language development.

There may be any number of obstacles. One of the most common is poor hearing. Children learn to speak by mimicking the sounds they hear. If they hear no sounds or only jumbled sounds, they cannot learn to speak in the same way children with normal hearing do. A hearing aid may improve hearing enough to allow them to distinguish sounds and begin to learn to speak. However, children with severe hearing handicaps usually need help from special teachers before they learn to speak.

If the child's hearing is normal, a physical examination may reveal some defect in the structure of the mouth or palate that can be corrected by surgery or therapy. Mental retardation may be another cause of slow speech development.

Early Life. Many children have no obvious physical or mental deficiencies, yet they cannot speak well. The cause may lie in their early life at home. Were these babies cared for by persons who were deaf, or ill, or retarded? When they were just beginning to make cooing sounds, were these babies ignored? Were they left alone for long stretches without hearing human voices or seeing friendly faces?

Were these speechless children shocked by some terrifying event that took place as they were learning to speak? The death of the mother or another loved person could cause speech difficulties. The shock of a disaster, such as an earthquake or flood, could cause a young child to become mute. Harsh toilet training during which the child was shamed or even punished for soiling his or her pants has been known to interfere with speech development.

Many speech problems are not so severe. Some, like Marlene's, may be easily corrected. "My mommy 'ays I'm a baby so I'v oo 'alk li' a baby." This was her explanation for refusing to repeat words after the teacher who was trying to help her pronounce her words more clearly. The teacher told Marlene's mother why the four-year-old girl was still talking baby talk. She suggested that if Marlene's mother stopped treating her like a baby, Marlene might want to talk like a four-year-old. An improvement in Marlene's speech showed up in a few weeks, and she continued to improve until soon everyone could understand her.

Stuttering. This is another common problem among small children. In the early years of speech, it is normal for a child to repeat words or have difficulty getting a word out. A child is likely to stumble on words because his or her tongue and lips have had very little practice in speaking. When a child is excited or frightened, he or she is even more likely to stutter.

Many adults lose patience with a stuttering child. "Slow down!" "Start over!" "Now say it without stuttering!" they sometimes scold. This response only upsets the child more so that his or her stuttering gets worse.

Here are a few simple suggestions for preventing stuttering and for helping children develop good speech:

- Do all you can to be the kind of listener children like to talk to.

- Give them time to talk without pressure to say the words correctly.

- Don't expect too much of them. Remember, they are very young. Accept childish speech, fumbling skills, and high-spirited and sometimes noisy behavior.
- When children stutter, take this as a sign that something in the surroundings may be worrying them. Make every day as simple and dependable as you can.

- Prepare them ahead of time for new experiences by talking about what is going to happen so that they feel more secure.

- Be sure they have plenty of rest.

- Speak to them in normal tones—not too loud nor too soft—and not too fast.

- Listen when they speak, even though it takes them a long time to express a thought.

If stuttering is handled in a relaxed way at the age of three or four, it will probably disappear as the child grows older. However, if the adults around the child put too much pressure on him or her to stop stuttering, the habit may continue into adulthood.

Silent Home Life. Sometimes children do not speak well because they do not hear much conversation at home. In some homes the adults are tired or sick and do not feel like talking with children. They may say a word or two to tell the child it is time to eat or time to get ready for school. There is no conversation about what the child did in school or about the other children the child plays with. There are children in child care centers who have a rich vocabulary of curse words but do not know how to ask for a drink of water.

When a child's experience is narrow, his or her speech has to be narrow as well. If Roberto has never seen nor tasted a peach, he will not know the word "peach." Children who are surrounded by many objects and who are taken to see new places and are encouraged to try out different materials usually learn the words for the things they are doing and seeing.

Shyness. Teachers will find that some shy children will not speak for the first few weeks they are at a child care center. This does not necessarily mean they have speech difficulties. They may simply be too bashful to talk to strangers. Give the newcomer lots of attention and make him or her feel welcome. If the child still does not speak after a month or so, the teacher and staff members may be wise in looking for a deeper reason.

Select two children whose levels of language development you want to observe. Use the language checklist to record your observations. Allow yourself one week to observe the two children.

Language Checklist

Child: _____ Age: _____ Date: _____

		Yes	No
1.	Does the child freely communicate ideas and talk with others?	___	___
2.	Does the child speak clearly?	___	___
3.	Does the child speak in full sentences?	___	___
4.	Does the child have a good vocabulary?	___	___
5.	Does the child understand and respond to what others say?	___	___
6.	Does the child enjoy playing with words, making up rhymes?	___	___
7.	Does the child ask questions?	___	___
8.	Does the child show any evidence of speech difficulties?	___	___

If yes,

	Yes	No
Does the child tend to speak baby talk?	___	___
Does the child stutter?	___	___

Language Checklist

Child: _____ **Age:** _____ **Date:** _____

		Yes	No
1.	Does the child freely communicate ideas and talk with others?	___	___
2.	Does the child speak clearly?	___	___
3.	Does the child speak in full sentences?	___	___
4.	Does the child have a good vocabulary?	___	___
5.	Does the child understand and respond to what others say?	___	___
6.	Does the child enjoy playing with words, making up rhymes?	___	___
7.	Does the child ask questions?	___	___
8.	Does the child show any evidence of speech difficulties?	___	___
	If yes,		
	Does the child tend to speak baby talk?	___	___
	Does the child stutter?	___	___

When you have completed these two checklists, discuss your observations with your trainer. You will be using the information you collected while observing these two children in the next learning activity.

III. Helping Children Develop Communication Skills

In this activity you will learn:

- to recognize how important your role is in promoting children's language development;

- to set up an environment that supports communication; and

- to use various strategies and activities to help children learn communication skills.

Most preschool children have developed some communication skills before the age of three. They have gained these skills naturally, in the course of daily life. At home, their families talked to them from the time they were infants. Parents and teachers encouraged their early attempts to communicate and taught them by talking to them and caring for them each day.

During the preschool years, children's communication skills expand when teachers create a supportive and rich environment. Teachers also serve as language models. There are many effective strategies that teachers can use to promote communication skills during daily activities and routines.

Preparing an Environment That Supports Communication

Most children need to feel comfortable and relaxed before they will freely communicate their ideas and feelings. How you relate to each child—how easily each one learns that you can be trusted—will influence their openness to listen and talk. When children learn that you will accept them as they are, they are more likely to respond to your questions and to share their thoughts with you. Similarly, children need to feel at ease with other children in the group. You've probably noticed that the most verbal children are the ones who make friends easily. It's especially important to be aware of the shy children in the group. They need your help to feel accepted by their peers and to learn how to communicate their ideas and feelings.

Here are some specific ways in which you can create an environment that supports communication.

- Arrange the space so that children can be in small groups as they work at activities. Children are more likely to talk with each other when there are just a few children present.

- Keep interesting things in the environment to encourage children to explore, ask questions, talk about their ideas, and play with each other.

- Set out props that will lead to dramatic play. In pretend play children tend to practice their communication skills. Two telephones in the house corner can lead to many lively conversations.

- Plan some group projects such as a mural or cooking activities. Help the children plan projects together and carry out their ideas.

- Take trips and walks in the neighborhood to expand children's experiences and give them new things to talk about.

- Set out materials that promote communication, such as puppets, flannel boards, language games, and water play.

A room in which children feel free, relaxed, and encouraged to communicate is not a quiet room. Teachers must be willing to accept a certain level of chatter and noise in order to support communication.

Serving as a Communication Model

Young children are good imitators. They pay attention to how you talk, what you say, and how you communicate. In your everyday interactions you serve as a communication model. What does this mean?

First, serving as a model for communication means accepting what a child says and how he or she speaks. Even if the child's use of language is incorrect, resist the urge to correct what the child has said. Do not ask a child to say it again correctly. If you do so, rather than teaching the child the correct use of language, you are really communicating that his or her way is wrong. This negative message can weaken the child's self-esteem. Teachers who frequently correct children and make them repeat what they say correctly soon find that these children talk less.

Accepting children's communication means:

- encouraging all attempts at communication, verbal and nonverbal;

- never degrading what a child says;

- not forcing a child to speak if he or she is shy and not ready;

- getting down to the child's level and listening carefully;

- being patient—sometimes it takes a child a long time to explain something; and

- accepting how a child talks but modeling the correct language. If a child says "I goed to my friend's house yesterday," an appropriate response might be this: "Oh, you went to a friend's house. Which friend did you visit?"

Serving as a model also means talking with children, not at them, all day long. Teachers need to help children learn how to carry on conversations. This is especially important for those children who are less verbal. Teachers can serve as good language models by doing the following:

- **Naming things for children.** By describing objects a child is using, something a child is wearing, or what a child is doing, you are teaching language skills. For example:

  "You have on your bumpy corduroy pants today."

  "I see you're using all the yellow pegs first."

  "What a long road you made with the blocks!"

  "Sherrie is stirring the soup—round and round and round it goes."

- **Using full and complete sentences that describe details.** If a child asks you where something is, rather than saying "over there" and pointing it out, take time to say, "The magic markers are on the art shelf next to the drawing paper."

- **Using a soft tone of voice.** A harsh voice makes children tense. A loud voice makes them talk louder and creates unnecessary noise in the room.

- **Teaching categories as you talk to children.** When you talk to children, name the categories to which things belong. For example:

  "That **color** is blue."

  "We're having apples today for snack. What **fruit** did we have yesterday?"

  "Here are some **farm animals** for the block area: a horse, a cow, and a pig."

- **Using specific words to describe something.** Name the characteristics of an object when you talk to children. For example:

  "Roll the rubber ball to me" rather than "roll it."

  "Put the paint brushes in the sink" rather than "put the brushes here."

  "Look at how fast Kirsten is riding the tricycle" rather than "look how fast Kirsten is."

  "See how high the bird is flying—right up to the top of the tree" rather than "see the bird."

Encouraging Children to Talk

Teachers should take advantage of all opportunities throughout the day to encourage children to use language. Because this is a stage when children generally like to talk, you will find it fun and easy to encourage language development. Another reason this can be enjoyable is that children tend to use language creatively. A child may say things like "it's leaking outside" to describe a slight drizzle, or "she has old hair" to describe someone with grey hair. Children can be very imaginative with language. You can probably think of some good examples of things your children have said.

Some of the following strategies are helpful for encouraging children to use language.

- **Ask open-ended questions such as the following.**

  "What do you think will happen if . . . ?"

  "What else can fly besides a bird?"

  "Can you think of any other animals who live on a farm?"

- **When describing a topic, extend the conversation to encourage children to think of other ideas.**

  "What else is slow? Slow as a plant grows. Slow as a snail crawls." "Let's think of other things that are quiet. Quiet as a baby sleeping. Quiet as a whisper."

- **Talk to children about how things feel, smell, taste, or sound.** Because they use all their senses to learn, preschoolers tend to be aware of the sensory characteristics of the things around them. Encourage them to describe in words what they experience.

  "Yes, this rock is smooth. How smooth is it? Smooth as the table top. Smooth as skin."

- **Take time to talk about feelings.** Help a child who is upset to use words to explain how he or she feels. Sometimes you have to give a child the words.

- "I can see you're having a hard time waiting for your turn. It _is_ hard to wait."

- **Use a tape recorder to encourage talking.** Let children tape themselves telling a story and then play it back.

- **Allow some time for sharing in small groups.** Children like to talk about things that are important to them or something they did during free play.

- **Introduce topics during meal times.** These are great opportunities for conversations.

- **Collect pictures that will interest the children and provoke conversations.**

- **Act out stories familiar to the children.**

You will undoubtedly think of many other ways to encourage preschoolers to use language to communicate. The opportunities are endless.

In this activity you will draw on the information you obtained using the language assessment checklist to plan some strategies and activities for promoting the language development of the same two children. Use the suggestions offered in this learning activity or make up some of your own. The first step is to review the assessments you have completed and to identify the areas in which each child needs help. Then decide what strategies and activities you will try. First read the example that follows.

Planning for Language Development
(Example)

Child: _Debby_   **Age:** _4 years_   **Date:** _March 10_

What language areas do you want to work on?

Debby needs to have more confidence in using language. She rarely starts conversations with other children. She speaks so quietly it's hard to hear her.

Debby responds to questions with one word. She rarely asks questions. When she communicates, it's with many short sentences.

What strategies and activities will you try?

I will bring in puppets and use them with Debby to try to get her to talk more. I will ask her to join one other child in an activity and help them get started. I'll be sure she sits near me more often at mealtimes so that I can help her talk to other children.

I will model more language when I am around Debby. I can describe what she is doing, extend her sentences, and show a lot of interest in what she has to say.

What results do you notice after trying out your strategies/activities for two weeks?

The puppets were a big success. Debby talked more freely with me. I was able to involve another child with the puppets, and Debby started talking to her. Now they've been playing together more.

It's still hard to hear Debby. She talks more when she is playing with one other child. I need to do more language modeling.

Planning for Language Development

Child: _____ **Age:** _____ **Date:** _____

What language areas do you want to work on?

_____

_____

_____

_____

_____

_____

_____

What strategies and activities will you try?

_____

_____

_____

_____

_____

_____

_____

What results do you notice after trying out your strategies/activities for two weeks?

_____

_____

_____

_____

_____

_____

_____

Planning for Language Development

Child: _____ Age: _____ Date: _____

What language areas do you want to work on?

_____

_____

_____

_____

_____

_____

_____

What strategies and activities will you try?

_____

_____

_____

_____

_____

_____

_____

What results do you notice after trying out your strategies/activities for two weeks?

_____

_____

_____

_____

_____

_____

_____

Discuss the results with your trainer.

IV. Selecting and Using Books with Preschool Children[5]

In this activity you will learn:

- to appreciate why books are an important part of your child development program;

- to choose books that are appropriate for preschool children; and

- to use books effectively with children.

An important teaching goal when working with preschool children is to help them develop a love for books and stories. Good children's books (and there are many of them) should always be available in the classroom. Exposure to good books is one of the best ways to help children develop positive attitudes toward reading. When children see adults reading and enjoying books, they learn that books are important and fun.

Books written for preschool children can help them understand themselves and the world around them. Books about experiences familiar to a child—a new baby at home, making friends, starting a new school—can help children deal with their feelings. Books can also help teach and clarify new concepts and ideas.

When teachers take time to read to a child or a group of children, they provide a meaningful social experience. Sharing a story brings children together. They often react to the story and comment on a picture or what is happening. Sometimes they will correct you if you miss a word or leave something out of a familiar story. This doesn't mean you shouldn't read the same story over and over again. The ability to remember the words in a story is an important skill that children need to develop before learning to read.

Setting Up a Book Area

Every preschool room should have a book area. The best location is in a quiet corner of the room, away from noisy activities such as blocks and the house corner. The book area can also serve as a getaway place for children who want to be alone for a while. It should be a soft and comfortable place, clearly defined by shelves and partitions.

To create an attractive and comfortable book area, you may want to try some of the following suggestions.

---

[5] Based on Diane Trister Dodge, *The Creative Curriculum for Early Childhood* (Washington, DC: Teaching Strategies, Inc., 1988), pp. 281-324.

- **Include soft furniture.**

  ___ A soft rug on the floor

  ___ A bean-bag chair

  ___ An overstuffed chair or a rocking chair

  ___ Large pillows

  ___ A mattress covered with attractive and cheerful material.

- **Display books attractively.**

  ___ Use a shelf that allows each book to stand alone so children can see the covers.

  ___ Keep books in good repair—not torn or marked up.

  ___ Use clear contact paper to preserve the attractive covers on new books.

- **Include a table and chairs for two or three children.**

  ___ Some children like to sit at a table to look at books.

  ___ A colorful tablecloth and a small plant will make the reading table appealing.

- **Use pictures on the walls.**

  ___ Covers from books often make attractive wall decorations.

  ___ Pictures showing children and adults reading books are helpful.

  ___ Pictures of themes from the books displayed can also attract children's interest.

- **Good lighting is important.**

  ___ Natural light is the best for a book area—try to locate the area near a window.

  ___ A standing lamp or one hung from the ceiling can also be used.

An attractive, uncluttered book area tells children that you value books. The condition of the books also conveys a message to children. If you keep books in this area that are torn, falling apart, and marked with pencil or crayons, you are saying it is all right to misuse books. Remove books in need of repair and try to fix them. If pages are missing, there is little you can do. If they can be repaired, involve the children in helping you fix them. Helping to repair books teaches children to take better care of books. You might even keep a "book repair kit" in the area. An old cigar or shoe box will do, or a basket. Items to keep in the kit may include:

- transparent tape to repair torn pages;
- cloth tape to repair the spine of a book;
- erasers to remove pencil marks;
- correction fluid to cover ink and crayon marks; and
- a pair of scissors.

Older preschool children will soon learn to fix books on their own. Younger children will be more likely to report "hurt" books and ask for your help. Once children see the importance of caring for books, they may be more careful when they use them.

Selecting Books for Preschool Children

There are many wonderful and appropriate books for preschool children. There are also some books that are *not* appropriate. It is important for teachers to learn how to select the best books for their children. The first place to start is to think about the interests and skills of the children you care for.

Young preschool children (threes and early fours) are very centered on themselves, their families, their homes, and their friends. They like stories about characters they can identify with. Books that are appropriate for young preschoolers have the following characteristics:

- a simple plot about familiar experiences;

- colorful and bold illustrations;

- realistic illustrations that children can understand;

- lots of repetition in the story;

- wonderful-sounding words (rhymes, nonsense words, repetition) and good language; and

- happy endings to give young children a sense of security.

Older preschool children (fours and fives) tend to enjoy books with more of a story. They can sit for a longer period of time and appreciate a story with humor or imagination. Books that are appropriate for older children have the following characteristics:

- a plot they can follow;

- a story with humor and perhaps a surprise ending;

- imaginative stories about things that children *know* couldn't happen;

- stories that extend their understanding of the world around them; and

- colorful illustrations with lots of detail.

Listed below are examples of books that may interest the children in your classroom.

- **Books about everyday life**

    Hoban, Russell. The "Frances" books (New York, NY: Harper & Row, 1976). *Bedtime for Frances*. Going to sleep in a dark room creates problems. *A Baby Sister for Frances*. Frances runs away under the table because she feels neglected. *A Birthday for Frances*. It is difficult when your sister has a birthday. *Best Friends for Frances*. Friendships have problems, too.

Flack, Marjorie. *Angus and the Ducks* (Garden City, NY: Doubleday, 1930). This is a simple adventure story about a boy who is curious.

Hutchins, Pat. *Titch* (New York, NY: Macmillan, 1971). Children can relate to the theme of being little.

Rockwell, Harlow. *My Nursery School* (New York, NY: Greenwillow Books, William Morrow, 1976). This is especially good for the beginning of the year.

Simon, Norma. *What Do I Do?* (Chicago, IL: Albert Whitman, 1969). This can be the basis for questions and answers about simple daily situations, and it has good drawings.

- **Books with simple text and lots of repetition**

Bemelmans, Ludwig. *Madeline* (New York, NY: Viking Press, 1939). The text is simple and rhymes.

Birnbaum, A. *Green Eyes* (New York, NY: Golden Press, 1968). The text is simple and the illustrations are beautiful.

Brown, Margaret Wise (Clemont Hurd, illustrator). *The Runaway Bunny* (New York, NY: Harper & Row, 1942). This is a very reassuring book for children. The illustrations are fun.

De Regniers, Beatrice Schenk (Paul Galdone, illustrator). *It Does Not Say Meow* (New York, NY: Seabury Press, 1972). This guessing book is about animals.

De Regniers, Beatrice Schenk (Beni Montresor, illustrator). *May I Bring a Friend?* (New York, NY: Atheneum, 1964). This story is great fun; the text is in rhyme and very humorous.

Ets, Marie Hall. *In the Forest* (New York, NY: Viking Press, 1944). This imaginative story with a simple refrain is about a boy and his make-believe animals.

Ets, Marie Hall. *Play with Me* (New York, NY: Viking Press, 1966). The story of a child looking for playmates. Pictures fit the text.

Lionni, Leo. *Inch by Inch* (New York, NY: Ivan Obolonsky, 1960). The text is simple with beautiful illustrations and a surprise ending.

Slobodkina, Esphyr. *Caps for Sale* (Reading, MA: Young Scott Books, Addison-Wesley, 1940). This is a humorous story with lots of repetition. It can be easily acted out.

- **Books depicting real situations that help preschoolers deal with their feelings and problems**

Blaise, Marge. *The Terrible Thing That Happened at Our Home* (New York, NY: Parents Magazine Press, 1975). The children find out what happens when a full-time mother goes back to work.

A series of books written by Miriam Cohen and illustrated by Lillian Hoban. All the stories take place in the same nursery school and deal with common feelings and problems. *Best Friends* (1971). *Tough Jim* (1974). *The New Teacher* (1972). *Will I Have a Friend?* (1967) (New York, NY: MacMillan).

Sendak, Maurice. *Where the Wild Things Are* (New York, NY: Harper & Row, 1963). There is no doubt that the boy in this story controls the wild creatures and is always safe himself.

Simon, Norma (Dora Leder, illustrator). *I Was So Mad!* (Chicago, IL: Albert Whitman, 1974). This book can lead to a good discussion of what makes each child mad.

- **Stories about a new baby at home**

  Alexander, Martha. *Nobody Asked Me If I Wanted a Baby Sister* (New York, NY: Dial Press, 1971).

  Greenfield, Eloise (John Steptoe, illustrator). *She Come Bringing Me That Little Baby Girl* (Philadelphia, PA: Lippincott, 1974).

  Keats, Erza Jack. *Peter's Chair* (New York, NY: Harper & Row, 1967).

  Vigna, Judith. *Couldn't We Have a Turtle Instead?* (Chicago, IL: Albert Whitman, 1975).

Reading with Preschool Children: Choosing the Right Time

Books should be used every day in a preschool room. The schedule should include time for reading to the whole group or to two smaller groups if two teachers are available to read. Young children can generally listen to a story for five to ten minutes. Older children are able to listen for a longer time, between ten and fifteen minutes. Reading to one child at a time is also important. This allows you to hold a child on your lap and gear the story to that child's special needs and interests. During free play the book area is one of the many choices available to preschool children. If you visit the book area for a few minutes during free play, children will be more likely to use the area.

Preparing for Story Time

Why, you might ask, should teachers plan and prepare for reading a story? The answer is that story time is so important that you don't want to leave it to chance. In terms of holding the attention of a group of active preschoolers, a little preparation can make a big difference. First, you will need to carefully select the books you will read. Use the criteria suggested in this module and consider the interests and abilities of your group. Second, read the story yourself and become very familiar with it. As you read through a book you are considering for your group, ask yourself the following questions:

- How long will it take to read the book, and can the children sit for that length of time?

- Are there places where the children can join in (for example, repeated phrases or questions posed in the book)?

- Are any of the concepts or ideas in the book likely to be unfamiliar to the children? How can I explain them?

- Is there anything special about the illustrations that I want the children to notice (for example, tiny details, hidden surprises)?

- Are sound effects (for example, animal noises or sirens) part of the story? How shall I make them?

Introducing the Story

To gain the attention of a group of preschool children, you will want to give some thought to how you will introduce the story. You want to do something that will help them focus their attention on you and the book. You also want to give them a reason to listen. Here are some suggestions:

- Tie the theme to something the children have recently experienced.

  "We all have angry feelings sometimes. If there's no room on the swings, or we can't find our shoes, we may feel angry. So I thought I'd read a book about being angry. It's called *I Was So Mad!*"

  "We all felt sad yesterday when our fish died. The story I'm going to read today is about a little boy whose cat died. It tells how he felt. It's called *The Tenth Good Thing About Barney.*"

- Show the children the cover of the book or the first illustration and talk about what they see. "What do you think this boy is doing?"

- Bring in an object that is an important part of the story and talk about it. "Here's a nice round stone I found on the playground. Do you think we could make soup from this stone? Let's see what happens in this book called *Stone Soup.*"

Reading the Story

If children can't see the pictures in the book, you may lose their attention. Some thought should be given to where you and the children sit. Children should be facing away from the light so they can see better. If the group is small, a semi-circle is a good way to ensure that everyone can see. Be sure everyone has a comfortable place to sit. Seat yourself on one of the child-size chairs so the children don't have to strain to see the book.

Here are some suggestions for successful story reading:

- Hold the book to one side so the children can see the pictures as you read.

- Start as soon as you have the children's attention.

- Speak clearly and vary your voice to suit the story—loud/ soft, fast/slow.

- Be dramatic—change your voice for different characters and pause at key places.

- If some children are having trouble listening, ask questions to get their attention ("What do you think will happen next?").

- Invite children to join in whenever possible with refrains and responses.

When you have finished the story, find a way to complete the experience or to extend it. Here are some examples:

- Discuss something in the book and ask the children to share their own experiences.

  "Have you ever felt like Andrew did? Did people not listen to you when you had something important to say to them?"

  "It was really hard for Frances when it was her sister's birthday. Did you ever feel like Frances?"

- Act out the story as a group or provide props so children can do it on their own.

- Make flannel board cutouts of favorite stories so children can retell the story themselves.

- Always leave the books you have read on the shelves so children can look through them again and again.

Most of all, enjoy children's books yourself. There are so many wonderful books for preschool children. Use the library to find new ones. You will enjoy reading more, and so will the children.

In this learning activity you will assess the books in your room using the criteria on the following pages for selecting books for preschool children. You will identify books that meet the criteria for good books. Then you will identify any problems you have had reading stories. Using the suggestions in this learning activity, you will try new ways to read books. Finally, you will evaluate your results.

Criteria for Reviewing Books for Young Preschool Children

If you work with young preschool children (threes and early fours), use the following criteria for reviewing each book in your room.

- Is the plot simple and about familiar experiences?

- Are the pictures colorful and realistic?

- Is there lots of repetition, or is a pattern repeated in the story?

- Are the words appealing (nonsense, repetitions, rhymes)?

- Do the pictures reflect the children's ethnic and cultural backgrounds?

- Is the story comforting (is there a happy resolution to a problem)?

List below at least eight books in your room that meet three or more of these criteria

Criteria for Reviewing Books for Older Preschool Children

If you work with older preschool children (fours and fives), use the following criteria for reviewing each book in your room:

- Is there a plot that the children can follow?

- Does the story have humor or a surprise ending?

- Is it imaginative?

- Does the story extend the children's understanding of the world around them?

- Do the pictures reflect the children's ethnic and cultural backgrounds?

- Are the illustrations colorful and filled with details?

List below at least eight books in your room that meet three or more of these criteria

_____

_____

_____

_____

_____

_____

_____

_____

_____

_____

_____

_____

_____

_____

_____

_____

If you cannot find eight books that meet these criteria, discuss this problem with your trainer. It may be time for the center to order new books. Until then, visit a local library and borrow books that meet these criteria.

Reading to Children

Think of your experiences reading books to preschool children. List below any problems you have encountered.

_____

_____

_____

_____

_____

_____

_____

_____

Review the suggestions for reading books given in this learning activity. List several strategies you want to try out.

_____

_____

_____

_____

_____

_____

_____

_____

Did using these strategies help? Write about your experience below.

_____

_____

_____

_____

_____

_____

Discuss this learning activity with your trainer.

V. Preparing Children for Reading and Writing

In this activity, you will learn:

- to identify the kinds of skills and understandings that help children prepare for reading and writing; and

- to create an environment that promotes the development of these skills and understandings.

Most people would agree that language development begins long before a child can speak in sentences. But if you ask people when children begin to read and write, they often say "in first grade." In fact, the ability to read and to write has its foundation long before first grade. Although formal attempts to teach young children to read and write are inappropriate, a rich environment that exposes young children to print and to writing is the beginning of literacy.

The developmental process through which children become literate is referred to as emerging literacy—how children learn to use language. Young children learn to read and write through regular exposure to literacy activities in their homes and child development programs. They learn about the importance of written language when they see their parents and teachers reading print in a variety of places—books, charts, the bulletin board—and writing—shopping lists, greeting cards, notes to each other. It takes a long time for children to make sense of language. They need to figure out for themselves: "What is the difference between drawing and writing?" "What does it mean when my teacher uses a different tone of voice?" "What do the symbols in books have to do with the words that people say out loud?"

The Foundation for Reading[6]

The most important factor in a child's ability to learn to read is a strong desire to read. Children who have been read to regularly in their early years, and who are given a rich assortment of good books to look at, are more likely to want to learn to read.

Children develop many important understandings by being exposed to books throughout the preschool years.

- They learn what books are like and how they should be handled. They also learn that books have a beginning and end and that they are read left to right and top to bottom.

- They learn that the print on the page makes sense and that it represents words. If young children are exposed to many firsthand experiences, these experiences also help them learn that print makes sense. The events in the stories and the ideas discussed will be more familiar to them.

---

[6]Based on Judith A. Schickedanz, *More Than ABCs: The Early Stages of Reading and Writing* (Washington, DC: National Association for the Education of Young Children, 1986), pp. 37-51.

- They learn that books are enjoyable and satisfying. This discovery encourages a positive attitude toward reading.

As in all areas of development, children go through predictable stages in understanding what reading is all about. Knowing about these stages will help you to recognize typical behaviors and encourage children's development. These stages are described below.

- **Learning to retell a story.**

    The more children are exposed to books and encouraged to retell stories, the more accurate they become in recalling the details and the correct sequence of events. The ability to retell a story is an important skill in learning to read. Two factors that help children develop this skill are hearing favorite stories repeatedly and hearing stories that are predictable so that they can anticipate what comes next.

- **Understanding that the print, not the pictures, contains the actual story.**

    You can tell if a child has not reached this stage if he or she expects you to read a page with no print, or if the child holds the book, covers up the print, and wants you to read. More experienced children will say things such as "now you can start reading again" when you get back to a page with print on it.

- **Attempting to match spoken words with the printed text.**

    At this stage children may run their fingers along the text as you read. They may also point to individual words as you read, though not necessarily the ones you are reading. This behavior tells you that the child is beginning to understand that each set of letters represents a word.

- **Increasing interest in the text itself.**

    Children at this stage are likely to ask questions about the print on the page. They may ask "what does this say?" or "where does it say that?" You may notice at the same time that these children are starting to pick out words in their environment. They may recognize signs such as "Stop" or "Exit." They can probably read their names and sometimes the names of other children in the class.

Although these stages are typical, it is important to note that how a child reacts to a particular story may vary depending on several factors, including:

- how often the child has been exposed to stories and books;

- whether the child has heard the story before and how often; and

- the appropriateness of the story itself.

The Foundation for Writing

Preschool children tend to be fascinated with writing. They love to use pencils, pens, crayons, and other writing tools. They enjoy imitating what adults do with these tools. If you make a shopping list, a three-year-old is likely to make one, too. If you write a letter, a four-year-old may decide that he or she needs to write a letter as well.

Young children attempt to write long before they begin to make recognizable letters or numbers. Their early attempts at writing are an important first step. Just as in learning to read, children go through predictable stages in writing. These stages are described below.

- **Scribble Writing.**

   Preschoolers' first attempts at writing are scribbles. But if you look closely, you will begin to see that they distinguish between drawing and writing. In the drawing below, which is a good example of this distinction, the child's writing is at the bottom left of the picture.

- **Making recognizable letters.**

   As children gain more experience with writing, they begin to make actual letters. Often these letters are part of a series of marks, some of which are not letters at all.

- **Doing more organized writing.**

  Children begin to understand that writing has to be organized on the page. Rather than placing the marks haphazardly on the page, they begin to understand that writing goes from left to right and that they have to leave spaces between words.

- **Grasping the connection between speech and writing.**

  As children begin to recognize letters, they also start to understand that each letter represents a sound. At this stage they may begin writing words and making up their own spelling—for example, "kt" for "cat." There is no need to correct this; it is an important step in their understanding of reading and writing.

Creating an Environment That Supports Reading and Writing Skills

Children who are exposed to an environment filled with interesting materials learn from their daily interactions in the environment. Teachers who include props and materials that inspire preschoolers to pretend and to experiment with reading and writing are promoting literacy skills through daily experiences.

Listed below are some examples of how teachers can prepare an environment that supports children's interest in learning about reading and writing.

- **Make signs, labels, and charts a part of the environment.**

  Picture labels for materials can include written words as well. Children can help you make the labels. Cubbies should have each child's name. Charts that are used by the whole group—helper charts, daily attendance charts, the daily schedule in pictures, a birthday chart—all encourage literacy skills.

  Lists can be posted for taking turns to use a popular item. Children can write their names and cross them off after their turn. Making recipes—writing and illustrating the ingredients for a recipe for a food-preparation activity—is a fun and engaging activity.

- **Point out signs and labels outdoors.**

  Show children traffic signs and explain what they mean. Read signs in store windows to children as you walk. Point to the words on juice and food containers.

- **Add props to dramatic play areas that encourage children to read and write.**

  In the house corner, include props such as magazines, telephone books, and pads and pencils to make lists. Add props when they can be appropriately used by the children. For example, if doctor play is evident in the house corner, prescription pads and an eye examination chart might be added. In the block area include cards,

353

magic markers, and masking tape that can be used to make signs for the buildings that children construct. Some of the props you can buy, such as wooden traffic signs, have writing on them.

- **Include some games with words and numbers.**

  Games such as Lotto, matching games, and number games that have words and numbers as well as pictures are all useful.

  Magnet letters and numbers can be available for experiments with ordering numbers and letters.

- **Record group stories.**

  Write on a large piece of paper what children have to say after a trip or a shared group experience. Read the story to the children.

- **Encourage children to draw and paint.**

  Paints should be available at the easel during free play.

  Markers, pencils, and crayons with plain drawing paper should always be available.

- **Maintain an attractive book area.**

  Use the ideas presented in the previous learning activity to set up an appealing book area. Visit this area and spend time there with one or two children. Keep rotating books so there is always something new for the children to look at.

- **Set up a writing center.**

  Identify a place in the room where children can go when they want to write. Furnish the area with a table and chairs and a shelf. Set out writing tools and paper so children can write signs, stories, and messages. Visit the writing center and use it for your own writing as well as to help children who need assistance.

These ideas are designed to make reading and writing a natural part of preschool children's daily living. In this way children will not feel pushed to read or write. They will be inspired to take their own steps toward becoming literate when they are ready.

In this learning activity you will observe the story-reading and writing skills of one child in your group. You will then assess your environment for literacy. Begin by reading "Props for Reading and Writing." Then do your observation. Finally, examine your environment and determine how you can make it richer to inspire children's interest in reading and writing.

Props for Reading and Writing[7]

Print props to add to children's dramatic play.

House play

Books to read to dolls or stuffed animals.

Empty food, toiletry, and cleaning containers.

Telephone books. (Make them with children's names, addresses, and telephone numbers. Cover pages with clear plastic adhesive.)

Emergency numbers decal to attach to the play phone. Write in numbers for doctor, ambulance, fire station, and police.

Cookbook. (Can be made with children's favorite recipes.)

Small notepads and a container with pencils.

Wall plaques with appropriate verses.

Stationery and envelopes.

Magazines and newspapers.

Food coupons.

Grocery store food ads.

Play money.

Doctor's office play

Eye chart posted on the wall. (Make one with rows of different size letters.)

Telephone book.

Message pad and pencils.

Signs such as *Doctor is in/Doctor is out, Thank you for not smoking, Open/Closed.*

Magazines and books for the waiting room.

Pamphlets for children about health care (brushing teeth, eating good foods, wearing safety belts).

File folders and ditto sheets for health charts.

Index cards cut in quarters for appointment cards.

Grocery store play

Empty food containers.

Labels for store departments: dairy, produce, etc.

Food posters. (Ask a supermarket for old ones.)

Brown grocery bags with the name of the store written on them.

Signs for store hours.

Numeral stamps and stamp pads to price foods.

Play money, cash register.

Grocery store ads.

Restaurant play

Menus.

Magnetic letters and board to post specials.

Placemats. (Cover construction paper with the name of the restaurant written on it in clear plastic adhesive.)

Note pads and pencils for taking orders and writing checks.

Play money, cash register.

Open and closed signs.

Transportation play

Recipe cards cut in half for tickets.

Maps or an atlas.

Suitcases with luggage tags.

Travel brochures.

Little notebooks for record keeping.

Post office play

Envelopes of various sizes.

Stationery supplies, pencils.

Stickers or gummed stamps.

Stamp pad and stamp to cancel.

Office play

Typewriter or computer terminal and paper.

Telephone book.

Ledger sheets.

Dictation pads, other note pads.

3-ring binders filled with information.

Sales brochures.

Business cards made from file cards.

Filing supplies.

Date and other stamps and stamp pad.

---

[7]Reprinted with permission from Judith A. Schickedanz, *More Than ABCs: The Early Stages of Reading and Writing* (Washington, DC: National Association for the Education of Young Children, 1986), pp. 112-113 and 122-123.

The writing center

Because children often wish to make greeting cards or books; write notes, letters, or stories; or experiment with various writing materials, they need a place in the classroom for these activities. This area, like the literacy skills materials area discussed earlier, need not be large. Because it will be available every day during the activity period, when children may choose between it and many other centers, space for three or four children to work comfortably will be adequate. A table and several chairs, plus a shelf for storing writing materials, will provide the basic setup for the area. Writing supplies will vary, but might include a selection of items such as those listed in Table 5.2.

Table 5.2.

Writing supplies for the writing center.

Pencils. (Thin lead with eraser. Thick lead without eraser. Colored pencils. Wax pencils if appropriate surfaces are available.)
Markers. (Both wide- and fine-tipped, available in a variety of colors, all watercolor.)
Magic slates and wooden pencils.
Alphabet letter stamps and ink pads.
Typewriter or computer with word processing.
Paper. (Plain newsprint, white and colored construction paper, typing, or mimeo paper, computer print-out paper, carbon paper.)
Acetate sheets and wipe-off cloths.
Letter and design stencils.
Index and computer cards.
Stapler.
Hole punch.
Scissors.
Paste and glue.
Pencil sharpener.
Book of wallpaper samples for use as book covers.
Stationery, perhaps created with stickers.
Envelopes.
Old magazines.
Chalk and chalkboard.
Bits of string and yarn.

Children will be attracted to the writing center if it is appealing, if materials are kept in good working order (no dried-out markers), and if you visit the center to offer encouragement and help to the children, and to do some writing yourself from time-to-time.

Beginning Reading and Writing Skills
(Example)

Child: _Jennifer_   **Age:** _4-1/2 years_   **Date:** _June 1_

When looking at books, this child demonstrates the following pre-reading skills:

With familiar books, she likes to turn the pages and tell herself the story. She occasionally goes to the library area and looks at favorite books. Sometimes she tells the story to another child.

When listening to a story being read, this child demonstrates the following beginning reading skills:

She corrects the teacher reading a familiar story when the text is not read exactly. Once she pointed to a page with no text on it and said, "There's no talking on this page."

Using writing tools (e.g., crayons, markers, pencils, paint brushes), this child demonstrates the following beginning writing skills:

She can write her name correctly. In the block area, she likes to make signs for her buildings. She will ask a teacher to write down what she wants to say, and then she likes to copy it herself. Sometimes she adds letters to her paintings.

Beginning Reading and Writing Skills

Child: _____   Age: _____   Date: _____

When looking at books, this child demonstrates the following pre-reading skills:

_____
_____
_____
_____
_____
_____
_____

When listening to a story being read, this child demonstrates the following beginning reading skills:

_____
_____
_____
_____
_____
_____
_____

Using writing tools (e.g., crayons, markers, pencils, paint brushes), this child demonstrates the following beginning writing skills:

_____
_____
_____
_____
_____
_____
_____

Now assess the environment of your room to see how it encourages children's literacy skills.

Assessing Your Environment for Literacy

Signs, Labels, and Charts

Do you have:

_____ Picture labels as well as pictures on the shelves?

_____ Cubbies with each child's name?

_____ Charts (helpers, daily attendance, etc.)?

_____ Lists (for taking turns)?

_____ Recipes (for cooking activities)?

_____ Others?

_____

_____

_____

What props are included in the house corner to engage children in writing or reading activities?

_____

_____

_____

_____

What props are included in the block area to engage children in writing or reading activities?

_____

_____

_____

_____

What table toys do you have that give children opportunities to see written words?

_____

_____

_____

_____

Do you have a writing center? If so, what is in the center?

_____

_____

_____

When you have completed this assessment, identify five new ways in which you can add literacy materials to your room. After listing these additions to your room, observe how children use the materials and record the results below.

1. _____

_____

2. _____

_____

3. _____

_____

4. _____

_____

5. _____

_____

How children used these materials:

_____

_____

_____

_____

_____

_____

_____

_____

_____

_____

Discuss this learning activity with your trainer.

Summarizing Your Progress

You have now completed all of the learning activities for this module. Whether you are an experienced teacher or a new one, this module has probably helped you develop new skills in promoting preschoolers' communication. Before you go on, take a few minutes to summarize what you've learned.

- Turn back to Learning Activity I, Using Your Knowledge of Child Development to Promote Communication, and add to the chart specific examples of what you learned about promoting children's communication skills during the time you were working on this module.

- Next, review your responses to the pre-training assessment for this module. Write a summary of what you learned and list the skills you developed or improved.

_____

_____

_____

_____

_____

_____

_____

_____

_____

_____

_____

_____

_____

_____

_____

_____

_____

If there are topics you would like to know more about, you will find recommended readings listed in the orientation.

Your final step in this module is to complete the knowledge and competency assessments. Let your trainer know when you are ready to schedule the assessments. After you have successfully completed these assessments, you will be ready to start a new module. Congratulations on your progress so far, and good luck with your next module.

Answer Sheets

Promoting Children's Communication

Interacting with Children in Ways That Encourage Them to Communicate Their Thoughts and Feelings

1. How did Ms. Kim know what Jerry wanted?

    a. She interpreted his nonverbal communications (pointing, pulling her to the block corner, nodding his head).

    b. She went with him to the block area and asked questions to find out what had happened.

2. How did Ms. Kim help Jerry communicate his feelings and thoughts using words?

    a. She said what she thought he wanted, giving him the words for his nonverbal communication.

    b. She told him what to say to David.

    c. She respected his wishes to make his own garage, again giving him a full sentence for his one-word response.

    d. She gave the boys a way to work together and promised to return to check on them.

Providing Materials and Activities That Promote Communication Skills

1. How did Mr. Lopez use a walk to promote communication skills?

    a. He asked Kara and Grace what they saw on their walk.

    b. He suggested that they write a story about their walk.

2. How did Mrs. Green promote communication skills as she helped Grace and Kara write a story?

    a. She encouraged them to write even though they couldn't write letters yet.

    b. She wrote the words that the girls dictated to her.

    c. She read the girls' words aloud to them.

Helping Children Develop Listening and Speaking Skills

1. What did Ms. Williams do to interest children in hearing the story?

   a. She talked about the story before reading it and said that there was something special about it.

   b. She asked if anyone remembered how the peddler carried his caps.

   c. She paused at different parts of the story to let the children join in with phrases they knew.

   d. She read the story with a lot of expression.

2. How did Ms. Williams use story time to promote listening and speaking skills?

   a. She introduced the book by asking children questions that made them interested in listening.

   b. She encouraged them to join in with answers and phrases whenever appropriate.

   c. She had the children reenact the story themselves using props she brought.

Using Your Knowledge of Child Development to Promote Communication

WHAT PRESCHOOL CHILDREN ARE LIKE	HOW TEACHERS CAN USE THIS INFORMATION TO PROMOTE COMMUNICATION
They sometimes talk to themselves—not for the purpose of communicating with anyone but simply to practice talking and to amuse themselves.	Notice when children are doing this. Talk to them about what you observe. "You were really enjoying digging with that shovel in the sandbox. You even made up a song about it.
Then tend to use language freely and creatively in dramatic play.	Put out props familiar to the children to encourage dramatic play. Help shy children enter the group so they can learn to communicate more and feel a part of the group.
They are able to remember stories and retell them, sometimes in correct sequence.	Repeat favorite stories. Select some story books with simple themes that include a lot of repetition. Talk to children about the stories and help them recall events so they improve their communication skills.
They like to make up stories of their own.	Be a good listener. Write the stories that preschoolers dictate and read them back so the children are encouraged to make up more stories.
They use language creatively; like to make up words, and enjoy rhymes and nonsense words and poems.	Select some books to read for the pure enjoyment of the words in the book. Notice rhymes and words children make up and repeat them for fun and to encourage them to use language creatively.
They ask lots of questions.	Be a good listener. Respond in ways that help children extend their thinking.
They draw pictures and create other representations that look like something. They often name what they make.	Encourage children to talk about what they have made. "Would you like to tell me something about your drawing?" After they have spoken, write what they say to show them that written words capture what they say.

WHAT PRESCHOOL CHILDREN ARE LIKE	HOW TEACHERS CAN USE THIS INFORMATION TO PROMOTE COMMUNICATION
They like to share experiences—things that have happened to them.	Take time to listen to what each child has to say. Comment on what they share to show you are interested.
They commonly make mistakes in grammar.	Do not correct children. Accept their way of speaking to encourage them to talk more. Serve as a model by speaking correctly.
They enjoy songs, poems, and finger plays and can learn increasingly complex ones.	Teach children new songs, poems, and finger plays. Select ones for which they can make up verses to encourage their language development. Use these as part of daily routines.
They are beginning to understand written symbols—letters, numbers, and some words.	Make labels with pictures and words for materials in the room. Offer games such as Lotto with pictures and printed words and numbers. Use job charts to expose children to written words and numbers as part of daily experience.
They are beginning to show interest in writing.	Keep writing materials available to children to encourage them to try writing.

Glossary

Communication   The act of expressing and sharing ideas, desires, and feelings.

Emerging literacy   The developmental process through which children become literate, including speaking, reading, and writing.

Language   A system of words and rules for their use in speaking, reading, and writing.

Nonverbal communication   The act of conveying feelings or ideas without using words.

Reading skills   Visual and perceptual skills needed to read, including following sequences from left to right and recognizing differences and similarities among things.

NOTES

NOTES

NOTES

NOTES